WOMEN'S
MINISTRY
HANDBOOK

WOMEN'S MINISTRY HANDBOOK

**EDITED BY CAROL PORTER
AND MIKE HAMEL**

VICTOR BOOKS®

A DIVISION OF SCRIPTURE PRESS PUBLICATIONS INC.
USA CANADA ENGLAND

Unless otherwise noted, Scripture references are from the
Holy Bible, New International Version, © 1973, 1978, 1984,
International Bible Society. Used by permission of
Zondervan Bible Publishers. Other references are from the
Authorized (King James) Version, and the *New American Stan-
dard Bible,* © the Lockman Foundation 1960, 1962, 1963,
1968, 1971, 1972, 1973, 1975, 1977. Used by permission.

Copyediting: Barbara Williams
Cover Design: Scott Rattray

Library of Congress Cataloging-in-Publication Data

Women's ministry handbook / by Carol Porter, Mike Hamel,
editors.
    p.   cm.
    Includes bibliographical references.
    ISBN 0-89693-885-9
    1. Women in church work. 2. Women — Religious life.
I. Porter, Carol. II. Hamel, Mike
BV4415.W647   1992
253'.082 — dc20   91-42082
                                              CIP

---

1 2 3 4 5 6 7 8 9 10 Printing/Year 96 95 94 93 92

CONTENTS

85548

PREFACE

This book began in the mind of Bruce McNicol, the President of Interest Ministries, in Wheaton, Illinois. The purpose of Interest Ministries is to equip leaders, encourage believers, and enable congregations to be healthy, growing, and reproducing. Mr. McNicol realized that if these purposes were to be achieved, Christian women needed to be effectively mobilized.

Since my husband, Mark, and I work in the field of Church Consulting for Interest Ministries, I was asked to take on this task. Mark has been my primary mentor through the years; I have seen him climb seemingly insurmountable mountains to complete a task he began. Though I often did not know what to do next, I knew that if this book was indeed God's project it would be accomplished through Him.

Networking began in the summer of 1988 and led a year later to a group of twenty-one women from churches across America and Eastern Canada who met for a weekend of work and inspiration. This book represents the combined experience and wisdom of these women. We range in age from late twenties to mid-seventies. We live in Canada and across the United States; attend inner-city and suburban churches; are African-American and Hispanic as well as melting-pot white. We are tied together by a common passion to see God's Word become incarnate in the hearts and lives of women: non-Christian women finding their Savior and believers walking in obedience. It is to this end that we have all written, prayed, and I have edited. A bibliography is included to further your knowledge in the individual areas of ministry. This manual is for your use. You may adapt it freely to your own situation.

The following women have contributed significant portions of the handbook:

Ruth Barton	Marilyn Hoekstra	Dora Rios
Rosie Bauman	Olive Liefeld	Cheryl Smith
Peg Burdick	Marie Little	Pat Smith
Naomi Cole	Mary McCallum	Felecia Thompson
Beverly Hislop	Joann McCoy	Grace Thornton

In addition to these women many others contributed their ideas and insight. Some were members of the initial conference in May 1989, while others have helped through contributing advice or material since then.

Heather Andrews	Susan Holton
Winnie Christensen	Ruth Conard
Yolanda Moreno	Lisa Ferro
Heather Rausch	Lois Fleming
Ella Flowers	Jan Seiker
Gloria Gossett	Linda Webb
Debbie Logan	Beverly Yates

Without the help of Mike Hamel, Resource Center Director at Interest Ministries, this book would not exist in its present form. He spent many hours tightening my original editing and organizing the handbook. When I was discouraged with the project, he cheered me on. Barbara Williams of Victor Books took up where Mike left off. Together we present this book to you for the glory of God.

Carol Porter
Pleasanton, California

CHAPTER ONE

Why Have a Women's Ministry?

We were sitting at a little breakfast nook having muffins and coffee together, gently probing each other's spirits to see if we could make a connection. Sue had just started coming to our church and I had invited her for Saturday morning coffee.

For my part, I wondered if Sue was a real believer. She was pondering whether she could find a niche in this church. Bit by bit we got acquainted. Yes, she was a believer, a believer in love with the Lord, but also a believer who hurt. She was the daughter of an alcoholic. Her husband was a successful accountant whom she longed to see become a believer. In spite of her own hurt and needs, she wanted to minister significantly to others.

She had accepted my invitation for breakfast with the hope I could help her become involved at our church. Not knowing how long she would stay with us — she had moved every two years — she wanted to quickly find a way to use her gifts.

Sue confided she had felt like an outsider at the last several churches she had attended. "All the women knew each other already and they just didn't seem to be interested in me. When I asked if there was any way I could help, all they could suggest was that I sign up on the nursery schedule."

Sue had a career as an account executive for a large advertising company. While she really didn't object to working in the nursery, her passion just wasn't babies. Her eyes lit up as I shared the desire of our women's ministry council to start a support group for women whose husbands were not believers. She would later find her place as a discussion leader in that ministry.

Sue is typical of many Christian women today well educated, wanting

13

to be used by God in her church, and uncomfortable with being limited to traditional forms of ministry. They are willing to do the necessary things women do in a church, realizing that they need to be done, but wanting to do so much more. This is where an organized women's ministry comes in; to facilitate traditional and nontraditional ministries of women.

A Women's Ministry Can Help Churches Grow
Churches should grow. Growth can be divided into several overlapping categories. *Biological growth* comes when the children of believers become believers themselves. *Evangelistic growth* comes when someone other than a child of a member becomes a new believer. *Transfer growth* occurs when a family or individual starts attending. The fourth type of growth is *growth in spiritual maturity* — the natural result when a believer is fed nourishing food. Women's ministries can contribute to growth in each of these areas.

For biological growth to occur a family must be attending the church at the time when their children are ready to become an active part of the fellowship. The women's ministry council can plan events and activities that will help keep the family in church during this crucial time period.

Women's ministries can provide a suitable environment for conversion and for subsequent growth. In a later chapter you will find specific directions on how to ground new believers in the basics of the Christian life. A big factor in growth is having supportive relationships with other believers. Christians just don't grow well in a vacuum; God places us in Christian families called churches. Within those churches women can form relationships to encourage that growth.

A church also grows through the transfer of believers from other churches. For various reasons a person decides to leave one church and go looking for another. This individual usually has specific reasons why she left the first church. She may point to the preaching, the music, or the lack of a specific program. Often, the real reason revolves around relationships. Either she could not break through the clique in the first church and felt like an outsider, or she had clashed with a specific individual within that congregation.

Other times the issue is philosophy of ministry which is worked out in the style of music, type of preaching, or even particular lists of do's and don'ts. Rarely is a doctrinal issue involved. In any event, when she visits the new church she is asking herself, "Can I make friends here?" or to put it another way, "Is anyone here like me?"

We all need acceptance; growth is hard without it. Women's ministries create a climate where acceptance does not have to be achieved, but is automatically granted. Church-hoppers are likely to stop looking when they find genuine love combined with sound teaching.

Transfer growth can also come from outside the community. When a Christian family moves into a new area one of the first orders of business is to find a church. The first Sunday we moved to California from Massachusetts we visited a church in our new town. The next night two women from the church appeared with enough food for a week, including homemade cream puffs for dessert that evening.

In other churches an outreach arm of the women's ministry prepares a basket of all the things a newcomer might need: maps, restaurant guides, public transportation schedules, and hints about the best places to shop and drops it by the newcomer's home. This attention to detail says, "We're glad you visited our church; come again."

Women are one of the most underused resources in the average church. No matter what size your church is, it should be a growing church and women can make strong contributions to that growth.

A Women's Ministry Can Open Doors to Relationships

Scripture instructs women to minister to each other. In Titus 2:4-5 we are told to "train the younger women to love their husbands and children, to be self-controlled and pure, to be busy at home, to be kind, and to be subject to their husbands, so that no one will malign the Word of God." The Divine Author of Scripture knows women need other women to help light the way through life.

Women of all ages are looking for women who are ahead of them in life experiences. The young businesswoman needs input from the career woman on how to be a Christian in the marketplace. Meanwhile the new mother at home needs the reinforcement of like-minded women with older children to stay at home with her children even though it may mean a reduced standard of living.

The empty-nest woman also needs help. The natural pressures and tensions of this mid-life period destroy marriages that were thought to be indestructible. Being at this stage myself, I look for role models. It's not just any empty-nester I want to talk to, but one who is transparent about her own life and who can share with me how to rely on God through yet another of life's transitional periods.

Women are specifically designed by God to meet the needs of women. Dee Brestin in her book, *The Friendships of Women* (Wheaton, Ill.: Victor Books, 1989, p. 14) notes that women are natural nurturers because they're more comfortable with same-sex intimacy than men. We instinctively know how to volley in conversation and express interest by asking questions.

Our ability to perceive emotions and empathize with others enables us to sense problems and understand the heart cries of another person. In addition, we tend to focus more on relationships than on things and activities.

A Women's Ministry Can Minister to the Women of the '90s
The woman of the 1990s is a different type of woman from her grandmother. *Megatrends 2000* (John Naisbitt and Patricia Aburdene, New York: Wm. Morrow and Co., 1990) calls the 1990s the "Decade of Women in Leadership." Even though the thrust of this book is secular many of the observations impact the local church.

The "ideal" nuclear family, husband as breadwinner, wife home with 2.5 children, represents only 7 percent of the population today. Many churches are still gearing programming to reach this population. The times are changing and church ministries need to change to compete for the little discretionary time available today.

Working women

The most important and obvious change is the large number of women who are working outside of the home. Seventy-nine percent of women with no children under eighteen work as do 67 percent of women with children. Fifty percent of women with small children are in the marketplace.

Both parachurch and local church ministries are affected. Scheduling and the type of programs offered must change to accommodate the new needs of these women.

The number of two-income families has increased significantly. Although two incomes may help alleviate financial stress, they create their own set of problems. These difficulties impact first the woman herself and then the ministries in the local church.

One of the first effects of the two-career home is the delayed birth of the first child. In the 1980s many couples had their first child in their mid-thirties. Now more and more couples are in their early forties when they start families.

These late mothers aren't as available to participate in women's ministries. If the older mother has returned to work after the birth of her child, then time with the child and husband is precious to her. Time is a scarce commodity so the programs she will attend need to be specifically tailored to her needs or she won't come. The day is past when a woman will be at a function just because the function exists. There are not enough hours in the day for everything; a fact fully understood by the working woman.

Donna is a perfect example of the previous description. She is an older first-time mother who is experiencing her own personal energy crisis. She loved her teaching career and put off having children until after she was thirty-five. She's now over forty and has preschoolers. Having enough energy for each day is a major issue. She attends school herself, works in her son's co-op preschool, tries to spend time with aging parents as well as keeping up with ongoing housework. Despite her husband's good intentions, most of the chores are Donna's responsibility.

One event on the women's ministry calendar Donna does enjoy is a monthly evening open house at which she can sit and talk with several women. The evening requires little from her intellectually or emotionally, but replenishes her soul. She can take without having to give back.

Educated women

Another factor to consider is that women are better educated than ever before. More women are in college than men. Fifty-four percent of adult working women (ages twenty-five to fifty-four) are college-educated, compared with 20 percent in 1965. One-third of all computer scientists are women. Forty-nine percent of all accountants are women, compared with 1.7 percent in 1972. In 1975 women received 11 percent of the MBA degrees, today they receive 33 percent.

Today's women have more skills, though not necessarily more spiritual depth, to give the church. They expect higher quality programming. The church which hopes to grow in a demographically upwardly mobile environment must focus on doing everything well. If your women's ministry is used to being casual about standards of excellence, you'll need to upgrade your approach to attract today's educated women. An educated woman is as spiritually needy as an uneducated woman, though the veneer of education may cover the depth of her need.

Singles and single moms

Over 50 percent of today's society is single. Gradually this percentage is being reflected in the church. Many churches have singles ministries, or band together with other like-minded congregations for a singles ministry. Section 4 suggests specific ways to minister sensitively to the single woman. But for now, just remember that she is there, and her needs must be addressed.

The increase in single moms is another factor to consider when planning women's ministries. These single mothers are hungry for fellowship and have little time to receive it. Since most of them work, the programs for them must be during the evening and be of sufficiently high value to them so they will make the effort to attend. The single mom will usually make more of an effort to attend an evening event than will the working wife. She is driven by her need for Christian adult companionship.

Seniors

We are going to be blessed with more older women. Life expectancy for women is now seventy-six. Not only is life expectancy greater, those in the leading edge of the baby boom (those born between 1946 and 1964) will reach fifty in the mid-1990s. Women's ministries need to program for and utilize these women. Section 4 suggests ways for ministering to and utilizing these women in ministry.

Organizing for Ministry

Before we go any farther we need to define ministry. I like the definition Dorothy Dahlman, Director of Women's Ministries for the Baptist General Conference, uses. She writes in her helpful book, *A Designer's Guide for Creative Women's Ministries* (Arlington Heights, Ill.: Harvest Publications, 1988, p. 11): "Ministry is the act of expressing God's love in meeting needs of people who know Him or could be reached for Him."

A definition I often use is even simpler, "Ministry is any action that brings another person closer to God." Ministry then, can be a variety of activities, many of which will have nothing to do with the organized women's ministry in your church.

This book is not just about women doing ministry. It's about a group of women in a local church who organize so that they accomplish their ministry more efficiently. Organization is not a bad word; it is an enabling word. Organization of the women's ministry is not designed to organize away the Holy Spirit, or to replace His prompting, but to facilitate the ministry He inspires.

In a small church, under fifty in total attendance, there is little need for an organization to facilitate relationships. The women all know each other. Perhaps a few join together for prayer, Bible study, and fellowship. These meetings can be arranged by phone and announced on Sunday morning.

But in order to meet the variety of needs present in a larger church, prior thinking and adequate publicizing must be done. This takes planning, planning takes organization, and organization means a group empowered to do the organizing. The larger the number of people involved the more organization needs to take place.

In their book, *Strategy for Leadership* (Old Tappan, N.J.: Fleming H. Revell, 1979, 21), Ed Dayton and Ted Engstrom note that in a church with 250 members there will be a total of 31,125 possible relationships. No wonder a growing church benefits from organization! In chapter 6

I'll suggest exactly *how* to get organized.

Organizations must have a recognized reason for existence as must each specific ministry. In too many churches the purpose for which women get together is not clear, so little is done that specifically meets anyone's needs.

A friend told me about a women's meeting in her church where the women met once a month on Thursday evening. Some would bring handwork, others would bring a letter from a missionary to read, and occasionally, someone would share some insight from the Bible. To those older women who had been doing this for years, it was a perfectly acceptable meeting. But to my friend it was a purposeless waste of time. Today's women are just too busy to attend something that doesn't meet a felt need.

Organizations exist in relationship to other organizations. Does your church have a clearly stated purpose? If so, then that can be a starting point for the development of a purpose for your women's ministry. If a church has as its purpose: "To exalt the Lord, to evangelize the community, to edify and equip the believer," then the women's ministry in that church should embody these same goals.

Women's Ministry and Church Leadership

Just how women's ministries interact with the rest of the church will depend to a great extent on the attitude of the primary leadership of the church. In many churches the men are as excited about women's ministry as the women. In fact, they are great encouragers of the women, realizing that an active women's ministry means more people are being reached for the Lord.

However, there are still many churches where the male leadership questions the value of an organized women's ministry. Their hesitancy may be based on one or more of the following misunderstandings.

• Women want to take over the church. They want to make all the major decisions, if not from actual leadership positions, from background manipulations. They're hungry for power and will lobby or nag until they get their way.

• Women will take off on their own without consulting the men. If a problem arises the leadership won't know what's happening and will be unable to deal with it in a positive, helpful manner.

• Women will do a better job with their ministries than the men and thus, unwittingly make the men look bad by comparison.

• Women don't have the spiritual gifts of teaching, preaching, and organizing. Jill Briscoe deals with this problem in a humorous fashion in, *Yes God, I Am a Creative Woman*, edited by Dorothy Dahlman and Bob

Putman (Arlington Heights, Ill.: Harvest Publications, 1985, 73–83). If this is the case in your church, do as Jill suggests and pray for the first opportunity where you can use your gift. It may mean, as in Jill's case, that a teaching gift meant for adults is first used with second-graders.

A sensitive, Holy Spirit empowered, women's ministry will do all in its power to prevent any of the above from happening. There are several ways smooth interaction with others in leadership can be accomplished.

First, establish how much authority over committees the staff leadership desires. Then, follow the guidelines they suggest. Guidelines could include sending a copy of the agenda and the minutes to the pastor or the person designated as the liaison with women's ministries. A pastor may prefer that a representative from women's ministries meet with him on a regular basis. As a church grows past the 500–750 point, it's advisable to have a representative from the women's ministry meet regularly with the rest of the staff to facilitate planning of programs and events.

Together

A church should work together as one organism with men and women encouraging one another:

> The body is a unit, though it is made up of many parts; and though all its parts are many, they form one body. . . . The eye cannot say to the hand, "I don't need you!" And the head cannot say to the feet, "I don't need you!" On the contrary, those parts of the body that seem to be weaker are indispensable, and the parts that we think are less honorable we treat with special honor. . . . God has combined the members of the body . . . so that there should be no division in the body, but that its parts should have equal concern for each other (1 Cor. 12:12-25).

If women get behind the ministries of the entire church, then it becomes easier for the men to allow them increased freedom in their own decision-making. God is glorified and His work is advanced when we work harmoniously side by side to build up His kingdom.

Bibliography
Exman, Gary W. *Get Ready . . . Get Set . . . Grow! Church Growth for Town and Country Congregations.* Lima, Ohio: CSS Publishing Co., 1987.

Logan, Robert. *Beyond Church Growth.* Old Tappan, N.J.: Fleming Revell, 1989.

Schaller, Lyle E. *44 Ways to Revitalize the Women's Organization.* Nashville, Tenn: Abingdon Press, 1990.

Schaller, Lyle E. *Growing Plans, Strategies to Increase Your Church's Membership.* Nashville, Tenn.: Abingdon Press, 1984.

Schaller, Lyle E. *The Small Church Is Different.* Nashville, Tenn.: Abingdon Press, 1982.

Tucker, Ruth A. and Walter Liefeld. *Daughters of the Church.* Grand Rapids, Mich.: Zondervan Publishing House, 1987.

Van Leeuwen and Mary Stewart. *Gender and Grace.* Downers Grove, Ill.: InterVarsity Press, 1990.

Wagner, C. Peter. *Your Church Can Grow: Seven Vital Signs of a Healthy Church.* Ventura, Calif.: Regal Books, 1976.

CHAPTER TWO

The Inner Life of the Leader

A Heart for God

Sharon called me several months ago. She was bubbling over with excitement. A few minutes into the conversation she said, "God is talking to me about living more for Him. I think I'm supposed to be reaching out to women where I work." I knew God had been talking to her; there were several new believers already as a result of her changed life. But best of all she was listening to Him.

Her excitement reminds me of Robert Boyd Munger's description in *My Heart Christ's Home* (Downers Grove, Ill.: InterVarsity Press, 1954, 5). "What an entrance He made! It was not a spectacular, emotional thing, but very real. It was at the very center of my life. He came into the darkness of my heart and turned on the light. He built a fire in the cold hearth and banished the chill. He started music where there had been stillness and He filled the emptiness with His own loving, wonderful fellowship."

When Jesus comes into a heart He does build a fire. John, writing from the Island of Patmos refers to the experience as one like "first love." Someone in the first stages of a love relationship can think of nothing other than the object of her love. The same is true in a spiritual sense. Sharon has a fire burning, and the glow from that fire attracts others to the Lord.

However, that fire must be tended, for your sake and for the sake of those whom your life impacts. Time must be spent with the One who kindled the flame. He knows just what logs to put on and how to regulate the oxygen so it burns brightly, but does not burn out. (This word picture comes from Gail MacDonald's, *High Call, High Privilege* [Wheaton, Ill.: Tyndale House, 1983, 18].)

Spending time with God has many facets. How do you describe your relationship with your best friend? You don't divide it into artificial categories: listening, talking, or spending time with them. When you are together, the relationship just flows. Communication involves listening, talking, and times of silence — sometimes the most profound form of fellowship.

As a leader, your life must be centered in God. Do you have a devotional time with the Lord each day? A devotional time is time spent in God's presence listening to Him speak through His Word and speaking to Him in prayer. It may include reading, memorizing, and meditating on the Bible, as well as praying and singing. The goal is to worship God and set the stage for obeying His voice throughout the day.

Establishing God's Word in Your Life

Here are some suggestions on how to establish God's Word in your life. There is no one way to do it; different ways suit different women. What is effective when you work outside the home may not meet your needs when you are home with small children. Experiment to establish a pattern that allows the Word to speak most clearly and consistently to you.

1. *Pray*. Ask for help in understanding what you are reading. "Open my eyes that I may see wonderful things in Your Law" (Ps. 119:18).

2. *Read*. Systematic reading is helpful. Here are some suggestions:

• Read through the Bible in a year. Many excellent formats are available. Try starting at the "Four Great Beginnings." On January 1 read Genesis 1, Ezra 1, Matthew 1, and Acts 1. On January 2, read the second chapters of each of the books. I first heard this suggestion from John Stott, Rector Emeritus of All Souls Church in London. Though this order seems chaotic, it provides a new perspective on God's work throughout history. It has become one of my favorite ways to read through the Bible in a year.

• Read through a book of the Bible paragraph by paragraph or chapter by chapter. Take notes on what God is saying to you. Focus on how you can apply the Word to your own life.

• Read your Bible until you discern the Lord speaking to you. This may mean three verses or several chapters. Then pray about what He is saying. (For a discussion of this process, see *"Lord, Change Me!"* by Evelyn Christensen [Wheaton, Ill: Victor Books, 1975].)

• Use a monthly reading program such as *Daily Walk* (available from the Navigators, P.O. Box 20, Colorado Springs, CO 80901). Your denomination may publish similar helpful tools. Or try *Encounters with God*, published by Scripture Union, 7000 Ludlow Street, Upper Darby, PA 19082. It will take you through the entire Bible in five years.

3. *Study*. Meditate on what was read.

● Follow an acrostic study scheme (SPECS). Read a passage and find:

> S — sin to forsake
> P — promise to claim
> E — error to avoid
> C — command to follow
> S — some new thought about God

(Not all passages will contain each of the five points.)

● Focus on just one verse and:

> A — apply it to yourself
> E — emphasize each key word (usually nouns and verbs) and what it means to you
> I — illustrate the verse
> O — other verses that add to the thought
> U — use it in your life

● Use a concordance to trace a particular subject throughout the Bible.

For variety you may also want to try:

● Asking the Lord to place a specific Scripture book and chapter in your mind. Then read it and look for specific treasures.

● Read the chapter of Proverbs corresponding to the day of the month. If you accompany that with five psalms, you will complete the Books of Proverbs and Psalms in one month.

● Supplement your Bible reading with a classic devotional diary. One of the best is *My Utmost for His Highest* by Oswald Chambers (Westwood, N.J.: Barbour & Co., 1963).

● Purchase a "promise box," available at many Christian bookstores. Pull one out of the box at intervals: mull over the verse as you walk through your day.

● If you have young children around and it's almost impossible to find regular Bible reading time, try leaving a Bible open to specific passages in a strategic location around the home. The kitchen counter, your bedroom, the bathroom, or laundry area are possible places.

And don't forget memorization. It's one of the best ways to put God's Word into your life.

The Source of Power

A leader's life must be characterized by prayer. Prayer is our power source. No matter how well organized a program is, if it is not bathed in prayer, it will not achieve its full potential. Pray regularly for those women with whom you work. You may be the only person praying for them.

There are many biblical examples of men and women who prayed in connection with a specific ministry.

Daniel is a great example of preceding ministry with prayer. He asked his friends to pray that the God of heaven would reveal the mystery of the king's dream to him (Dan. 2:14-19). King Darius decreed throughout his kingdom that God was the true God as a direct result of Daniel's unceasing commitment to prayer even in the face of possible death in the lions' den (Dan. 6).

Nehemiah prayed his way through the rebuilding of the wall around Jerusalem (Neh. 1:4).

Esther requested all the Jews in Susa to fast and presumably pray for her as she went to the king to request clemency for the Jews (Es. 4:16).

Jesus went off into the mountain to pray prior to the calling of the twelve disciples (Luke 6:12-16).

Years ago, an older woman who was my mentor in many areas said, "Carol, never engage in more ministry than you can actively support in prayer." I agreed in principle, but I often took on more ministry than I could possibly support in prayer.

It's still a struggle to keep a balance between ministry activities and prayer time. However, I know from personal experience the difference between working for the Lord with and without adequate prayer support. The difference is the impact of that ministry on the lives of others.

Do you want the Holy Spirit's power flowing out through you? Then PRAY! Humble yourself to enlist others to pray for your ministry, and faithfully pray for theirs.

Making Prayer Important in Your Life

Prayer is more than coming to God with a shopping list of requests. It is communion with God. In addition to intercession, it should involve thanksgiving, confession, and especially worship.

In his helpful study, *True Worship* (Chicago, Ill.: Moody Press, 1982), John MacArthur, Jr. defines worship as honor paid to a superior being. He describes proper worship as a matter of discipline — we must train ourselves to meditate on God. "True meditation is based on information. . . . When you discover a great truth about God, begin to meditate on that truth until it captivates every element of your whole thinking process. Then meditation will give rise to worship" (p. 88).

Brother Lawrence, in *The Practice of the Presence of God* (Old Tappan, N.J.: Fleming H. Revell, 1963, 14, 17, 30–31), writes of this same process:

> . . . we should establish ourselves in a sense of God's presence by continually conversing with Him . . . that in order to form a habit

of conversing with God continually, and referring all we do to Him, we must first apply to Him with some diligence; but that after a little care we should find His love inwardly excite us to it without any difficulty. . . . The time of business does not with me differ from the time of prayer, and in the noise and clatter of my kitchen, while several persons are at the same time calling for different things, I possess God in as great tranquility as if I were upon my knees at the blessed sacrament.

As growing, serving, Christian women, we too should experience the same joy in conversing with God while engaged in our personal equivalent of scrubbing pots and pans.

The following ideas will help you maintain a heightened awareness of God's presence. They will also help you intercede more effectively. Satan will fight to keep us from daily worship and deliberate intercession. Don't be discouraged. If you become bored with a particular prayer project lay it aside and try something else. The important thing is that you pray!

1. *Choose a time and place free from distractions.*
   - early in the morning or in the evening after the house is quiet
   - when the children are at school or are napping
   - in your car during your lunch hour at work
   - while walking

Find a place that works for you. If that place becomes the place where you worship, the very act of going "there" will set the stage for communion with the Lord.

Vary your positions when you pray: sit, kneel, lie on the floor, walk, raise your hands. You want to express humility, openness, and dependence on God.

2. *Focus your thoughts on God.* Begin with worship. Reflect on who God is and what He has done. He is a holy God for whom nothing is impossible. Worship takes time; you can't expect to rush into God's presence and feel as if you are there right away.

Begin by reading a psalm. Read slowly, meditatively. Think about the meaning of each of the key words. In worship, your goal is not to read large portions of Scripture. You will develop your own list of favorites. Try Psalms 3, 27, 40, 51, 86, 90–91, 100, 111, 145.

You may want to incorporate music into your worship. Use hymns and praise songs. Songs that speak directly to God are good for worship. (See the references at the end of the chapter.)

3. *Have a framework for your prayers.* You may want to try something like this acrostic.

A — adoration of God.

C — confession of sins. Review your day and acknowledge any sinful attitudes or actions. Keep short accounts with God so your worship and intercession won't be hindered.

T — thanksgiving, especially for answered prayer. Feeling grateful isn't enough. We should express our appreciation in words of thanksgiving and praise.

S — supplication. Supplication or intercession is often a large part of prayer. The following points will help you be more effective:

4. *Use Scripture as a pattern for prayer.* Pray with your Bible open. Insert your name or others' names into the passages. Pray the content of the verse into the life of the one you are bringing before God. Examples:

Ephesians 6:13 — "I pray that (person's name) will put on Your full armor, God, so that when the day of evil comes she may be able to stand her ground, and after she has done everything, to stand."

Colossians 1:10 — "I pray that (person's name) may live a life worthy of You and please You in every way: bearing fruit in every good work, growing in the knowledge of You."

5. *Keep a written, dated prayer list.* In the margin note when God answers your prayers. You can develop this into a notebook divided into various sections:

● family needs

● local church needs: pastor, staff, key women leaders, women's ministries activities

● church needs worldwide: glean from denominational newsletters and nondenominational publications

● missions: use your church's list of missionaries or a day-to-day guide for praying for the world like, *Operation World* (Fort Washington, Penn.: WEC International, 1978)

● evangelism; unsaved friends and family

● national and local leaders

● current events; glean from newspaper headlines

● workplace concerns

You may want to write out some of your prayers and include them in the notebook. Writing prayers can help you keep your mind focused. It also gives you a record of your spiritual growth in prayer.

6. *Develop a pattern that helps you be consistent.*

● Pray for specific concerns on specific days of the week.

● Pray about three key events and three key people each day

● Pray through your church directory, interceding for different families each day.

7. *Be sensitive.* Maintain a listening spirit throughout the day so you

hear the Spirit speak to you about people needing immediate prayer.

8. *Do a Bible study on prayer.* A particularly good workbook for this is Kirkie Morrissey's, *On Holy Ground* (Colorado Springs: NavPress, 1983).

Journaling

Many women find it helpful to use a devotional diary, often referred to as a journal, in which to jot down thoughts from the Lord. Effective leadership depends on knowing yourself as well as knowing God. One of the best ways to know yourself and God is through active journaling. Putting your thoughts into words will help you untangle them; you will know what you are thinking.

When I first began journaling, I didn't realize I would also use my journal in ministering to others. Writing it seemed a very private, personal thing to do. But now there is so much useful material to share with others. Many times the very passage and subsequent thoughts written in the morning are exactly what I need to share with a hurting woman later in the day. The Holy Spirit will operate through you as you write in your journal. Pay attention to certain themes He is developing in you.

Give journaling a try. Don't connect it with writing papers in school. No one is going to grade it.

Let's Begin

Buy a spiral-bound notebook, a composition book, or a bound "blank" book. Write the year in the front of the book. Before you make a day's entry, write the date at the top of the page. Always write in ink for neatness and to preserve what you write. Keep your pen with your journal.

Try to write daily. Write when you are the most spiritually alert. In a year you will have developed a lifetime habit. Save your journals. They form a record of your spiritual journey as well as your personal biography.

What to Journal

- what you did the previous day, people you met, lessons you learned, sins you recognized and confessed
  - thoughts that come to you during your quiet time
  - musing on what God may be doing in your life
  - thoughts and feelings that flood your inner spirit
  - your relationship with your family and friends
  - your fears and sense of weakness
  - your wrestling with God over specific areas of obedience or disobedience

- prayers when your mind can't concentrate on praying
- your exaltation in the nearness of God
- passages of Scripture during special study times
- poetry you write or copy from elsewhere
- meaningful quotes from books you read
- sketches you draw to illustrate Scripture in your life

Choices

In the old poem, "Invictus," William Henley concludes with, "I am the master of my fate: I am the captain of my soul." The truth is we are *not* the master of our fate; that is in the hands of God. Yet to us God has committed the responsibility of making choices that can determine our eternal future and, to a great extent, the direction of our lives on earth.

The most important decision we make concerns our relationship with God. Have I been born into His family? Will my inner being be filled with His Spirit? Will the very tenor of my existence reflect the fact that I belong to the Lord? Will I be fully available to God to be all that He wants me to be and all that I need to be for the women around me?

Bibliography

Briscoe, Jill. *Running on Empty*. Dallas, Texas: Word Publishing, 1988.

Brother Lawrence. *The Practice of the Presence of God*. Old Tappan, N.J.: Fleming Revell, 1958.

Chambers, Oswald. *My Utmost for His Highest*. New York: Dodd, Mead and Co., 1963.

Christensen, Chuck and Winnie. *How to Listen When God Speaks*. Wheaton, Ill.: Harold Shaw Publishers, 1978.

Foster, Richard. *The Celebration of Discipline*. New York: Harper and Row Publishers Inc., 1978.

Foster, Robert. *Seven Minutes with God*. Colorado Springs: Navpress.

Klug, Ronald. *How to Keep a Spiritual Journal*. Nashville, Tenn.: Thomas Nelson Publishers, 1982.

MacArthur, John. *True Worship*. Chicago: Moody Press, 1982.

MacDonald, Gail. *High Call, High Privilege*. Wheaton, Ill.: Tyndale House Publishers, 1981.

Mayhall, Carole. *From the Heart of a Woman*. Colorado Springs: Navpress, 1976.

Packer, James I. *Knowing God*. Downers Grove, Ill.: InterVarsity Press, 1973.

Sanders, J. Oswald. *Spiritual Leadership*. Chicago: Moody Press, 1980.

Terabassi, Becky. *Releasing God's Power, Let Prayer Change Your Life*. Nashville, Tenn: Thomas Nelson Publishers, 1990.

White, John. *Daring to Draw Near*. Downers Grove, Ill.: InterVarsity Press, 1977.

Winward, Stephen. *How to Talk with God*. Wheaton, Ill.: Harold Shaw Publishers, 1973.

The following books contain music which directs the Spirit to worship and praise.

Worship Him. Compiled by Jesse Peterson and Mark Hayes, distributed by Alexandria House, P.O. Box 300, Alexandria, IN 46001, 1983.

Praise Worship. Compiled by Dan Burgess, Integrity Music, Inc., P.O. Box 16813, Mobile, AL 36616, 1988.

Exalt Him! Songs for Celebration and Praise. Compiled by Tom Fettke, Word Music, P.O. Box 1790, Waco, TX 76796, 1988.

Scripture in Song. Compiled by David and Dale Garratt, Scripture in Song, P.O. Box 550, Highway 55, Virgil, ONT L0S 1T0, Canada.

CHAPTER THREE

Equipped for Ministry — Part One

This chapter focuses on God's part in preparing you for ministry. The next chapter deals with your part. God's part began before your birth. He told Jeremiah, "Before I formed you in the womb I knew you, before you were born I set you apart" (Jer. 1:5). He planned your body and personality (see Ps. 139:13-16). During the course of your life He has allowed a variety of experiences, those you have considered good as well as those you have thought unpleasant, to further mold you. Then at new birth He gave you spiritual gifts with which to minister.

Let's take a look at these three areas.

- temperament
- life experiences
- spiritual gifts

God Wants to Use Your Temperament

When God made you, He carefully knit you together so that your personality would mesh with the spiritual gift you would receive at your new birth. The right sperm and egg, carrying the precisely correct genetic information joined to form each one of you. Your personality is no surprise to God. Psalm 139:15, NASB refers to you "(being) skillfully wrought."

At new birth you became a new creature (2 Cor. 5:17) and were indwelt by the Holy Spirit (1 Cor. 3:16). All the potential that the Creator built into you in the beginning can now be realized through the sanctifying process of the Holy Spirit. He wants to fully indwell you and use you, releasing you from the chains of your past. (Florence Littauer, in her book, *Your Personality Tree* [Dallas, Texas: Word Publishing, 1986] has a good discussion of how family relationships and circumstances can mask and thwart your natural temperament.)

There is an excellent diagnostic tool available from the Carlson Learning Company called the *Performax Personal Profile*. It's inexpensive and self-grading. It will be helpful to you as an individual, but is even more powerful when used in a group context.

The following synopsis of this test, referred to as the DISC, will give you a feel for its helpfulness. At the end of the chapter is an adaptation of the DISC material included by permission of the Carlson Learning Company.

Overview of the four temperaments

The "D" stands for "DRIVER." This woman is a task-oriented, stick to business, individual who thrives on difficult assignments and wants immediate results. In her push to get results she may offend more sensitive individuals.

Her preferred work environment includes power, authority, prestige, a wide scope of operations and freedom from controls and supervision. In addition, she is likely to get bored unless there are many new and varied activities to challenge her. She will help your women's ministry organization run with any new project. Provide her with checks and balances even though she may chafe under them.

The "I" describes the "INITIATOR." She initiates with people and works through them to get results. Surround her with lots of people, assure her of having fun in the project, and she will do anything within her power for the team. She is verbal, generates enthusiasm, loves participating in a group, and truly desires to help others.

The work environment which will let her accomplish the most includes social recognition, freedom of expression, group activities, democratic relationships, and use of counseling skills. She needs others who will concentrate on the task at hand, take a logical approach, and insist on timely follow-through with her projects.

These first two temperaments are both initiators, the "D" with projects, the "I" with people. The last two temperaments are primarily responders, the "S" to people, the "C" to projects.

The "S" stands for "STEADY." As a team member she usually concentrates on one task, is a great listener, and responds well to sincere appreciation. "Steadies" are usually highly skilled in specialized areas and are a blessing to all on a committee. Often your best decorators and craft women are of this temperament. They have the patience and stick-to-itiveness to see intricate tasks to completion.

To keep her working happily assure her that you will not rock her boat by changes without lots of warning signals. She does not like work infringing on home life, as home relationships are of great importance to her. She prefers traditional procedures and opportunity to maintain long-term relationships.

The "C" describes the "COMPLIANT." But she is anything but compliant to another's wishes. Her goal is for others to comply to her high standards. For that reason, many refer to her as "COMPETENT."

The Competent woman likes a clearly defined task, stability, and limited risk-taking. She's diplomatic, a critical thinker, always checking the accuracy of others. She can be very assertive, or competitive if combined with the "I" trait. When in combination with the "D," this lady can set the world on fire.

Her best work environment will include standard operating procedures, reassurance that things are being done right, others who are personally responsive to her effort, and door openers who will call attention to her accomplishments. I have seen this temperament pushed aside and wasted on committees because C's will not force their strengths on others.

At the end of the chapter is an instrument that will help you identify your temperament. It is an adaptation of the DISC. Check the appropriate boxes to identify your strengths and weaknesses. Through the years God will work in you to maximize your strengths and minimize your weaknesses. Give Him free rein to work for His glory in your life.

Using the DISC in a team context

The DISC lends itself well to a team context, since its focus is on interpersonal relationships. An entire group of women (like the women's ministry council) can take it and then discuss what they discovered about themselves, and how they interact in a group. Write the Carlson Learning Company (P.O. Box 59159, Minneapolis, MN 55459) for their tool or use the chart at the end of this chapter. Set aside several hours to share your findings with one another. Discuss what traits you checked and how you responded to what they showed. After an individual shares, the others should provide insight from their past interactions with her which either confirm or question the conclusions. The tone of the whole discussion should be supportive and helpful. Pray for each other before and during the sharing.

Use this temperament information to place the right women in the right position in your women's ministry council. More will be accomplished and each member will be happier if her role is consistent with her personality strengths. I am an "I" type individual who has often served in a "D" or "C" capacity as a detailed organizer. I have recently been replaced in a key ministry area by someone who has great God-given ability to administrate details. Praise God we are created differently.

Let's celebrate those differences and use them for the glory of God.

However, don't box yourself in and say you can only function in one particular mode. God may need to use you in ways that aren't consistent with your basic temperament. Stay flexible. Things-oriented "Drivers" can pay attention to details as well as to people. People-oriented "Initiators" can stay home and write books. "Steadies" can adjust to change and work at a faster than normal speed. "Competents" can leave a job less than perfectly done to meet the needs of people around them.

God Can Use Your Life Experiences

God is the divine Author of all of our lives. Psalm 139:16 says, "All the days ordained for me were written in Your book before one of them came to be."

All that you experience is meant by God to receive double use. First in producing maturity in your life and then by being worked out in the lives of others. The Apostle Paul was able to help others based on all that he had been through (2 Cor. 11:23-29). He told the Corinthians that God comforts us in all our troubles, so that we can comfort those in any trouble with the comfort we ourselves have received from God (1:3-7).

Be transparent. Let your life provide light for other women. I know this is hard, particularly in the difficult areas of your life. Yet it is precisely in the difficult areas that other women need to see how God has been the Rock of Refuge for you. A new friend of mine is bringing women to Christ because she is open about how He is helping her deal with some enormously difficult things in her life.

Look over the list of life experiences below. Check those you have been through. Ask God to use each one for His glory. (This list can also be used as a tool by your women's ministry in developing a pool of women able to comfort and encourage others who are going through similar difficulties.)

____ Death of your husband
____ Divorce or marital separation
____ Death of a close family member or friend
____ Remaining single
____ Your own illness or injury
____ Losing a close friendship
____ Fired from your job
____ Dissatisfied with your current job
____ Having a husband who travels a great deal
____ Retirement — you or your husband

_____ Major change in a family member's health
_____ Pregnancy
_____ Unwanted pregnancy
_____ Miscarriage
_____ Stillborn infant, or sudden infant death
_____ Older parents moving into your home
_____ Son or daughter leaving home
_____ Trouble with in-laws
_____ Unresolved bitterness within your family
_____ Absence of romantic love in your marriage
_____ Low self-esteem
_____ Problems with teenagers (drugs, rebellion, pregnancy)
_____ Chronic fatigue
_____ Loneliness
_____ Menstrual, physiological problems
_____ Aging
_____ Depression
_____ A major geographical move
_____ Alcoholic parents
_____ Abused as a child
_____ Relative/friend with AIDS

God Gave You Spiritual Gifts

(This section was adapted from material by Ruth Barton.)
God has given each of us spiritual gifts which He intends for us to use in building up the body of Christ, "But to each one of us grace has been given as Christ apportioned it . . . to prepare God's people . . . so that the body of Christ may be built up" (Eph. 4:7, 12). These gifts are supernatural abilities given by the Holy Spirit for the purpose of ministering to one another.

According to 1 Corinthians 12:7, 11, they are given arbitrarily and for the good of all. The Holy Spirit does not give us spiritual gifts for the purpose of serving our own egos, but to serve God and one another.

You have at least one spiritual gift. The key to identifying your gifts is your willingness to try new areas of service and to grasp opportunities which the Lord brings your way. As you serve willingly and faithfully, you will begin to identify areas in which the Lord has gifted you. Ministry is service; it is giving of your time and energy to meet the needs of others. One gift/ministry is not more important than another.

That has been abundantly clear as I've watched our new church grow over the last four years. Since we are renting a school, the church must be set up and taken down weekly. We are as dependent on the set-up crew as we are on the preacher. The coffee servers are as key as the door greeters. We celebrate the different ways God has gifted us.

I rank at the bottom of the scale in the gift of serving. This lack of serving gift became crystal clear to me one morning six years ago. My husband was teaching an all-day Saturday seminar at church. Someone had to go early, start the coffee, and lay out fruit and sweet rolls. Not wanting to ask someone else to plug in the coffee at 7 A.M. (I also do not have the gift of administration) I decided I would do it.

All week long my family lived with a grumbler. It wasn't the hour that annoyed me, I'm an early riser anyway, it was the task I disliked. When I lay out food, it just looks "laid out" not "an inviting feast to the eye and palette." Had I been going to counsel, teach, or encourage another person, I would have been thanking the Lord all week for the opportunity. Knowing and using your gift makes such a difference in your attitude toward ministry as well as its results.

Discovering your spiritual gifts

The best way to discover your spiritual gifts is by trying lots of different ministries. After you have had considerable experience, ask yourself:

- What types of ministry do I enjoy most?
- What types of ministry weigh heaviest on my heart?
- In what types of ministry have I seen positive results? Not so positive results?
- What spiritual abilities do others see in me?
- Which ministry am I asked to do again and again? Never asked to do again?
- Which of my natural abilities could be used in a spiritual capacity?
- What types of ministry mesh with my God-given temperament?

The Spiritual Gifts Inventory at the end of this chapter can help you discern or affirm your giftedness.

Developing your spiritual gifts

Though you might not realize it, you will begin developing your gifts while you are in the process of finding them. Once you do know your gift, then focus on it. Don't waste it by trying to develop your weaknesses instead of concentrating on your strengths. Ask the Lord to open a door or show you a place to serve where your gifts can be developed. Pray for the discipline needed to use your gifts to their fullest potential.

In chapter 4 of *The Making of a Leader* (Colorado Springs: NavPress, 1988, 81) Robert Clinton discusses the need to develop spiritual gifts. "The need to do a responsible job in ministry leads to awareness of the need to expand ministry skills. . . . The potential leader . . . recognizes a gift or two and has some skills for exercising his gifts. He gravitates toward new ministry challenges and assignments that allow him to use his gifts more effectively." Clinton continues (p. 89), "Leaders who plateau early reveal a common pattern. They learn new skills until they can operate comfortably with them, but then they fail to seek new skills deliberately and habitually. They coast on prior experience."

Don't let this happen to you. Attend seminars relevant to your gifts. Ask the Lord to give you mentors who are several steps ahead of you. (Authors can mentor you through their writings.) Expect God to give you experiences which will develop your gifts.

If each person in a church, or on a women's ministry council, develops and then uses her gifts generously, several positive things will occur. Everyone will have a sense of worth and purpose knowing that God has a unique contribution for them to make (1 Cor. 12:15-21). Each person will be more enthusiastic and less frustrated and discouraged because they are serving where they are gifted rather than struggling where they aren't.

The body will be healthier and God's design for the equipping and maturing of the saints will be accomplished.

> Speaking the truth in love, we will in all things grow up into Him who is the Head, that is Christ. From Him the whole body joined and held together by every supporting ligament, grows and builds itself up in love, as each part does its work (Eph. 4:15-16).

Bibliography

Berry, Jo. *The Priscilla Principle, Making Your Life a Ministry.* Grand Rapids, Mich.: Zondervan Publishing House, 1984.

Heim, Pamela Hoover. *The Woman God Can Use.* Denver, Colo.: Accent Books, 1986.

Littauer, Florence. *Your Personality Tree.* Dallas, Texas: Word Publishing, 1986.

Mayhall, Carole. *Lord of My Rocking Boat.* Colorado Springs: Navpress, 1981.

MacDonald, Gail. *Keep Climbing.* Wheaton, Ill.: Tyndale House, 1989.

McRae, William. *The Dynamics of Spiritual Gifts.* Grand Rapids, Mich.: Zondervan Publishing House, 1976.

Mitchell, Marcia. *Giftedness: Discovering Your Areas of Strength.* Minneapolis: Bethany House, 1988.

Senter, Ruth. *Beyond Safe Places and Easy Answers*. Nashville, Tenn.: Thomas Nelson Publishers, 1987.

Wagner, C. Peter. *Your Spiritual Gifts Can Help Your Church Grow*. Ventura, Calif.: Regal Books, 1979.

STYLE OF MINISTRY INDICATOR

DIRECTIONS: In each of the following rows of four words across, place an X in front of the one word that most often applies to you. If there are two words that both clearly describe you, then mark them both, but select no more than two. If you reach a row of words that does not seem to apply to you at all, then skip that row. After completing the sheet, add up all the Xs in each of the four columns.

STRENGTHS

1. ____	Adventurous	____ Animated	____ Adaptable	____ Analytical
2. ____	Persuasive	____ Playful	____ Peaceful	____ Persistent
3. ____	Strong-Willed	____ Sociable	____ Submissive	____ Self-Sacrificing
4. ____	Competitive	____ Convincing	____ Controlled	____ Considerate
5. ____	Resourceful	____ Refreshing	____ Reserved	____ Respectful
6. ____	Self-Reliant	____ Spirited	____ Satisfied	____ Sensitive
7. ____	Positive	____ Promoter	____ Patient	____ Planner
8. ____	Sure	____ Spontaneous	____ Shy	____ Scheduled
9. ____	Outspoken	____ Optimistic	____ Obliging	____ Orderly
10. ____	Forceful	____ Funny	____ Friendly	____ Faithful
11. ____	Daring	____ Delightful	____ Diplomatic	____ Detailed
12. ____	Confident	____ Cheerful	____ Consistent	____ Cultured
13. ____	Independent	____ Inspiring	____ Inoffensive	____ Idealistic
14. ____	Decisive	____ Demonstrative	____ Dry Humor	____ Deep
15. ____	Mover	____ Mixes Easily	____ Mediator	____ Musical
16. ____	Tenacious	____ Talker	____ Tolerant	____ Thoughtful
17. ____	Leader	____ Lively	____ Listener	____ Loyal
18. ____	Chief	____ Cute	____ Contented	____ Chartmaker
19. ____	Productive	____ Popular	____ Permissive	____ Perfectionist
20. ____	Bold	____ Bouncy	____ Balanced	____ Behaved

WEAKNESSES

21. ____	Bossy	____ Brassy	____ Blank	____ Bashful
22. ____	Unsympathetic	____ Undisciplined	____ Unenthusiastic	____ Unforgiving
23. ____	Resistant	____ Repetitious	____ Reticent	____ Resentful
24. ____	Frank	____ Forgetful	____ Fearful	____ Fussy
25. ____	Impatient	____ Interrupts	____ Indecisive	____ Insecure
26. ____	Unaffectionate	____ Unpredictable	____ Uninvolved	____ Unpopular
27. ____	Headstrong	____ Haphazard	____ Hesitant	____ Hard-to-please
28. ____	Proud	____ Permissive	____ Plain	____ Pessimistic
29. ____	Argumentative	____ Angered Easily	____ Aimless	____ Alienated
30. ____	Nervy	____ Naive	____ Nonchalant	____ Negative Attitude
31. ____	Workaholic	____ Wants Credit	____ Worrier	____ Withdraw
32. ____	Tactless	____ Talkative	____ Timid	____ Too Sensitive
33. ____	Domineering	____ Disorganized	____ Doubtful	____ Depressed
34. ____	Intolerant	____ Inconsistent	____ Indifferent	____ Introvert
35. ____	Manipulative	____ Messy	____ Mumbles	____ Moody
36. ____	Stubborn	____ Show-Off	____ Slow	____ Skeptical
37. ____	Lord-Over-Others	____ Loud	____ Lazy	____ Loner
38. ____	Short-Tempered	____ Scatter-brained	____ Sluggish	____ Suspicious
39. ____	Rash	____ Restless	____ Reluctant	____ Revengeful
40. ____	Crafty	____ Changeable	____ Compromising	____ Critical

TOTALS ____ (D)   ____ (I)   ____ (S)   ____ (C)

SPIRITUAL GIFT INDICATOR

Check off all statements which are true of you or reflect your feelings.

1. _____ I do not think it is helpful to show sympathy to one who has sinned.
2. _____ I'm always looking for practical ways to help.
3. _____ I enjoy public speaking and teaching.
4. _____ I find it easy to motivate people to do the right thing.
5. _____ I feel people who don't tithe are missing out on a lot of blessing.
6. _____ I am a take charge person who can usually bring order out of chaos.
7. _____ I am very sensitive to the emotional state of others.
8. _____ It is wise to get the truth "out on the table," no matter how painful.
9. _____ When people are in my home, I like to wait on them "hand and foot."
10. _____ People often tell me that I helped them understand things.
11. _____ I get irritated with preachers who are always scolding the people.
12. _____ I am willing to personally sacrifice in order to meet someone's need.
13. _____ I can organize people and I delegate easily.
14. _____ I am an easy mark for stray animals, especially if they are hurt.
15. _____ I am greatly disturbed by sin in a person's life.
16. _____ I often stop to help motorists in trouble (if not dangerous).
17. _____ I prefer systematic Bible teaching over a series of unrelated topics.
18. _____ When people ask my advice, I suggest a definite course of action.
19. _____ God sometimes tells me how much to give and what to give it to.
20. _____ I enjoy a team effort more than doing the work myself.
21. _____ People in emotional distress often come to me for comfort.
22. _____ I can usually tell when someone is lying.
23. _____ I sometimes get irritated when others don't jump in to help.
24. _____ I find it easy to illustrate spiritual truths and make them clear.
25. _____ I tend to be optimistic — always giving hope.
26. _____ I can't understand why wealthy Christians don't give more.
27. _____ People who talk about problems, but never take action, irritate me.
28. _____ I am sometimes accused of being too soft on sin.
29. _____ Others sometimes accuse me of being blunt and undiplomatic.
30. _____ I find it almost impossible to say no to others.
31. _____ Disorganized messages (which have no outline) irritate me.
32. _____ Even in failure, I see the potential in people.
33. _____ It is exciting to give and see God give back so I can give again.
34. _____ I am a goal-oriented person.
35. _____ I am reluctant to confront people; I don't want to hurt them.
36. _____ The goal of preaching should be repentance, not enlightenment.
37. _____ I prefer a "behind the scenes" role. I am not an "up-front person."
38. _____ I get upset with people who use verses out of context.
39. _____ I am able to encourage others, even when I am suffering.
40. _____ I want to make more money to financially support the Lord's work.
41. _____ I am considered "pushy" and demanding — driving people to the limit.
42. _____ I love ministering to the sick, the poor, and the handicapped.

43. _____ I am impatient with preachers who fail to give an invitation.
44. _____ I find it difficult to delegate; it is usually easier to do the job myself.
45. _____ People kid me about being a "bookworm."
46. _____ People kid me about being a "cheerleader."
47. _____ I trust God to supply beyond my needs so I can give to others.
48. _____ Some say projects are more important to me than people.
49. _____ Others tell me I'm a good listener.

Now, transfer checks to the corresponding blanks below and add up the totals in each column. The highest possible score in a dominating gift would be 7.

1 _____	2 _____	3 _____	4 _____	5 _____	6 _____	7 _____
8 _____	9 _____	10 _____	11 _____	12 _____	13 _____	14 _____
15 _____	16 _____	17 _____	18 _____	19 _____	20 _____	21 _____
22 _____	23 _____	24 _____	25 _____	26 _____	27 _____	28 _____
29 _____	30 _____	31 _____	32 _____	33 _____	34 _____	35 _____
36 _____	37 _____	38 _____	39 _____	40 _____	41 _____	42 _____
43 _____	44 _____	45 _____	46 _____	47 _____	48 _____	49 _____
_____	_____	_____	_____	_____	_____	_____
Prophet	Server	Teacher	Encourager	Giver	Leader	Mercy Shower

This instrument was designed by Dr. Mark Porter, Church Growth Consultant with INTEREST MINISTRIES.

CHAPTER FOUR
Equipped for Ministry — Part Two

In the last chapter we looked at God's part in preparing you for ministry. This chapter is about your part; what you do with what He's given you. How you select your goals and priorities and manage your time will control the extent to which God can use you. The desire to be available to God for His use can be a great motivator in letting God make the most of who He has made you.

Let's think through these three areas together:

- setting your goals
- selecting your priorities
- managing your time

Setting Your Goals

Your goals will determine the direction of your life. You can be like the person James describes as "like a wave of the sea, blown and tossed by the wind . . . double-minded . . . unstable in all he does" (James 1:6, 8). Or you can set and trim your sail so that the ship of your life catches the wind of the Holy Spirit. Decide to set your sail!

Luke 2:52 forms a helpful framework when considering goals. Jot down a few personal goals in the four spheres mentioned in this verse.

- intellectual (increasing in wisdom)
- physical (increasing in stature)
- spiritual (increasing in favor with God) ·
- social (increasing in favor with people)

If goals will be reached they must be *measurable*. You must think about the time frame for reaching your goals. Without a specific time framework to check your progress the chances are you won't make any. If you have a spiritual goal to begin more way-of-life witnessing, then decide how many people you want to share with per week or month.

Goals must be *realistic*. We can get discouraged because we set ridiculously high goals. I have a pastoral care list assigned to me by our church elders. If I tried to call or see personally each woman on the list weekly, I would be totally discouraged. But I know that I can make six calls a week and usually see two women for coffee so I set my goal accordingly.

Your goals should be apparent from your behavior. If a goal is really a goal, it's going to affect your priorities and how you use your time.

Make sure you set goals for yourself only, not for those you live with or for other people in your church!

Selecting Your Priorities
Jesus' priority was doing the will of God, "I seek not to please Myself but Him who sent Me" (John 5:30). Doing the Father's will meant making people a priority. "When He saw the crowds, He had compassion on them, because they were harassed and helpless, like sheep without a shepherd" (Matt. 9:36). Your priorities should also involve people.

There is no such thing as a foolproof, once and for all way of looking at priorities. It sounds deceptively simple to say God first, family second, and others last. But life doesn't always go according to plan.

My plan and firm intention is to have a quiet time with God as soon as I return from walking early in the morning. However, since I do most of my husband's secretarial work, sometimes his deadlines override my schedule and it's late in the day before I have time alone with God. Is this good? No. Does it happen? Sure.

My primary priority at church is to meet first-time visitors and greet those new to the church. However, when my elderly mother is with me, taking care of her needs and sitting with her overrides the other priority.

My friend, Carol Treachler, has a helpful way of looking at priorities. She envisions three spheres, an inner core, a middle layer, and an outer crust. Each is free to move in relation to the other.

The *inner core* consists of our personal relationship with God. We could label it with Matthew 6:33: "But seek first His kingdom and His righteousness, and all these things will be given to you as well." When the core is solid it provides strength for the outer layers — otherwise we are stuck with Ping-Pong-ball thin priorities. When the outer layer gets dented, there is no resilience.

The *middle layer* is family and home. It includes you, your husband, and your children. If you are single your relationships are in this layer. If you don't take care of yourself and those close to you, physically, emotionally, and spiritually, you will have nothing to give to others. Unless you are handling your own home well you won't be equipped to manage the household of God (1 Tim. 3:1-6).

Finally the *outside crust* is the world around us. Each person's outer layer is unique. It's made up of job, friends, church, and ministry contacts. We can handle the outer crust well only when the inner two cores are stable. When trouble strikes any outer areas, it can be absorbed by a strong, resilient inner core. Our lives should resemble a baseball — able to be hit for a home run without being dented.

Managing Your Time

Unless there is some reason to use our time well most of us will live from day to day rather aimlessly. It's not until we want to use our time for some special purpose that we will concentrate on making the most of the hours God gives us.

When I was a young mother, it seemed all I could do to get through each day. I had no plan and little reason for doing any activity at a specific time of day. One morning a neighbor called to see if we could go shopping together. It was only 9 A.M. and I could tell from her conversation that all her basic household responsibilities were done. And she had one more child than I did! I was struck with the fact that I could do much better in managing my time if I really wanted to.

Some eight years later I heard the voice of God, as well as the voice of friends, speak to me about managing my time because it was of value to Him. He wanted to bring people into my life who either needed Him as Savior, or who needed help growing spiritually. To have time for ministry I would have to identify what was important in my life and then decide to do those things *whether I felt like it or not*. It's hard to make yourself do things you don't feel like doing. The essence of self-discipline is putting off self-gratification until later. The first step in managing your time better is being willing to deny yourself things that in themselves might be acceptable.

Jesus is a prime example of someone who was in perfect control of His time, yet never appeared hurried or harried. He had time for teaching (Matt. 5:1-2), for praying (14:23), for being alone (Mark 1:35-37), and for ministry (John 13–16).

When you get involved in women's ministries, every hour becomes precious. The idea of time management is not to work yourself into a frenzy but to properly use each minute God has given you.

Here are several small steps you can take to put your available hours to better use. Try the ones that appeal to you. Don't get overwhelmed or discouraged, just start where you are and allow God to work in your life so that your time is His time.

Carry a calendar notebook with you. I prefer the "month-at-a-glance" format as it encourages spreading the load out more evenly. Look at your calendar or check with other family members before agreeing to do something.

Spend a few minutes prayerfully planning a day's activities, either the night before or early in the morning. Take into account the 80–20 principle. Eighty percent of the job is done in the first 20 percent of the time. Don't waste time over-completing a task.

When you have lots to do, make a list. Assign priorities: A (top priority), B (medium priority) and C (lowest priority). You may be able to permanently put off Cs or delegate them. Delegate items you can't do, items that others can do better, or things you shouldn't be doing.

Keep a centralized "to do" list instead of pieces of paper and backs of envelopes in your purse. I use the back of my calendar notebook for this purpose. As you execute your list concentrate on one thing at a time. If you're sidetracked, get right back to the task at hand as soon as possible. If you think of other things you need to do, don't let them interrupt you. Jot them down on your "to do" list for later action.

Discipline your telephone time. If you suspect you're spending too much time on the phone, keep a record of the time spent on the phone for one week. When the phone rings, and you are too busy for what appears to be a lengthy call, say so, and reschedule the telephone call. Make telephone appointments just as you schedule other things. (Note: always ask when you are the caller, "Is now a good time to talk?")

Schedule relaxation days. If possible use them positively as days of reflective solitude with the Heavenly Father. Make Him Lord of your Sabbaths. Do whatever recharges your batteries. Read a good book. Take a walk with a neighbor. If you work outside the home, it might be relaxing to tear into that messy closet or clean the garage, if it relaxes you.

Get regular exercise. Your energy level will be higher because of it. You will sleep better, and need less sleep time. I can cut one hour from my required sleep by walking for thirty minutes in the early morning.

Take into account your natural energy highs and lows. I am normally a morning person so that's my time for high energy creative tasks and important problem-solving.

Keep your clothes mended and ready to wear. Go through your closet at least yearly and give away what you don't wear. Coordinate clothing around several key colors. If you don't know your best colors ask someone to help you discover them.

Define "neatness" in each area of your house. You need to know your goal when cleaning so you don't spend time over-cleaning. Each household item should have its own place so you'll know where to find it. When putting it away, you will also know where "away" is.

Plan your menus. This helps prevent last-minute trips to the store.

Clean your refrigerator before you go shopping. This will facilitate putting food away. Arrange your shopping list according to the order of items on the shelves at your market. Don't shop with anyone else. If possible do your shopping when you aren't hungry and the store isn't crowded.

Balance

We have briefly covered six life components in the last two chapters. The first three: *temperament, life experiences,* and *spiritual gifts* come from the hand of God. The last three: *goals, priorities,* and *time management* are our responsibilities. The ability to knit all these together in a balanced life comes from the Lord, who "in all things . . . works for the good of those who love Him" (Rom. 8:28).

Bibliography

Adeney, Miriam. *A Time for Risking, Priorities for Women.* Portland, Ore.: Multnomah Press, 1987.

Alexander, John W. *Managing Our Work.* Downers Grove, Ill: InterVarsity Press, 1975.

Barnes, Emilie. *More Hours in My Day.* Eugene, Ore.: Harvest House Publishers, 1982.

Dahlman, Dorothy. *Yes, God, I Am a Creative Woman.* Arlington Heights, Ill.: Harvest Publications, 1985.

Ecker, Richard E. *The Stress Myth.* Downers Grove, Ill.: InterVarsity Press, 1985.

MacDonald, Gordon. *Ordering Your Private World.* Nashville, Tenn.: Thomas Nelson Publishers, 1986.

Moravec, Marilyn, Pamela Heim, and Roberta Collins. *Push Me Gently, Lord.* Arlington Heights, Ill.: Harvest Publications, 1988.

Ortlund, Anne. *Disciplines of the Beautiful Woman.* Waco, Texas: Word Books Publisher, 1977.

Porter, Mark. *The Time of Your Life.* Kansas City, Kan.: Walterick Publishers, 1988.

Young, Pam and Peggy Jones. *Sidetracked Home Executives.* New York: Warner Books, Inc., 1981.

Winston, Stephanie. *Getting Organized.* New York: Warner Books, 1979.

CHAPTER FIVE
Leading So Others Will Follow

Major contributors to this chapter include Bev Hislip, Pat Smith, Marilyn Hoekstra, Dorothy Arnold, and Dr. Pamala Reeves.

In *The Making of a Leader* (Colorado Springs: NavPress, 1988, p. 14) Robert Clinton describes leadership as, "A dynamic process in which a man or woman with God-given capacity influences a specific group of God's people toward His purposes for the group." A leader, then, is a person who influences others. God is in the business of growing leaders — not the overnight variety, like Jack's beanstalk, but strong, oak tree types, able to withstand life's storms. Clinton outlines the growth process like this:

- Sovereign Foundations — your genetic and family background
- Inner Life Growth — getting to know God in a personal way
- Ministry Maturing — beginning to use your spiritual gifts
- Life Maturing — mature fruitfulness flowing from right priorities
- Convergence — reaching full potential through correct responses to God's work in your life
- Afterglow — recognition and indirect influence at broad levels

This chapter is designed to help you in your leadership development, no matter what stage you're in. It deals with:

- the qualities of a leader
- leadership styles
- motivation
- handling criticism
- managing meetings

There are many ways to use this material. As you read it, first apply it to yourself, noting areas where change or growth are needed. Then use each section as an outline for leadership training sessions. You can take the first fifteen minutes of your women's ministry council meetings for these mini-training sessions.

Qualities of a Leader
Spiritual qualities

- *An intimate relationship with God.* God's priorities are the leader's priorities, whether popular or not, whether to her personal advantage or not. She knows God and clings to His values despite their possible unpopularity.
- *Jealous for God's honor, not her own.* She evaluates herself and her motives: "Am I serving for my own acceptance? My own good? To meet my own ends? Whom am I serving: God, self, others?"
- *Devoted to prayer.* Prayer is a priority in her life. Her leadership is built on her relationship with God. Only as she serves Him with a clean heart can she lead in a way people will trust and follow.
- *Committed to God and His Word.* Her dependence is on God, not on herself. She knows the reality of God's empowering Spirit. She lives in obedience to His commands and believes He is able to do what He says.

Personal qualities

- *Integrity.* She is sincere and honest, practicing what she preaches. Her behavior is consistent with her beliefs. She has high moral standards. Her private life is consistent with her public life. She influences by what she is as much as by what she says.
- *Courage.* She is committed to doing God's will even when she is afraid, disturbed, or hurt. She moves ahead in spite of fear.
- *Vision.* She sets short and long-term goals and develops steps to reach them. She keeps her ultimate goal in mind and isn't distracted from where she wants to go.
- *A positive self-image.* Her leadership requires some sense of ease with herself, her task, and others. She has inner peace in the midst of outer turmoil which allows her to focus on the needs of others.
- *A teachable spirit.* A leader is a learner. When she makes a mistake she uses it as an opportunity to grow. She is vigilant about little things that can make a difference.

In addition to these qualities a good leader is someone who:

- *Thinks before acting.* She considers options, consequences, and results before she takes action. However, her pioneer spirit makes her willing to take risks to achieve a desirable result.
- *Faces and deals with issues.* She is willing to take an unpopular course when necessary. She perseveres in the face of problems. She

takes steps to meet needs she sees, refusing to accept the status quo.

- *Serves others.* She knows that in serving others she is serving God. She appreciates and supports others' suggestions.
- *Motivates others.* She is a facilitator of other people's strengths and draws out the best in them. She offers direction, encouragement, support, and hope.
- *Delegates to others.* She is realistic about her own limitations and perceptive of another's strengths. She pursues excellence.

The above positive qualities don't develop unopposed in our lives. There are many obstacles to overcome, both internal and external, on the path to effective leadership.

- *Poor self-image and crippling sense of inadequacy.* A leader keeps her eyes on the Lord, not on her shortcomings. She isn't paralyzed by her own high expectations or those of others (1 Cor. 1:27; 2 Cor. 12:9-10).
- *Discouragement, disappointment, and fear of failure.* These emotions come from time to time. But overall a leader trusts in God and expects His help as she attempts new things for Him.
- *Spiritual dryness.* To minimize this a leader tries to maintain a regular schedule of Bible study and prayer even when she doesn't feel like it. She checks her priorities and believes that worship before work brings renewal.
- *Relational conflicts.* She repents of unloving attitudes and jealousy when they surface. She keeps in check any need she feels to be in control.
- *Overload or burnout.* To avoid these a leader must learn her limits; learn to delegate; learn to say no with confidence that she is saying yes to God's priorities for her. Rest and relaxation are vital!
- *Conflicts with those in authority.* Sometimes this is unavoidable. A leader chooses to follow the structure of authority over her, seeking to respect it, cooperate with it, and submit to it.

There are also bad habits which must be avoided because they lessen a leader's effectiveness:

- compulsive talking
- habitual lateness
- critical spirit
- pettiness — seeing molehills as mountains
- lack of emotional control
- strong individualism which stifles teamwork
- passivity — overly reserved, limp
- overcommitment to many things
- laziness
- poor time management and priorities

Finally, here are four wrong motivations to be in leadership:
- because of pressure from others to become involved
- to receive prestige and admiration
- to fulfill a personal need for acceptance and approval
- to have power and authority over others

Leadership Style — Task or Relational

The more self-understanding we possess the better we will lead others. People have very different leadership styles based on their personality and experience.

A *task-oriented* person thinks, "I'm a goal-oriented person. It's important to me to complete a job I've started. For that reason I try not to waste time. I have a strong desire to do things better, to improve my performance constantly."

A *relationally oriented* person thinks, "I'm a role-oriented person. I'm very aware of what others are feeling and have strong emotional responses myself. It's important to me that people get along harmoniously. I've a strong desire to be with and enjoy people. I don't want to be left out."

Every group needs both styles of leadership. This test will reveal your leadership style. On the line in front of the questions, write

4 — if you always behave that way,
3 — if you frequently behave that way,
2 — if you seldom behave that way,
1 — if you never behave that way.

When I am a member of a group:

_____ 1. I give facts, ideas, opinions, information to help the group in the discussion.

_____ 2. I encourage the quiet members to participate. I am open to all the ideas in the group, and I let the members know I really value their contributions.

_____ 3. I ask for ideas and information from other group members.

_____ 4. I use good communication skills, and I help everyone understand what others have said.

_____ 5. I help keep the group moving and do not get sidetracked. I ask others to carry out certain things we have discussed.

_____ 6. I help the group enjoy working together. I will tell a funny story or do something to break the tension when it arises.

_____ 7. I sum up what's been said, pulling together various ideas and opinions.

_____ 8. I observe the way the group is working and point out to them what's happening so we can work together better.

_____ 9. I keep the group motivated to work toward its goals.

_____ 10. I bring out into the open any conflicts between members and try to help them resolve them so we can have more group unity.

_____ 11.I ask others to summarize group discussions and decisions to be sure they understand what's been said and done.

_____ 12.I express my appreciation for other group members and for their contributions. I let people know I accept them.

Add the scores from the odd numbered questions to get your task-action total. Add the scores from the even numbered questions to get your relational-action total.

To help you identify with each question they can be personified as follows:

Task-oriented

1. *Information and opinion giver:* Offers facts, opinions, ideas, feelings, and information. "Before we continue, let me tell you how other groups have solved this task."

3. *Information and opinion seeker:* Requests facts, opinions, ideas, feelings, and information. "I don't understand? What do you mean?"

5. *Direction and role definer:* Uses observations of how the group is working to discuss how the group can improve. "We need a timekeeper. Patricia, why don't you do that?"

7. *Summarizer:* Pulls together related ideas or suggestions and re-states them. "Linda's idea is related to Ruth's. I think they could be combined."

9. *Energizer:* Encourages group members to work hard to achieve goals. "I think we'd find a solution if we put a little more work into it."

11. *Comprehension checker:* Asks others to summarize discussion to make sure they understand. "Sue, tell us what we've said so far so we can see if we all understand it correctly."

Relationally oriented

2. *Encourager of participation:* Lets members know their contributions are valued. "Helen, I'd like to hear what you think about this. You have such good ideas."

4. *Communication facilitator:* Makes sure all group members understand what each other says. "Does everyone understand Pam's idea?"

6. *Tension releaser:* Tells jokes and increases the group fun. "I think Carla should sing her report on how the children's choir is coming along."

8. *Process observer:* Calls attention to needed tasks and assigns re-

sponsibilities. "We seem to be suggesting solutions before we're ready. Let's define the problem first."

10. *Interpersonal problem solver.* Helps resolve and mediate conflicts. "I think we should discuss the conflict between Doris and Linda in order to help resolve it."

12. *Supporter and praiser:* Expresses acceptance and a caring attitude toward group members. "I really enjoy this group. I especially enjoy Kayla's sense of humor."

Knowing and accepting your leadership style can help you maximize your strengths. It can help you understand those who are different from you. And it can also help you build a balanced leadership team.

Leadership Style — Autocratic, Democratic, or Laissez-faire
Beyond being task or relationally oriented there are other distinct leadership styles. Each of us is most comfortable operating within one of the following. Evaluate yourself and the needs of your group as you read this section. Pray for God to mold you and use you according to the need of the hour.

Autocratic
An autocratic leader dictates policy and makes major decisions. She gains obedience from the group by using formal authority, rewards, and punishment.

Autocratic leadership is most effective in emergencies and new projects. Groups with autocratic leaders have these characteristics:
- strong organization
- rigid standard operation procedures
- rigidity of control increases with group size
- information and ideas mostly confined to the leader
- most effective in emergencies
- fastest achievement, fewest errors

Democratic
A democratic leader allows group members to take part in policy-making by drawing ideas and suggestions from the group and encouraging mutual participation in decision-making (even though she may reserve the final decision for herself).

Democratic leadership is most effective in changing opinion. Groups with democratic leaders have these characteristics:
- high level of cohesiveness
- more mutual respect
- more social-emotional interaction

- most original effort
- individual's ideas are encouraged
- fewest complaints, highest member satisfaction

Laissez-faire

A laissez-faire leader is a facilitator who allows the group to make decisions. (This type of leader works best with a mature group.) She plays down her role in the group's activities and acts primarily to provide information, materials, and facilities for the group to accomplish its objectives.

Laissez-faire leadership is most effective in a group needing a facilitator. Groups with laissez-faire leaders have these characteristics:

- marked lack of organization
- more humor
- least hostility
- least productivity
- more group-minded activity
- group can feel abandoned, tuned out, or frustrated

There is no right or wrong leadership style, but there is a right or wrong style for a specific task which needs to be accomplished. To determine the leadership style your group needs, think through the circumstances it finds itself in. Assess its maturity, skills, and experience.

An autocratic leader usually is required at the beginning of a work. For example, Dawson Trotman founded the Navigators and Bill Bright founded Campus Crusade for Christ using autocratic leadership. These men had a vision, specific goals, and a strategy to accomplish those goals.

After a project's groundwork is in place, a democratic leader can step in to lead the group to growth.

If a group of mature, skilled people simply need a facilitator, a laissez-faire leader is the best choice.

Motivation

Motivation is that something within a person that excites her to action resulting in high energy output, commitment, and creativity. The leader's role is to provide a motivational climate that stimulates an individual's intrinsic motivation.

To be motivated people need a:

- sense of belonging
- share in the planning
- clear understanding of what is expected
- genuine responsibility and challenge

- feeling progress is being made toward original goals
- desire for recognition when it is due
- reasonable degree of security

Beyond these common basics, people are motivated by different things. Three drives which prompt people to action are the need for *achievement*, the need for *affiliation*, and the need for *influence*. A leader should know how to recognize these motivations in a person and how to work with her accordingly.

People motivated by the need for *achievement* spend time thinking about:

- doing their jobs better
- accomplishing something unusual or important
- reaching their goals
- overcoming obstacles

They are characterized by a:

- concern for excellence
- desire to do their best and to achieve unique accomplishments
- willingness to take personal responsibility for finding solutions to problems

Their goal is success as measured by improved performance and excellence.

People motivated by the need for *affiliation* spend time thinking about:

- wanting to be liked and how to achieve this
- consoling or helping people
- warm and friendly relationships
- their feelings and the feelings of others

They are characterized by a:

- preoccupation with being liked and accepted
- need for friendly relationships and interaction
- fear of being separated from other people (definitely not "loners")

Their goal is spending time with others and enjoying mutual friendships.

People motivated by the need for *influence* spend time thinking about:

- gaining influence over others
- using this influence to win arguments, change people, gain status and authority

They are characterized by a:

- concern for their reputation and position
- tendency to give advice (sometimes unsolicited)
- desire to have their ideas dominate

Their goal is having an impact or influence on others.

(The above material was adapted from Marlene Wilson's book, *How to Mobilize Church Volunteers* [Minneapolis: Augsburg Publishing House, 1983], 30–32.)

Here is a helpful tool you can use to assess your own motivational inclination.

Motivational Needs Survey

1. Describe a recent situation in which you experienced a sense of satisfaction and fulfillment.

Which statement most closely identifies this situation?

_____ a. a specific goal was accomplished
_____ b. a warm, fulfilling relationship was established
_____ c. a group of people was influenced

2. Which project would you most enjoy?

_____ a. a project in which you have the responsibility of finding the solution to a chronic problem in your organization
_____ b. a project requiring a cooperative effort with your peer group
_____ c. a project requiring you to direct and control the efforts of a group of people

3. Which option is the most satisfying to you?

_____ a. taking a calculated risk and seeing it pay off
_____ b. being accepted and liked by the group
_____ c. giving direction and supervision

4. Which option do you most enjoy?

_____ a. finding solutions to problems which prevent goals from being reached
_____ b. promoting harmonious relationships among those in your work group
_____ c. using persuasive skills to influence the work of others

5. Your closest friend would describe you as a person who:

_____ a. looks for greater challenges
_____ b. makes friends and acquaintances easily
_____ c. likes to participate in a good argument

6. What would be the most important factor in helping you accomplish your job or tasks?

_____ a. concrete feedback about how you are doing
_____ b. an opportunity to interact with others
_____ c. the amount of authority you can exercise

7. Describe the ingredients you would build into your ideal job assignment or task.

Which choice below most closely matches the most important ingredient you listed above?

_____ a. offers an opportunity to accomplish something significant
_____ b. provides an opportunity to work as part of a team
_____ c. offers an opportunity to influence significantly the efforts of others

8. At the end of a project, what type of reward would you prefer?

_____ a. personal satisfaction in knowing that a goal has been reached
_____ b. respect and admiration from your work group
_____ c. recognition and advancement through the formal organization

9. What do you think about when you daydream?

_____ a. accomplishing new and challenging goals
_____ b. warm, friendly relationships within the organization
_____ c. rising to the top of the organization

10. In a group situation, which would you prefer?

_____ a. to make the greatest contribution to the group
_____ b. to be the best liked person in the group
_____ c. to be the leader of the group

To determine your own motivational needs tally the number of:

_____ a. responses for achievement motivated
_____ b. responses for relationship motivated
_____ c. responses for influence motivated
(Taken from Motivation Seminar, Walk Thru the Bible Ministries, Atlanta, Ga. All rights reserved.)

Handling Criticism

Part of leadership involves learning how to give and receive criticism in ways that produce positive character change instead of defensive resistance.

Giving constructive criticism

1. *Pray* for wisdom to know when to speak and for courage to not keep silent when something needs to be said. Pray that you won't sow discord.

2. Express your criticism *directly to the person involved.*

3. *Go privately.* Matthew 18:15-17 gives good directions on how to confront a person. Don't criticize in a public setting unless there's no other way to solve the problem. If she fails to respond, inform her you may involve a third person. If it's impossible to convey the criticism verbally, use a letter. Always make a copy of a letter or any other written communication.

4. *Double-check your motives.* Ask yourself: Has my ego been hurt? Is my concern truly to help the other person and strengthen our Christian ministry?

5. *Speak the truth in love.* Loveless negative criticism is a prime component of worldliness. First Corinthians 13 says love should characterize all our relationships.

6. *Be honest.* Communicate accurately the needed information and your feelings. Honesty doesn't mean expressing all we think or feel. Don't say one thing to a person's face and another thing behind her back.

7. *Be objective and specific.* Objective means evidence which anybody can observe, evidence that's the same no matter who views it.

8. *Be as positive as possible.* Find two or three positive things to say for every negative you have to share. Don't attack. Allow the one being criticized to explain her position.

9. *Suggest alternatives.* Always accompany criticism with remedial suggestions. Volunteer at least a little assistance in helping to correct the situation.

Receiving negative criticism

1. *Ask God to guide* your response to the criticism: *to teach* you through it and *to help* you control your temper.

2. Don't *become defensive.*

3. *Let the critic finish.*

4. *Ask for evidence* upon which the criticism is based.

5. *Identify the real problem.* Also determine what are the underlying issues, the hidden factors.

6. *Identify your weaknesses and blind spots.*

7. *Determine why the critic has criticized.* Does she have needs which are revealed by her criticism?

8. *Discuss the criticism* with God and a friend.

9. *Learn* through the criticism. Ask yourself, "What is the Lord trying to teach me?" "How do others perceive me?"

10. *Decide what sort of response is needed.* Commit yourself to do whatever needs to be done to resolve the issues raised.

11. Carefully determine *how you should respond* (in person, letter, or telephone).

(This material was adapted from John W. Alexander's, *Practical Criticism: Giving It and Taking It* [Madison, Wis.: InterVarsity Press, 1976], 10–28.)

Handling Problem People

Meetings can be disrupted by problem personalities. Here are four a leader might encounter. There are times when any one of us might fit one of these descriptions, but these suggestions apply to situations where the action is a habitual characteristic.

Talkative Tess

Possible causes:

- overly eager
- show off
- overly talkative
- insecure

What you can do:

- Let the group take care of the person as much as possible.

- Wait until the person takes a breath, thank her for her input, and refocus the subject according to the agenda.

- Talk with her outside the meeting. Try to discover the real reason behind her behavior and deal with it.

- Final option; confront her directly with her problem.

Late Linda

Possible causes:

- doesn't think the meeting is important
- doesn't think the meeting will begin on time

What you can do:

- Begin the meeting on time.
- Don't stop the meeting to bring the late arrival up to speed.
- Talk with the person outside the meeting and encourage her to be prompt.

Silent Sue

Possible causes:

- shyness
- insecurity
- boredom
- superiority complex

What you can do:

- If she seems shy or insecure, compliment her when she talks.
- If she seems bored, arouse her interest by asking for her opinion on what's being discussed.
- If she seems to have a superiority complex, indicate your respect for her experience before asking her opinion.

Argumentative Alice

Possible causes:

- enjoys needling others
- insecurity

What you can do:

- Don't get upset.
- Try to find merit in one of her points.
- Express your agreement and then move on to something else.
- If she makes an obvious misstatement of fact, turn it to the group and let them correct it.

A Call to Action

Leadership is a call to action. It's also a call to hard work. But the labor has its rewards, like seeing people become believers and seeing disciples grow in their faith. The excitement of spiritual leadership is seeing lives changed.

Let God continue to use and develop your leadership abilities. Be content with what He's doing but eager for Him to do even more. Paul stated it well in Philippians 3:12 where he wrote, "Not that I have already obtained all this, or have already been made perfect, but I press on to take hold of that for which Christ Jesus took hold of me."

Press on!

Bibliography
Barber, Cyril J. *Jeremiah and the Dynamics of Effective Leadership.* Neptune, N.J.: Loizeaux Brothers, 1987.

Clinton, J. Robert. *The Making of a Leader.* Colorado Springs: Navpress, 1988.

Dayton, Edward R. and Ted Engstrom. *Strategy for Leadership.* Old Tappan, N.J.: Fleming Revell, 1979.

Eims, Leroy. *Be the Leader You Were Meant to Be.* Wheaton, Ill.: Victor Books, 1975.

Gangel, Kenneth O. *Competent to Lead.* Chicago: Moody Press, 1974.

Gangel, Kenneth O. *So You Want to Be a Leader.* Harrisburg, Penn.: Christian Publications, 1973.

Inrig, Gary. *A Call to Excellence.* Wheaton, Ill.: Scripture Press, 1985.

LePeau, Andrew. *Paths of Leadership.* Downers Grove, Ill.: InterVarsity Press, 1983.

MacDonald, Gordon. *Restoring Your Spiritual Passion.* Nashville, Tenn.: Thomas Nelson Publishers, 1986.

Sanders, J. Oswald. *Spiritual Leadership.* Chicago: Moody Press, 1980.

CHAPTER SIX
Starting a Women's Ministry

Major contributors to this chapter were
Bev Hislip and Marilyn Hoekstra.

Lay the Foundation

The purpose of a women's ministry is to provide vision and coordination for the outreach and inreach ministries of women in the local church. Through the smooth functioning of the women's ministry council women with gifts are connected to people with needs so that the body functions to the glory of God.

The council works under the authority and direction of the pastor/elders in the church. The fields of service of the council might include: evangelism, new believer follow-up, Bible studies, general pastoral care (both in crisis and in ongoing life problems), and service to the body (e.g., church dinners, nursery care, community outreach, and foreign missions).

The first step in developing such an organization is for either the church leadership or a concerned woman to ask God for a small group of godly, ministry-oriented women to lay the groundwork. These women may become the council or act as a pre-council steering committee. Final selection of the council should be made in agreement with the pastoral leadership. Avoid taking a vote among the ladies as a method of selecting leadership. Feelings will get hurt and the best women may not be selected.

The most efficient council size is between three and seven members. A term of office of two to four years will allow opportunity for many women to serve on the council. In addition it will give women an opportunity to rotate off without feeling like they are quitters.

The steering committee should communicate frequently with the church leadership in the early stages of planning. This is particularly important if the original motivation for the ministry came from women alone instead of from the overall church leadership team. Identify a specific individual on the pastoral staff as liaison with the women's ministry. This might be the senior pastor, an elder, or deacon depending on your church structure.

At the inception of the ministry determine how it will be funded. This might occur in any of the following ways:

● Through regular church offerings. In this case the appropriate financial officer reimburses the women for expenses submitted.

● Through fees built in for each project. Examples include dinners, seminars, and retreats.

● Through special offerings taken at the time of the event plus amounts needed from the church budget.

Qualifications for Council Members

Women should be selected on the basis of character, leadership, ability, and age. Use the material in the previous chapter to help you identify potential leaders. Be realistic in your appraisal; no one is perfect, we're all in process.

If possible the following leadership/personality styles should be represented on the council.

● a *driver/doer* who is able to initiate projects, delegate wisely, and monitor progress.

● an *initiator* who is outgoing and knows the women in the church.

● a *good listener* who will work hard to maintain personal relationships and likes to specialize in specific ministries.

● a *quality-controller* who likes working with details and will see that a standard of excellence is maintained in the ministry.

Resist the temptation to form a council of women with similar temperaments. The council might get along better, but it would lack balance. I am an "initiator." I love people and want to have a good time. However, I have trouble with follow-through in projects and I don't always accurately evaluate people's motives and abilities. I tend to see people in light of what they *could* become instead of what they currently are. Too many women like me on a council and the job would not be well done.

It's ideal to have a wide range of age/experience on the council. Include career women, mothers of young children, and older women. Younger women may not have as much experience or maturity, but their perspective is needed.

Council Structure

Select a coordinator. She should be an organizer and diplomat, with sufficient time to give to the ministry. How much time will depend on the stage of development of the ministry, its complexity, and the size of the church. In the larger church this individual often serves in a staff position.

Appoint a secretary to take minutes and remind people about responsibilities. She is responsible to take clear notes and distribute the minutes within a week of the council meetings.

Your third selection should be a treasurer. This task can be combined with the secretary in a small church. She will oversee expenditures of monies and submit a budget to the church financial officer. She should see that a budget is prepared for each event. Include such expenses as child care, promotion, postage, decorations, speakers fees, and transportation. Balance these expenses with the ticket cost of the event, anticipated offerings, or amounts provided from the general fund of the church. Make every effort to stay within your budget. This effort will be appreciated by your church treasurer and be rewarded by God who requires us to be good stewards.

The treasurer might also establish a policy regarding scholarships. You may have women who would benefit from attending a particular event but cannot afford it. On the other hand some of your women may have extra money and desire to help others attend — protect the anonymity of receivers and givers.

Next plan the organizational structure of the council. Each woman should select a particular area of responsibility according to her interests and experience, even though at times the council will work on projects and ministries as a unit. The coordinator, secretary, and treasurer might also lead key ministries, depending on their interests and time available.

In her helpful book, *How to Grow a Women's Minis-Tree* (Regal Books, 1986, 55–60), Daisy Hepburn, likens the structure of a ministry to a tree. The image of a tree has the following advantages:

- It is a live image.
- It has unlimited growth potential.
- It is designed to produce desired fruit.
- The branches are interdependent.
- It is easily understood.
- It provides a place of refreshment.
- It grows upward, taking the major responsibility off the director.
- It has a stable root system.
- It is extremely versatile.
- It allows for pruning without in any way damaging the other

branches. Pruning one branch allows greater strength to flow to other branches.

In her model the *roots* serve as the authority for the ministry. In your church this might include the Bible, board of elders, deacons, pastor, or other governing group. The *trunk* represents the administration — the officers of your council. The *branches* are the general areas of your ministry. They might include: outreach, spiritual growth, service, missions, hospitality. On the branches are the *twigs*. Here are the actual ministries — the activities of your ministry. For example, Bible studies, prayer, and discipling are on the spiritual growth branch.

Many councils find it easier to work with a more traditional organizational chart, but I think it is helpful to maintain a tree mind-set even if your organizational chart is traditionally drawn. (See Figures 1 and 2.)

The Work of the Council
Importance of Prayer in Planning

This ministry must be saturated with prayer. You are developing a ministry, a vehicle for the Holy Spirit to touch lives, not organizing a business venture. Spend as much time as possible in prayer. Begin and end your meetings with each of you praying. If you come to a point in your meeting when you are frustrated and do not know what the next step is, stop and pray. God promises wisdom; we do not need to flounder along without His specific help. "If any of you lacks wisdom, he should ask God, who gives generously to all without finding fault, and it will be given to him" (James 1:5). God does not expect us to get along without His help; it is abundantly available when we ask in faith.

Closely tied to prayer is the issue of waiting on God. Our timing is not always His timing. When we wait on the Lord, we gain new strength (Isa. 40:31). One of the reasons for this added strength may be that in God's timing we do not have to bang our heads against a brick wall. When His light is green, energy is not drained away in fruitless effort. If you run into overwhelming resistance when beginning a new women's ministry in your church, or in reorganizing an existing ministry, back off, continue to pray and wait for God's timing. However, even when done on God's timetable expect roadblocks that need to be overcome through much prayer and effort.

Work with, not against your church's philosophy of ministry

Determine from your church leadership what style of ministry is suitable for your women's ministry. The style depends on the overall philosophy of ministry. Every church has a philosophy of ministry. It may be precisely stated or it may exist as a general understanding. A philosophy of

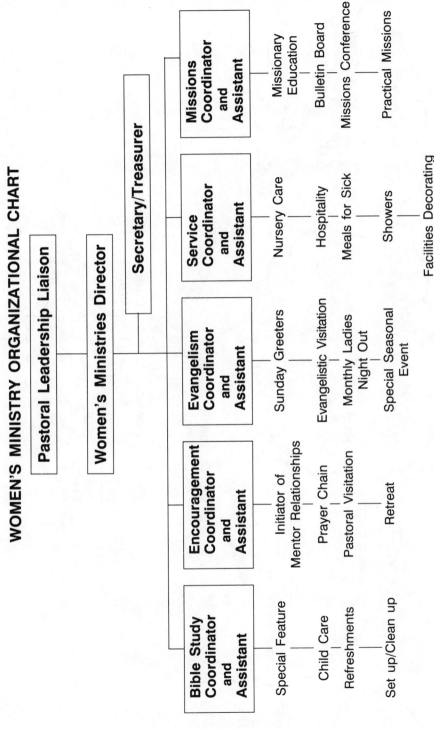

WOMEN'S MINISTRY ORGANIZATIONAL CHART

Pastoral Leadership Liaison

Women's Ministries Director

Secretary/Treasurer

Bible Study Coordinator and Assistant
- Special Feature
- Child Care
- Refreshments
- Set up/Clean up

Encouragement Coordinator and Assistant
- Initiator of Mentor Relationships
- Prayer Chain
- Pastoral Visitation
- Retreat

Evangelism Coordinator and Assistant
- Sunday Greeters
- Evangelistic Visitation
- Monthly Ladies Night Out
- Special Seasonal Event

Service Coordinator and Assistant
- Nursery Care
- Hospitality
- Meals for Sick
- Showers
- Facilities Decorating

Missions Coordinator and Assistant
- Missionary Education
- Bulletin Board
- Missions Conference
- Practical Missions

Figure 1

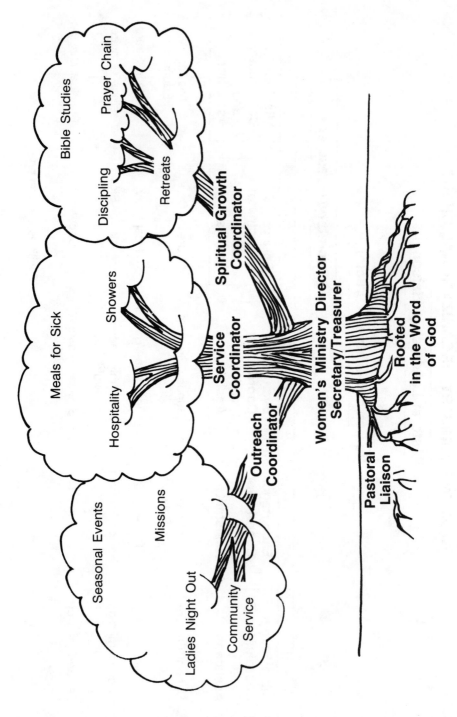

Figure 2

ministry answers the question, "Why do we conduct ministry as we do?" It determines the direction and style of ministry.

If your church does not already have a clearly stated philosophy of ministry, talk to your leadership about it. A women's ministry should not run on a third track headed by its own engine. It is a car pulled down the same track as the rest of the church. The train engine is guided by your pastoral staff and is fueled by the philosophy of ministry.

Examples of philosophies of ministry include the following:

- The classroom church

Focus: Bible lecture

- The life-situation church

Target: unbelievers

- The tall steepled, liberal church

Focus: Eucharist, formality, social issues

- The rock generation church

Target: baby boomers, contemporary, informal

- The "spiritual high" church

Target: Believers who need a strong emotional experience on a weekly basis

The philosophy of ministry will affect the following elements of your women's ministry:

- Leadership style — Is it authoritarian or participatory, or somewhere in between? Leadership style will affect how much freedom the women have to make their own decisions.
- Felt need of attenders — Consider: socioeconomic profile, culture, educational level, occupation, hurts, interests. The average educational level may affect the selection of Bible study material. The socioeconomic profile may affect community services offered such as food pantry or clothing closet.
- Charismatic viewpoint — Is your church charismatic, non-charismatic, open, anti-charismatic?
- Pastoral care structures — Especially if your church is larger than a single cell (more than 100) it is important to know where the pastoral care takes place. Is it within your home groups, special interest groups, Sunday School classes? To what extent will women's ministry be responsible for the pastoral care of women attending its programs?
- Evangelistic strategy — Is it structured around a specific evangelism program, such as Evangelism Explosion? Is your Sunday morning service planned with the unbeliever in mind? Will your women's ministry be responsible for training or encouraging evangelism? Should a clear Gospel be presented at women's events? Is a public invitation given? How is follow-up of new believers handled?

(This section was developed from "The Pastor's Update," vol. 1, no. 10, July 1990 published by Charles E. Fuller Institute of Evangelism and Church Growth.)

All of these issues do not need to be addressed at the inception of the ministry, but you need to be aware of them and how they will impact your ministry development. When you develop a new ministry, ascertain that it fits within the guidelines established by your church's philosophy of ministry.

Determine a Tentative Plan of Action

After receiving a green light from your leadership and understanding the philosophy of ministry, determine a general plan of action. Ask, "What will we do first?" "What additional ministries might we add next year?" Start small. The best place to begin is usually with a Bible study. Then you might add one or two outreach events, such as a mother/daughter brunch, or a dinner with a holiday theme. Add a retreat and begin to develop a one-to-one discipling ministry as leadership becomes available. Add ministries according to the needs. Later chapters will describe organizational steps for key ministries.

If your church has had a women's ministry for many years that needs revitalizing, your "first step" may be to talk to those currently in charge. Don't disparage the existing ministry. Encourage and get behind its programs where you can. They might want to become a part of the new council, or continue as they are apart from your new organization. Be flexible. Your way is not the only way to get things done! Above all, be willing to change things slowly. A battleship takes fifteen miles to reverse its course. The average church takes three years to develop a full women's ministry. Even then, because the body of Christ is a living organism, change will continue to occur.

Council Meetings

In the initial stages of the new ministry you'll want to meet frequently, perhaps weekly. Eventually, when the various branch committees are functioning well, monthly meetings should be sufficient. (In a small church the ministry can be carried out by the council itself without the additional branch structure.) Plan your meetings at a time convenient for everyone involved. Some councils meet in a businesslike setting in a committee room at church. Others prefer the informality of a home — perhaps including a meal. Many will need to meet in the evening to accommodate working women.

Assign a portion of each meeting to leadership training. This might include book reports, videos, studies on pertinent Bible passages, or reviews of seminars attended by a group member. Encourage one another to grow in leadership ability as well as in the Christian faith. Some councils might build in accountability for such things as Scripture memorization, personal quiet times, pastoral care, or lifestyle witnessing. Plan to attend any area seminars that will provide new vision and increase your ability to minister to the women in your church. Avoid stagnation.

Include some friendship-building activities in your times together. You will profit from letting your hair down and becoming real with one another. If your church is large the council members may not even know one another. Even in a small church it's possible for individuals who have attended for years to not know each other well. Plan a yearly retreat for the council where you can lay out plans for the coming year, do more intensive leadership training, and have fun together.

Managing Meetings

Meetings are an integral part of the life of a council. They are essential for communication and team-building. But they can also create frustration and waste valuable time.

It's the responsibility of the council coordinator to set the tone of the meeting before it even begins, to keep it moving in the right direction, and to end it on time. Follow these steps for a productive meeting.

1. *Set the agenda* before the meeting and mail it to the committee members (see sample agenda).

2. *Set the stage with your opening comments.* State clearly the purpose for the meeting and write the key agenda items on a display board or overhead projector.

3. *Prioritize the agenda* into A's and B's. Place A-1 beside the most important item, A-2 beside the next, and so forth. All A's must be covered at this meeting. Place B-1 and so forth beside items that can wait.

4. *Always deal with A's first.* Juggle the agenda, but deal with the A-1 while fresh. Don't be diverted by believing the B-15 consideration will "just take a minute."

5. *Assign time limits.* Post a discussion time limit for each item. This keeps members focused on important issues and helps discourage digressions.

6. *Appoint a timekeeper.* Necessary equipment: a watch and a voice to announce, "We've already spent ten minutes on the potluck and we have posted only two minutes."

7. *Refer to committee whenever possible.* Assigning tasks to a committee, with plans to report back at a future meeting, is sound management practice. It expands spiritual service, saves valuable time, and keeps meetings moving.

8. *Cross off each item when completed.* As each item is decided, deferred, or dismissed, cross it off the agenda, allowing everyone to see progress and to note unfinished business.

9. *Make allowances for uniqueness.* For some committee members making decisions produces anxiety. They always want more information before arriving at a decision. For others, anxiety is created by what appears to be "endless hashing and rehashing of a subject." Keep your meeting moving by carefully managing the needs of both groups. Remember, those who are cautious keep a committee from making hasty, imprudent decisions; those who are decisive help a committee take action.

10. *Be kind to yourself.* Only so much can be accomplished in any one meeting. Meetings move when there is structure and encouragement for presenting and exploring ideas. A perfect answer does not need to be found for every problem. Don't force every issue to a conclusion.

11. *Draw to a close on a constructive note.* During the course of the meeting remind the group of its progress. Give clear summaries often. When time is almost up, give directions for the final few minutes.

12. *End on time.* Sometimes even with A's defined, great time keepers, and willing committees, an important item remains uncovered by the designated ending time. Stop the discussion. Summarize the options. Do they want to continue or not? If there is no agreement, the coordinator assumes responsibility for deciding whether to continue, to schedule another meeting, or to appoint a committee. If you decide to continue, always allow those needing to leave a graceful exit. At the end of the meeting thank everyone for coming, set the next meeting date, and conclude with a time of prayer.

SAMPLE AGENDA

Women with Heart Ministries Meeting
7:30 P.M. July 9, 1990

Prayer Time

Principles of leadership from the life of Deborah — Judges 4–5

Branch Reports
Outreach Branch
- Evaluation of pool party
- Preview of plans for attending Pumpkin Festival
- Update on missions education and promotion
- Other items?

Spiritual Growth Branch
- Evaluation of summer Bible studies
- Preview of plans for fall studies and retreat
- Discussion of how to increase attendance at Sat. prayer meetings
- Other items?

Caring Branch
- Discussion of how to minister more effectively to new mothers
- Recruitment of new leader for Dial-a-Meal ministry
- Other items?

Service Branch
- Reorganization of coffee service on Sunday morning
- Preview of plans for Christmas craft day
- Other items?

Other items of business
- Do we need to expand our committee?
- Finalize plans for attending area seminar on biblical counseling

Prayer Time

Next meeting — Aug. 22 at Linda's. Bring a swimsuit and towel for the hot tub after the meeting.

Ministry Descriptions

These are several benefits to writing out ministry descriptions:

- It makes you carefully think through and crystallize the content of the ministry.

- It helps in the recruitment of volunteers and makes it easier for women to find ministries which fit their gifts and abilities.

- It provides a standard for evaluating performance.

This can be a lengthy task, particularly if you're starting from scratch or if you have a lot of descriptions to write. Don't tackle them all at once. Start with the most acute need or with the particular ministry you're currently trying to staff.

At the end of this chapter are some sample ministry descriptions of the positions suggested in the material above. Specific ministry descriptions will vary according to the size and administrative style of the church. The gifts, temperament, and experience of the women doing the ministry should also be reflected in the description.

MINISTRY DESCRIPTION
Women's Ministry Director

MINISTRY GOAL:
   To set the vision for and oversee the activities of women's ministry in the church ("The buck stops here.")

QUALIFICATIONS:
   • Public and private life above reproach
   • Consistent, vibrant walk with Christ
   • Faithful, available, and teachable
   • A minimum of three years membership in the church
   • Approval of the church elder/pastor(s)/staff and the blessing of her husband, if married
   • Prior experience on the Women's Ministry Council
   • Administrative skills — able to follow-through on details

RESPONSIBILITIES:
   • To set and maintain the vision for women's ministries
   • To oversee all of the women's ministry activities
   • To work closely with the pastoral leadership team and to keep them informed about women's ministries
   • To chair women's ministry meetings
   • To stay in contact with women's ministry coordinators and to pastorally care for them

ORGANIZATIONAL RELATIONSHIPS:
   • Responsible for: Women's Ministry Coordinators
   • Responsible to: Pastoral leadership of the church (a specific person — pastor, elder — should be named)

TIME REQUIRED
   (Time spent will vary greatly according to church size, complexity of programs, and availability of support help. The estimated time for YOUR church should be spelled out here.)

LENGTH OF MINISTRY:
   One year minimum (two years is better; she must train her replacement before she retires).

MINISTRY DESCRIPTION
Bible Study Coordinator

MINISTRY GOAL:
To coordinate the planning and implementing of weekly women's Bible studies.

QUALIFICATIONS:
- Public and private life above reproach
- Consistent, vibrant walk with Christ
- Faithful, available, and teachable
- A minimum of three years membership in the church
- Understands the needs of those who attend the studies
- Able to teach or supervise those who can
- Administrative skills — able to follow-through on details

RESPONSIBILITIES:
- To appoint committee members as needed to help organize women's Bible studies.
- To chair monthly committee meetings.
- To oversee the recruiting and training of teachers, discussion leaders, and others to work in this ministry.
- To plan study content (perhaps writing study material).
- To evaluate class mechanics and general effectiveness.

ORGANIZATIONAL RELATIONSHIPS:
- Responsible for: Bible Study Committee members
- Responsible to: Woman's Ministry Director

TIME REQUIRED
(Time spent will vary greatly according to church size, complexity of programs, and availability of support help. The estimated time for YOUR church should be spelled out here.)

LENGTH OF MINISTRY:
One year minimum (she must train her replacement before she "retires").

MINISTRY DESCRIPTION
Encouragement Coordinator

MINISTRY GOAL:
　To develop and oversee those areas of women's ministry which are specifically designed to encourage the believer in her walk with Christ.

QUALIFICATIONS:
- Public and private life above reproach
- Consistent, vibrant walk with Christ
- Faithful, available, and teachable
- Able to motivate people
- Able to delegate
- Administrative skills — able to follow-through on details

RESPONSIBILITIES:
- To appoint committee members as needed to help organize encouragement ministries.
- To chair monthly committee meetings.
- To oversee the recruiting and training of women to work in encouragement ministries.
- To stay alert to the spiritual needs of the women in the church and to plan ministries to meet those needs.
- To be aware of new women entering the church and to help them get involved in women's ministry.

ORGANIZATIONAL RELATIONSHIPS:
- Responsible for: Encouragement Committee members
- Responsible to: Women's Ministry Director

TIME REQUIRED
　(Time spent will vary greatly according to church size, complexity of programs, and availability of support help. The estimated time for YOUR church should be spelled out here.)

LENGTH OF MINISTRY:
　One year minimum (she must train her replacement before she "retires").

MINISTRY DESCRIPTION
Evangelism Coordinator

MINISTRY GOAL:
   To see people come to Christ through the evangelistic efforts of women's ministries.

QUALIFICATIONS:
   - Public and private life above reproach
   - Consistent, vibrant walk with Christ
   - Faithful, available, and teachable
   - Strong interest and personal involvement in evangelism
   - Able to work well with people
   - Administrative skills — able to follow-through on details

RESPONSIBILITIES:
   - To appoint committee members as needed to help organize evangelism ministries.
   - To chair monthly committee meetings.
   - To oversee the recruiting and training of women to work in evangelism ministries.
   - To stay aware of the needs and the evangelistic opportunities in the community.

ORGANIZATIONAL RELATIONSHIPS:
   - Responsible for: Evangelism Committee members
   - Responsible to: Women's Ministry Director

TIME REQUIRED
   (Time spent will vary greatly according to church size, complexity of programs, and availability of support help. The estimated time for YOUR church should be spelled out here.)

LENGTH OF MINISTRY:
   One year minimum (she must train her replacement before she "retires").

MINISTRY DESCRIPTION
Service Coordinator

MINISTRY GOAL:
 To develop and oversee those areas of women's ministry which are specifically designed to care for the practical needs of the body.

QUALIFICATIONS:
 - Public and private life above reproach
 - Consistent, vibrant walk with Christ
 - Faithful, available, and teachable
 - A heart for the hurting and needy
 - Able to recruit, organize, and delegate
 - Awareness of church and community needs
 - Administrative skills — able to follow-through on details

RESPONSIBILITIES:
 - To appoint committee members as needed to help organize service ministries.
 - To chair monthly committee meetings.
 - To oversee the recruiting and training of women to work in service ministries.
 - To stay aware of practical needs within the body and to create opportunities for women to give and receive practical expressions of Christian love.

ORGANIZATIONAL RELATIONSHIPS:
 - Responsible for: Service Committee members
 - Responsible to: Women's Ministry Director

TIME REQUIRED
 (Time spent will vary greatly according to church size, complexity of programs, and availability of support help. The estimated time for YOUR church should be spelled out here.)

LENGTH OF MINISTRY:
 One year minimum (she must train her replacement before she "retires").

MINISTRY DESCRIPTION
Missions Coordinator

MINISTRY GOAL:
   To help fulfill the Great Commission in its broadest sense by promoting and supporting in every way possible the missionary outreach of the church.

QUALIFICATIONS:
   • Public and private life above reproach
   • Consistent, vibrant walk with Christ
   • Faithful, available, and teachable
   • A heart for missions and an understanding of the life of a missionary (personal missions experience helpful)
   • Ability to organize and administrate programs, conferences, etc
   • Administrative skills — able to follow-through on details

RESPONSIBILITIES:
   • To appoint committee members as needed to help organize missions ministries.
   • To chair monthly committee meetings.
   • To oversee the recruiting and training of women to work in missions ministries.
   • To encourage prayer, communication, and financial support of the church's missionaries.
   • To work with other ministries within the church to promote missions through every means possible.
   • To assist missionaries on furlough.

ORGANIZATIONAL RELATIONSHIPS:
   • Responsible for: Missions Committee members
   • Responsible to: Women's Ministry Director

TIME REQUIRED
   (Time spent will vary greatly according to church size, complexity of programs, and availability of support help. The estimated time for YOUR church should be spelled out here.)

LENGTH OF MINISTRY:
   One year minimum (she must train her replacement before she "retires").

CHAPTER SEVEN
Staffing a Women's Ministry

Survey Your Women

After the initial planning and formation of the council, the next step is to survey all the women in your church. A survey will do two things. It will help you identify the ministry needs of your women and locate those who can meet the needs.

No one ever gets 100 percent return on a survey, but distribute to achieve maximum return. Try passing it out when many of the women are together, such as at a Bible study or church meeting. Have them complete and hand it in as they leave. Alternatively, you can mail it with a stamped return envelope. If your church is small, you can conduct the survey by telephone or in person.

Don't do a survey until you are ready to use the results. To do so will lead to credibility loss. Only solicit information you need for the next year, not for the indefinite future. Many churches take a survey yearly.

A good survey will tell you:

- *who* the women are
- *which* current ministries they are interested in
- *what* their needs are
- *how* they can minister to others

The survey can be short and to the point.

- Include a place for their name and phone number (both daytime and evening).
- List the current or anticipated ministries with a box to check whether they wish to attend or help (e.g., ladies Bible study, prayer chain).
- List specialized skills or interests needed in your ministries with appropriate boxes (e.g., craft skills, meal preparation and service, word processing).

- Ask about any special needs/interests they might have.

This information can be obtained on a single piece of paper.

A survey can also be longer and ask for more details about the woman herself as well as break down ministry areas into smaller segments. See samples of both types of surveys at the end of this chapter.

Stages in a Woman's Life and How They Affect Her Ministry

In addition to taking the survey it's important to understand the stages in a woman's life and to be sensitive as to how they affect her desire and ability to be involved in ministry. Even a small church will have women in many of life's stages. Some women will be in a particular stage by choice, others perhaps by unwanted circumstances. Take this into account in developing your programs, recruiting leadership, and encouraging attendance.

You want to include everyone who would like to participate in women's ministries without making anyone feel guilty if she's unable to be involved at certain stages in her life. The following section, written by Ruth Barton and Grace Thornton, both young mothers in greater Chicago, will increase your sensitivity as well as provide you with ministry ideas.

Here, then, are some of the stages, along with:

- possible limitations inherent in each stage
- ways to increase your sensitivity to the women experiencing these limitations
- possible ministries appropriate at that time of life

This list isn't exhaustive, but it's intended to stimulate your thinking. Instead of assuming that everyone fits precisely into one of these stages, get to know the individual women in your church so you can better understand their particular situations.

Single, Career Woman

Possible limitations

- She may be carrying tremendous responsibility alone: job, financial security, maintaining living quarters, and social life.
- She may feel she has no peer group in the church, particularly if she is over thirty and other singles in the church are young college students.
- She may feel a lack of intimacy in general, and especially with other women in the church. She may feel she has nothing in common with the other women in the fellowship.
- She may be struggling with accepting her singleness.

Growing in sensitivity

- Analyze your own feelings about singleness. Remember that the New Testament affirms singleness.
- Include singles in fellowship social gatherings.
- Treat singles as adults rather than as overgrown teenagers by offering them positions of real responsibility. This will help them to feel like a part of the fellowship.
- Remember that just because a single woman doesn't have a husband or children doesn't mean she doesn't have a social life. Don't overburden singles by delegating too many tasks to them.

Possible ministry opportunities

- Leading/attending an early morning Bible study/prayer meeting.
- Women's ministry lending librarian.
- Encourage her in any ministry she is interested in.
- Professional women may have high-level skills (attorney, accountant, board member, editor, investment banker) and may be more interested in nontraditional ministry roles. Encourage them to contribute their expertise. One such woman designed a computer program to follow-up all visitors at her church. Another who worked professionally in a Christian organization dealing with child evangelism did all her church's Sunday School leadership training.

Young Married Woman

Possible limitations

- She is making many adjustments.
- She may need to work outside of the home, which will take much of her time and energy.
- She, along with her husband, may not be ready for commitment to a particular church.

Growing in sensitivity

- Get to know young women and their husbands.
- Don't push them. Realize that they need time with their husbands and time in their home. Remember Israel's one-year rule for newlyweds!

Possible ministry opportunities

- Attending evening Bible studies.
- Working along with her husband in the Sunday School.
- Using craft skills with a decoration committee for special events.
- She is often better used in short-term rather than long-term commitments.

- Depending on spiritual maturity, she may be a candidate for discipling or able to follow-up new believers.

Mother of Young Children

Possible limitations
- She is under much stress just keeping her family and home running smoothly.
- She lacks time and energy for outside ministries.
- She lacks time for personal spiritual renewal or preparation for ministry.
- She may be experiencing marital difficulties.
- Her young children limit the types of ministries in which she can participate.

Growing in sensitivity
- Get to know a mother's individual needs. Realize that she may be experiencing feelings of inadequacy, frustration, and isolation.
- Encourage her in practical ways through notes, phone calls, baby-sitting, and so on. To help a mother with young children to participate in ministry, team a young mother with an older woman who would enjoy spending time with her children.
- Be flexible with her because she constantly must adjust to her family's changing needs.

Possible ministry opportunities
- Encourage her in short-term commitment ministries.
- Depending on interest and skill, use her on decorations, making name tags, or food preparation for special events.
- Encourage her attendance at the daytime ladies Bible study. Be understanding if her attendance is sporadic due to illness of children.
- If she is equipped by experience and temperament to be a discussion leader at a Bible study, use her, but give her a co-leader who will be regular in attendance.
- Help her discover her spiritual gifts, so that when she does minister, it is satisfying and fruitful.

Mother of School-age Children

Possible limitations
- This woman's biggest limitation is that she is so tied to her children's school schedules and extracurricular activities that her days are very segmented and she often feels like a taxi driver.

Growing in sensitivity

- Affirm her involvement in her children's school activities and her desire to be available to her children.
- Help her feel comfortable when she has to leave church functions early to pick up a child.
- Keep her schedule in mind as you schedule women's meetings.
- Resist the urge to suggest that she leave her children with a neighbor. This usually is much easier said than done.

Possible ministry opportunities

- Encourage her in all those listed for the mother of young children.
- Give her training in any gift areas discovered. These are her years to build for mature ministry when her children are gone.
- Encourage her to mentor/disciple younger mothers.
- Encourage her in hospitality to newcomers.
- If administrative, she might be available for committee leadership.

Working Mother

Possible limitations

- She is under so much pressure juggling two full-time jobs, career and wife/mother, that she may not have time or energy for outside ministry.
- She may not have time to build friendships with other women in the church so she may not feel like part of the fellowship.

Growing in sensitivity

- Realize she may be feeling guilty for not staying at home with her children. Don't increase her guilt by making judgmental comments, such as, "If your children were important to you, you wouldn't work."
- Understand her need to spend time with her family in the evenings and on weekends.
- Encourage her to be involved in women's ministry at whatever commitment level she's able.
- Acknowledge that she may have professional skills she can use within the church.

Possible ministry opportunities

- Encourage her participation in a low-commitment ministry such as telephone prayer chain.
- Provide Bible studies at a time convenient for her.
- Help her discover her spiritual gifts, so that when she does minister it is satisfying and fruitful.

Single Mother

Possible limitations
- She's so busy working outside the home and caring for her children alone that she may not have any time for ministry.
- She may feel judged by the people of the church. She also may feel guilty about the breakup of her marriage. These feelings may make her feel like an outsider in the church.

Growing in sensitivity
- Don't judge or condemn her because she's a single mother. Instead, be friendly, accepting, and supportive.
- Offer to baby-sit occasionally so she can have time away from her children. Watch her children while she attends the women's retreat and becomes spiritually renewed.

Possible ministry opportunities
- Encourage her to minister in short-term opportunities according to her interests.
- Provide opportunities to serve on a rotating basis in service ministries such as coffee preparation for Sunday morning.
- Ask her to bring food for special events. Make it clear that a bought dessert is satisfactory.
- Place her in responsibilities where she will have time to talk to other believers while she ministers. Christian friendship is one of her greatest needs.

Mother of Teen/College Children

Possible limitations
- She may be emotionally drained from coping with her child's rebellion and struggle for independence and from helping her children make important decisions.
- She may be juggling several stages at once: younger children, aging parents, working mother.
- She may be experiencing her own mid-life crisis.

Growing in sensitivity
- Know the individual situation. Don't judge availability by appearances only.
- Understand she may feel very inadequate to minister. Conflicts with her rebellious child may leave her feeling she has more questions than answers.

- To help mothers of teens realize they aren't alone, encourage women who have passed through this stage to share their own similar struggles.

Possible ministry opportunities

- If this woman isn't bogged down by difficult circumstances, she may be ready to accomplish significant ministry, either within the women's ministry or within another arm of the church.
- Beginning leadership in any aspect of ministry according to her gift/interest is most appropriate.
- Encourage training to enhance use of her gift. Give her good books to read.
- Disciple her into appropriate ministries.

Empty Nest Woman

Possible limitations

- She may be experiencing loneliness, personal identity crisis, or depression which is paralyzing her.
- She may be experiencing adjustments in her marriage now that the children are no longer at home.
- She may lack confidence in herself and doubt her self-worth.

Growing in sensitivity

- Don't assume she has it all together.
- Do be aggressive in drawing her in and letting her know she is needed. She has much time, energy, and experience to offer.
- Be understanding, but encourage her not to wallow in depression and waste this stage of relative freedom.

Possible ministry opportunities

- This is the group that will carry the bulk of your ministry load.
- Place them in charge of committees for all aspects of ministry.
- Encourage them to try new ministries. Help them keep growing.
- Watch for burnout in women at this stage. They are likely to take on more than they can accomplish.

Caregiver (woman caring for aging parents or husband)

Possible limitations

- She faces heavy physical responsibilities, difficult decisions, and emotional stress. She also may be mourning the loss of a parent, spouse, or other loved one.

- Her time and energy may be depleted.
- The pressure in her life may far outweigh her joy.

Growing in sensitivity

- Realize she may not be able to participate at all or may have to back off commitments she already has made.
- Give her plenty of space but be available for listening or providing practical help such as offering to stay with the ill family member so she can get a break.

Possible ministry opportunities

- Give her tasks that can be done in short segments of time. This might include phoning, sending out cards to remind others of ministry responsibilities, etc.
- If she's able to be regular in church attendance use her in ministry that does not require significant midweek preparation.
- Encourage her attendance at evening midweek Bible studies.

Senior Woman

Possible limitations

- She may be experiencing fatigue and/or illness.
- She may feel she has done her ministry duty in the church and now it's someone else's turn.
- She may be experiencing dissatisfaction regarding her own life.
- She may not have transportation to get to church.

Growing in sensitivity

- Treat her with respect.
- Plan activities especially for the senior women.
- Visit her, give her rides to and from fellowship activities, and listen with interest to stories from her past.

Possible ministry opportunities

- Help her feel wanted by affirming her ability to have a strong prayer ministry. Keep her informed about prayer needs and answers to prayer.
- She has much practical experience; ask for her advice on important issues.
- If health and energy allows she might take an important part in ministry to other seniors.

Staffing Your Ministries — Getting and Keeping Volunteers
Every church has occasional trouble staffing ministries. I was recently amazed to find that a large church in Southern California closed pre-school classes when they were not adequately staffed. An attractive sign on the door stated, "Due to understaffing of the preschool, this class will not meet. Please take your child into the worship service with you." Somehow, I had supposed this particular church had all their staffing problems solved! In a strange way I was encouraged.

Staffing may be less of a problem in Women's Ministries than else-where in the church. Particular programs can be initiated or terminated depending on interest level and availability of leadership. The tree mod-el for ministry structure discussed in the previous chapter makes it easy to both initiate and terminate ministries depending on needs, interests, and availability of leadership. The following guidelines will assist you in recruiting the best possible leadership:

Pray earnestly before recruiting. Pray in your council meetings before selecting key leaders. If you don't have almost unanimous agreement on a particular selection, postpone it until you do. Expect God to show you whom to ask to do what.

Observe the women in your church. Look for evidence that indicates they're ready to get involved. In my own church a woman is usually ready for some task after she has regularly attended for three to six months. The type of ministry will determine the qualifications you're looking for. Do not always look for the most mature person. Young women with potential are wonderful candidates for many leadership po-sitions. They will grow into maturity if they are guided by someone with more experience.

Interview the prospective ministry candidate. Do this in person, either at church or over coffee at a convenient restaurant. Ask her about her per-sonal needs and goals. Show concern for her as a part of the church. Let her know she's important and valuable whether or not she volunteers.

Give her time to respond. Allow adequate time for making an informed decision. Encourage the woman to check with her family, particularly her husband, if she's married. If temperament and gifting aren't clearly known, help her discover these. Find out what ministries she is best suit-ed for.

When a volunteer commits to a ministry it's important that you:

Define expectations. Clearly define ministry expectations and antici-pated length of service in a written job description. Go over it with the person to prevent surprises over time required or responsibilities involved. Build in enough flexibility so the individual can adjust the job to fit herself as she goes along.

Give adequate on-the-job support. Praise her work wherever possible. If she's a Bible study leader, provide her with enough information to fully prepare. If she organizes the food service for a dinner, publicly thank her at the time of the event and also send her a note of thanks.

Make meetings efficient. No one likes to attend meetings that accomplish little of real value. Meetings should include fresh input for personal growth, adequate prayer time, and an agenda that covers the necessary business (see chap. 6 for information on how to manage meetings).

Do a yearly review. In this review you may want to ask:

1. What is your overall impression about the ministry this past year? How do you feel about your specific role in it?

2. What fruit or personal blessing have you seen in your ministry? Did you discover or affirm any gifting or abilities?

3. What was the most helpful input or effective training you received?

4. What has been your family's response to the demands of this ministry?

5. What are your current personal and ministry goals?

6. Is God leading you to serve in this capacity next year? If not, what did you learn that you can pass on to others?

7. Is there a different ministry you would like to try next year?

This time should not be threatening to the individuals. Make it as affirming as possible and concentrate on planning for next year's ministry.

Summary

The real story is not how many women are ready for high levels of ministry today, but what you are doing to prepare tomorrow's leaders.

One year, my husband and I were giving a series of seminars in New Zealand — a land with far more sheep than people. Most sheep stations use dogs to work the sheep. At one of our seminars I overheard an old shepherd talking about one of his lead dogs, "She's pretty old, but she has enough energy left to train one more dog before she goes down." His comment has stayed with me. How many women will I train before "I go down?" How many will *you* train?

One way to train is to involve as many as possible in low levels of ministry. Ask two women to be responsible for dessert at your Bible studies instead of just one. Use ten women for book reports at a retreat instead of one woman giving ten reports. Use multiple lecturers in a Bible study. Yes, some will be better than others, but you must develop a reservoir of experienced leadership. Some churches have a gifted Bible teacher speaking weekly, but when the Lord calls her home, the ministry will die. Don't let this happen.

Another effective way is to have an understudy working with you. In the next chapter we will look at various structures for your ministry, including some examples from actual churches. In one church, each leadership position is filled by a team — an older woman paired with a younger woman. Whatever your particular approach to selecting women to lead ministries, choose with the future in view.

Bibliography

Hepburn, Daisy. *How to Grow a Women's Minis-tree.* Ventura, Calif.: Regal Books, 1986.

Hepburn, Daisy. *A Resource Manual to Be Used with How to Grow a Women's Minis-tree.* Ventura, Calif.: Regal Books, 1986.

Koop, Sandra, Melanie Margaron Bowden, and Mabel Pittman. *How to . . . a Packet of Involvement Skills.* Wheaton, Ill.: Conservative Baptist Association of America, 1990. (For a copy, write: Conservative Baptist Association of America, P.O. Box 66, Wheaton, IL 60189.)

McGinn, Linda R. *Resource Guide for Women's Ministries,* Nashville, Tenn.: Broadman Press, 1990.

MINI-SURVEY

Give me a call about attending or helping with the following ministries.

Name: _____

Address: _____

_____

Phone: (Days) _____ (Eves.) _____

Attend	Help	
☐	☐	Outreach Events
☐	☐	Getaways
☐	☐	Community Service Opportunities
☐	☐	Missions
☐	☐	Meals, transportation, etc. for the sick
☐	☐	New Moms Ministry
☐	☐	Heart to Heart (support group for wives with unequal yoke)
☐	☐	Secret Pal
☐	☐	Ladies A.M. Bible Study
☐	☐	H.E.A.L. (12-step support group)
☐	☐	Prayer Ministry
☐	☐	Ladies Annual Retreat
☐	☐	Discipling of Believers

I would like the following additional ministries:

_____

_____

_____

I would like and plan to attend workshops in the following areas:

_____ Adult Children of Alcoholics _____ Divorce Recovery
_____ Weight Control _____ Parenting (age of child_____)
_____ Other _____

I have the following skills and interests to share:

- ☐ Crafts
- ☐ Posters
- ☐ Drama
- ☐ Music (piano, organ, singing) _____
- ☐ Greeting/hostessing
- ☐ Word processing
- ☐ General clerical
- ☐ Administrative skills
- ☐ Making meals for those in need
- ☐ Taking meals to those in need
- ☐ Preparing/serving food for events
- ☐ Visitation
- ☐ Phoning
- ☐ Refreshment service on Sun. morning
- ☐ Preschool helper/teacher
- ☐ Grade school helper/teacher
- ☐ Other _____

Please turn in the survey to a member of the women's committee, an usher, or mail to the church office at (your church's address).

EXTENDED SURVEY

WOMEN'S MINISTRY SURVEY

Please answer the following questions and return the survey to the Women's Ministry Director.

Name: _____

Address: _____

Phone: _____

Age: _____ over 40   _____ 39 and under

MARITAL STATUS:

_____ single _____ married _____ married with children

_____ divorced _____ divorced with children _____ widowed

Names and ages of children: _____

_____

_____

_____

_____ I attend church sponsored functions *only* when child care is provided.

_____ I have a tight budget but can afford sitters for events which interest me.

PRIMARY WORK/CAREER FOCUS:

_____ full-time at home   _____ full-time outside home

_____ part-time in home   _____ student

_____ part-time outside home

SPECIAL INTERESTS AND ACTIVITIES

music (what type?) _____

art _____

crafts _____

drama _____

other _____

SPECIAL NEEDS

I would like workshops or a support group in the following areas:

_____ Adult Children of Alcoholics   _____ Divorce Recovery
_____ Weight Control   _____ Parenting
                                             (age of child) ____

Other: _____

I WOULD LIKE TO HELP
WITH THE FOLLOWING MINISTRIES

GETAWAYS (fun activities designed for outreach)
_____ Helping to plan the event
_____ Organizing transportation

SPECIAL OUTREACH DINNERS
_____ Program development
_____ Food service, etc.
_____ Decorations

COMMUNITY OUTREACH
_____ Assist in identifying worthwhile projects in the community
_____ Transport food/clothing to meet specific needs
_____ Volunteer at Crisis Pregnancy Center
_____ Volunteer at Shepherdsgate (a home for battered women)

PERSONAL EVANGELISM
_____ I would like some training

_____ I could help others in "way-of-life" witnessing

PRAYER MINISTRY
_____ Being on a prayer chain
_____ Being captain of a prayer chain
_____ Gathering requests for the prayer chains
_____ Assisting with day of prayer
_____ Hosting a weekly ladies prayer meeting

VISITATION
_____ Visiting newcomers
_____ Visiting those in need in the church
_____ I have experience in church visitation
_____ I would like to visit but would like some training first

BIBLE STUDY
_____ I would like more information about Bible studies
_____ I would like to lead a discussion group
_____ I would like to lead a discussion group, but need training
_____ I would like to lecture for the study
_____ I would like to lecture, but need training
_____ I would like to host an evening Bible study. I would prefer:
        Mon. ____ Tues. ____ Wed. ____ Thurs. ____ Fri. ____

LADIES RETREAT
_____ I would like to help in the planning of the next retreat

HELPING NEW BELIEVERS GROW
_____ I can help new believers begin to grow
_____ I would like to do this but need instruction
_____ I would like someone to help *me* grow

MEETING PRACTICAL NEEDS
_____ Taking food to new mothers or anyone ill
_____ Helping with a move
_____ Cleaning homes for the ill
_____ Emergency child care
_____ Providing short-term housing
_____ I would appreciate training in how to be of specific help

BABY AND BRIDAL SHOWERS
_____ Coordinating

_____ Hosting

SUPPORT MINISTRY FOR THE NEW MOTHER
_____ Available for visitation and encouragement

FOREIGN MISSIONS
_____ Serving on the Missions Committee
_____ Writing letters to missionaries
_____ Helping maintain the missions bulletin board
_____ Preparing practical gifts to send to the missionaries

GENERAL MINISTRY
_____ Child care
_____ Decorations for events
_____ Publicity, posters, etc.
_____ Contributing articles for the church newsletter
_____ Computer work
_____ Meals at church:
    Cooking _____ Serving _____ Set-up _____ Clean-up _____
_____ Coffee hour on Sundays
_____ Hosting church events in my home
_____ Greeting on Sunday morning
_____ General phoning
_____ Other: _____

CHAPTER EIGHT

Structure and Programs for Women's Ministry

The last two chapters contained information on how to start and staff women's ministries. This chapter describes a selection of programs a women's council may facilitate as well as possible council structures for different size churches. Your ministry and council organization will be similar to that in other churches, but will reflect the uniqueness of your own situation.

In North America we often categorize congregations according to denominations. We assume the churches within these denominations are essentially the same as one another and different from churches of other denominations. However, denomination affiliation can be a minor factor in determining the character of a church.

There are many factors besides background and denominational affiliation which contribute to the uniqueness of a particular church. In *Always Advancing: Modern Strategies for Church Growth*, R. Daniel Reeves and Ronald Jenson (San Bernardino, Calif.: Here's Life Publishers, 1984) talk about several of these factors. Three factors in particular will affect how you will develop your women's ministry. These key considerations are:

- age
- context
- size

The Age Factor

Infant churches (up to three years old) have only basic levels of programming. They often don't have their own building. Depending on the character of their parent church, they may be highly structured or fluid in nature. Change is easy to effect. If you are in this kind of church it will be easy to build an exciting women's ministry.

Childhood churches (three to twelve years old) are characterized by rapid growth mixed with sporadic tensions. Much of the planning is done by trial and error. New programs can be started and then scrapped if they don't work. The growth will bring in women who have experienced various types of ministries at other churches. Evaluate and learn from their experience and use what fits your church.

Adolescent churches (twelve to twenty years old) typically struggle with an identity crisis. Tension develops between the pioneers (those who established the church) and the homesteaders (those who have joined during the last five years). Enthusiasm for new programs diminishes with the age of the church. In this age church you need to take time to win the support of the key women before you institute new programs or unfamiliar practices.

Young adult churches (twenty to forty years old) may be at a plateau. A false sense of security can set in. Programs tend to be fixed in place whether they work or not. By significantly restructuring the women's ministry you can open new paths of entry into the church. Women's ministry can be a vital force for growth in a church at this stage of development.

Middle-age churches (over forty years old) and *Historic churches* (over two full generations old) are almost always plateaued or declining in membership. One reason may be ethnic changes in the community. Another may be a rise in the median age to above fifty years. These churches are growing and exciting places to be only if they have new and dynamic leadership or if they have experienced a spiritual renewal or a sociological transfusion. Women's ministries can be an active part in bringing any of these about.

The Context Factor

Included in this category are such variables as setting (urban, suburban, or rural), geographic location, and church image — is it a prestigious church? Does it exist in the shadow of such a church? Is it exclusive in nature with strict membership and rigid convictions concerning Christian practice?

These contextual distinctives will all affect women's ministries, with the rural, suburban, or urban setting being the most influential. Each of these three categories subdivides into further categories. (If you are interested in more specifics see *Always Advancing*.)

In general the urban church is under 300 people in size, with slow to moderate growth. Its ministries reflect the needs of its community: food pantries, clothes closets, support groups, and counseling for a variety of needs. If you minister in this type of situation you'll have to work to keep the heart of your programming Bible centered, evangelistic, and committed to discipleship. Do not get sidetracked from your major mission of proclaiming salvation through Jesus Christ.

The suburban church, depending on the age of the community in which it's located, often ministers to the baby boomers (people born between 1946 and 1964). Boomers are selective consumers who usually participate only in what meets their needs. Since they're the largest segment of the population today, most of the focus of this book applies to the needs of this group. Women attending suburban churches often have limited time to give or receive ministry due to at least part-time work outside the home. Take this into consideration if you are in a suburban church.

Rural churches on the other hand have their own problems. Churches in small towns or agricultural communities, are likely to have been around for a long time. There will be minimal growth unless the community undergoes radical changes brought about through land development. What was done in the past still strongly influences what is doable today and in the future.

If change needs to be made, make it slowly. Prepare the women in advance for changes in ministry programming. Take a good look at your community to locate needs that your women's ministry can address. There are lost, hurting people everywhere who need to be reached with the love of Christ. A good book on the rural church is *The Rural Church*, by Edward Hassinger, edited by Lyle Schaller, Abingdon Press: Nashville, Tenn.: 1988.

Whether you are in an urban, suburban, or rural church, fight the tendency to minister only to your own flock. Churches are lighthouses to be set on hills, not flickering candles giving light only under their own baskets.

The Size Factor — Ministry in the Small Church
(up to thirty women)

Churches which average below 40 people on Sunday morning comprise 25 percent of American churches. Those averaging between 50 and 100 people account for another 25 percent.

Leadership in this size church is controlled by lay people or part-time staff. The church functions like one big family. The smaller the church the more casual and intimate the programming. Little advance publicity is needed because of established lines of communication among members. Most rural churches are in this category.

The women's council in even a small church will benefit from a well-thought-out structure. Small does not need to mean unorganized!

Structure

Women's Ministry Director
She oversees all the women's ministry activities.

Bible Study Coordinator
She coordinates and delegates responsibilities for:
- teacher/discussion leader (she may be the primary teacher herself)
- prayer
- refreshments
- child care

Evangelism Coordinator
She coordinates and delegates responsibilities for outreach programs, including:
- speaker, testimony, devotional
- music, skit, craft demonstration
- decorations, refreshments
- child care
- invitation and follow-up

Service Coordinator
She coordinates and delegates responsibilities for:
- nursery
- meals/kitchen
- care of sick: visitation, flowers, meals, etc.
- bridal and baby showers

This four-member core team (Director, Bible Study Coordinator, Evangelism Coordinator, and Service Coordinator) should meet monthly for prayer, planning, and evaluation.

Programs

Bible Study and Encouragement
Think basic. Plan one weekly meeting including Bible study, prayer, and fellowship. Use published Bible study material.

If a large proportion of your women work outside the home choose a time when they can attend. Add special monthly features, demonstrations, or crafts as resources allow.

Provide child care. You can have your women take turns baby-sitting, or use sitters who attend another church. Another approach is to hire sitters. If you do so, pay them adequately.

Evangelism

Plan one or two programs a year designed especially for non-Christians. Develop seasonal outreach events, taking advantage of times like Christmas and Mother's Day. Do something special or adapt your regular midweek meeting for this outreach.

Service

Delegate services like nursery work, maintaining the kitchen, preparing and delivering meals to the sick, planning baby and wedding showers, etc., according to the individual gifts and ministry needs of your people.

Most churches begin as small churches. My own church, Valley Bible Church, in San Ramon, California, began as a church plant with a core group of about forty adults. We meet in a school, so all midweek activities are in a home or rented facilities. During the first year, our women's ministry was led by four women who had been part of the women's ministry council in our original church. We worked together as a unit without specific job descriptions, though one woman was our Coordinator and another took and distributed minutes.

The ministry was divided into three branches: Outreach, Building Believers, and Caring. Outreach included a doll-making workshop, trip to a historic town, and Christmas craft day. Two dinners were held with an evangelistic thrust, and we began to help the local Crisis Pregnancy Center.

Building Believers consisted of a morning ladies Bible study, personal discipling, a Day of Prayer, and yearly retreat. The Caring component of the ministry involved showers for new mothers, meals for those in need, and refreshments after the Sunday service. We kept the structure simple, and focused on evangelism and discipleship in a context of a caring community of believers.

The Size Factor — Ministry in the Midsize Church
(thirty to ninety-nine women)

Midsize churches average between 100 and 175 in Sunday attendance. (Twenty-five percent of American churches are this size.) Many consider this to be the optimum size. Programs can have some diversity, but are easily manageable. Members are able to relate to one another spontaneously.

Another 10 percent of American churches are in what's sometimes called the "awkward size" — between 175 and 225. They are in that difficult stage commonly referred to as "The Two Hundred Barrier." They're too small for multiple leadership and not usually comfortable with two worship services.

As a church grows, more ministry details are delegated to committees. These committees meet as needed and report to the women's council. Committees dealing with major ministry responsibilities should be attended by a member of the council. For example the retreat committee should be attended or chaired by the encouragement coordinator.

Westminster Presbyterian (Presbyterian Church of America) located in Clinton, South Carolina represents a midsized church which began with 35 adults in 1982 and now has 150 in attendance. The original women's ministry was a loosely organized circle which met once per month and studied a book, usually recommended by the denominational headquarters.

In 1989 a council was developed with a goal of getting younger women involved in various areas of ministry. Seven women ranging in age from twenty to seventy meet monthly to oversee two circle studies (morning and evening) which meet weekly, a yearly outreach dinner, support activities with a local Christian adoption agency, and a fall dinner for college students. They encourage women to participate with the church's Evangelism Explosion program and follow-up of new believers. A monthly newsletter which includes book reviews ties the ministry together.

Structure

Women's Ministry Director
She oversees all women's ministries.

Bible Study Coordinator and Assistant
They oversee a committee which is responsible for:
- teachers/discussion leaders, recruitment, and training
- follow-up of first-time attenders and new believers
- greeters/hostesses
- special features
- child care and programming
- refreshments
- prayer
- setup and cleanup

Encouragement Coordinator and Assistant
They oversee outreach ministries, which might include:
- Sunday greeters/hospitality
- women-visiting-women program

- monthly Ladies Night Out events
- seasonal special events

Service Coordinator and Assistant

They oversee ministries such as:
- nursery
- hospitality (meal preparation, service, and cleanup)
- flowers for the sick
- baby and wedding showers
- facility cleanup and redecorating (often done in conjunction with the deacons or other committees)
- food pantry and clothes closet
- community service volunteers (unless handled by Evangelism ministry)

Missions Coordinator and Assistant

They oversee functions like:
- contacting missionaries on the field
- identifying and meeting practical needs of missionaries
- promoting missions education and maintaining missions awareness via a bulletin board and other means of communication

Each of the five coordinators should meet with her team leaders monthly or as needed. The women's ministry council (five major coordinators and the Director) should meet quarterly or as needed. The frequency of these meetings will depend on the capability of the coordinators and the complexity of the planning.

The women's ministry council could begin the year with a day of orientation, training, prayer, and fellowship, perhaps as part of a weekend leadership retreat. They could end the ministry year with a day of praise and thanksgiving to God. All ministries and programs should be evaluated each year and suggested changes for the future should be made in writing.

Programs

Bible Study

Plan a weekly Bible study in which women can choose between one of two studies in a discussion format. You may want to have fifteen to thirty minutes of teaching for all the women, followed by small group discussion.

If many of your women work be sure to provide an evening study time for them.

Add a creative special feature to the program each week.

Provide child care with planned activities for the children.

Establish prayertime guidelines to be implemented by the prayer chairwoman in each group.

Use greeters or hostesses to welcome women as they arrive. Put your friendliest women in greeting positions. They can set the tone for the entire session. Encourage everyone to reach out to newcomers.

Use refreshments to help create a warm atmosphere for fellowship time. Newcomers feel safe hiding behind a coffee cup. If facilities allow, take refreshments into the study time.

Encouragement

Initiate mentoring/discipling relationships.

Establish a prayer chain and encourage prayer partners.

Plan a women's retreat. Even with a small number of women attending a retreat can have powerful spiritual impact!

Evangelism

Encourage way-of-life evangelism. Equip your women through literature and personal instruction to reach their families and friends for Christ. Make *Four Spiritual Laws* type booklets readily available.

Establish a women-visiting-women program. Make sure someone keeps track of relevant visitor information. Make a follow-up visit to everyone who attends your program. These visits need not be threatening to anyone — a cup of coffee together at a local restaurant is ideal.

Plan small group activities like a ladies' night out featuring a craft project — with or without a devotional or testimony. Plan larger group activities like seasonal special events. Use both as evangelistic opportunities.

Service

Organize service according to need and church structure. In addition to the things already mentioned under small churches, services may include: meals for church functions, new mothers, and those who are ill. Care of facilities — cleaning/redecorating — may come under this category. Meeting social needs within the community could be part of either your service or evangelism ministries.

Missions

Maintain contact with any missionaries from the church. Keep the church informed and educated about missions using a missions bulletin board. Plan a yearly missions event, perhaps in conjunction with other churches. Encourage practical projects to meet the specific needs of your missionaries.

The Size Factor — Ministry in the Large Church (100 to 349 women)
Large churches average between 225 and 450 in attendance and make up 10 percent of the churches in this country. New decision-making processes need to be implemented at this size. The task of administrating a strong women's program can become a part-time staff position.

An additional 4 percent of churches — with attendance between 400 and 750 — are classified by Reeves and Jenson as "Huge Churches." These churches are pacesetters in their communities and denominations. They are able to offer multiple ministry and service options and can minister to a wide range of needs among women. But they will be hampered by:

- problems in recruitment of volunteers
- squabbles over space
- lack of spontaneity
- scheduling conflicts with other ministries

Small and midsized churches can be administered by hands-on leadership with a shepherd mentality. But in larger churches the leader must become more of a rancher. A rancher works through other people to care for still more people. This involves training and trusting others with ministry. It also involves more ministry done through committees. The women's council deals primarily with leadership and planning, though they must not lose touch with individual women.

Eastgate Bible Chapel, located in Portland, Oregon, exemplifies such a church at the smaller end of the size-grouping. It was founded in 1959 and has an attendance of 300. Prior to 1985 there was a midweek study for women, consisting of lecture and refreshments, and a small missionary group. Some women began praying for change and in 1985 with the full backing of the church leadership, they began to develop EBC's Women's Ministry.

Their objectives are: REACH UP to be women in worship and prayer; REACH IN to be women in the Word, applying it to our lives and sharing it with each other in fellowship; REACH OUT to be women in the world who influence that world for Christ.

In order to implement these objectives they have developed the following structure and programs:

Bible Study Branch
- *Women's Fellowship* meets weekly and includes informal fellowship, discussion of the study questions, formal teaching time, and prayer.

Support and Encouragement Branch

- *Working Women* meet monthly for a Saturday breakfast which concludes with a fifteen-minute devotional.
- *Prayer* is a vital part of many of their ministries including: the Women's Fellowship, Women's Missionary Group, Prayer Chain, and specific prayer partners.
- *Women's Friendship Team* is made up of six women who are available for: friendship, counsel, accountability, regular time in God's Word, and prayer as well as finding or recapturing God's perspective in life's situations.
- *Yearly Ladies Retreat* designed as a getaway for believers is held in mid-fall from Saturday morning to Sunday afternoon.

Service Branch (Helping Hands)

- *Flowers* sent to hospitalized
- *Meals* for new or hospitalized mothers and following a funeral
- *Showers* for wedding and baby
- *Food Pantry* to provide temporary food assistance

This ministry is directed by a Coordinator and two assistance coordinators who comprise the Core Team and meet monthly. All the ministry leaders meet in August, November, January, and March for training and review of their ministry areas. Their year concludes in May with a "real Treat" — an overnight designed for fun and inspiration. Job descriptions are written for each position and used as a basis for recruitment as well as yearly review.

At the other end of the scale of large churches is Central Baptist of Sioux Falls, South Dakota founded in 1883 and affiliated with the Baptist General Conference.

In the late 1970s change was badly needed in the women's ministry. The missionary circle structure was not appealing to the younger women who were seeking ministry opportunities within parachurch organizations. These women were growing spiritually but not significantly contributing to the local church. At that point one of their members attended a meeting in Chicago with Dorothy Dahlman, the director of women's ministries for the Baptist General Conference.

A slow metamorphosis began when she returned. The initial step was education. The *what* and *why* of change were carefully presented. New leadership was *selected* instead of *elected*. Women in the parachurch organizations were challenged to shift their focus to the home base. Some older ladies wished to maintain the familiar circle structure so it was left intact and considered part of the new women's ministry organization. Finally a ten-member leadership team was organized including: President, Vice President, Secretary/Treasurer and seven Coordinators.

This team administrates a full slate of women's activities. Read through their programs looking for suggestions you can use in your own church.

Spiritual Growth Branch

- Weekly morning Bible study which includes fifteen minutes of special features. The older preschoolers attend an organized program
- Noon Bible studies meeting in a public library
- Two Saturday seminars per year on such topics as infertility, child-rearing, how to be a caregiver, time and home management
- Summer Bible study in homes, with four separate time slots offered
- Heart to Heart, a Titus 2 group which encourages older women to open their homes to younger women for an evening of "What I Have Learned" sharing

Evangelism

- Crafteas have become an excellent evangelistic tool. They are held three times per year at the church from 7–9 P.M. with preregistration preferred. The evening begins with a ten-minute devotional coordinated with the craft if possible.
- Christmas coffees are held in homes at a time and day selected by the hostess. Neighbors are invited with printed invitations to hear a brief testimony and share Christmas traditions. These coffees have been excellent entry points into other ministries of the church.
- New Life Bible Study is for women with little Bible background.

Service to the Community

- Baking for penitentiary inmates during the holiday season
- Participation in a picnic for a home for battered wives by providing food and crafts for sale
- Baking for the local Ronald McDonald house
- Providing meals for handicapped
- A "Sweaters for Someone" program. Warm clothing is collected in the fall. After Thanksgiving the needy are invited to the church to select what they need. Everyone is treated with care and respect; background music and the aroma of hot cider create a holiday mood. Each visitor receives a Christmas tract.

Special Events

- Four special events per year are planned. Tickets are purchased and an offering is taken to fund other women's ministries.

Missions
- The February special event is a missions evening with flair! A popular theme was "An Evening at a French Café."
- Other aspects of the missions program center on meeting the specific needs and wants of missionary wives and children.

Prayer
- Women's ministry organizes special "Concerts of Prayer" for the whole church.
- Prayer coffees are held in late summer to pray for the fall women's programs. Women can attend a brunch or dessert prayer session according to their own schedule.
- Planning is underway for a Moms in Touch ministry which prays for local schools.

After taking a look at some specific large churches, here is a generalized approach to women's ministry in the large church.

Structure

Women's Ministry Director and Assistant
They oversee all women's ministries.

Bible Study Coordinator and Assistant
They oversee the ministries of the Midweek Coordinator and the Working Women Coordinator.

Midweek Coordinator and Assistant. They oversee the committees for:
- teachers/discussion leaders, recruitment, and training
- follow-up of first time attenders and new believers
- greeters/hostesses
- special features
- music
- child care and programming
- refreshments
- prayer
- setup and cleanup

Working Women Coordinator and *Assistant.* They oversee the committees ministering to the special needs of working women.

Encouragement Coordinator and Assistant
They oversee ministries such as:
- discipleship
- prayer

- pastoral visitation
- support groups
- peer counseling
- Retreat Coordinator

Evangelism Coordinator and Assistant
They oversee outreach ministries, which might include:
- Sunday greeters/hospitality
- women-visiting-women program
- monthly Ladies Night Out events
- seasonal special events
- evangelistic Bible studies

Service Coordinator and Assistant
They oversee ministries such as:
- nursery
- hospitality (meal preparation, service, and cleanup)
- flowers for the sick
- baby and wedding showers
- weddings (Wedding Coordinator)
- facility cleanup and redecorating (often done in conjunction with the deacons or other committees)
- food pantry and clothes closet
- community services volunteers (unless handled by evangelism ministry)

Mission Coordinator and Assistant
If this comes under women's ministry they oversee:
- missions communication
- missions education
- missions publicity
- missions conferences
- missions projects
- assistance to returning missionaries

If missions is not under women's ministry they can still help in these areas.

The Director and the five major coordinators and assistants should meet monthly. The meetings should include prayer, planning, and other business. Leadership training can be incorporated into this meeting (see chap. 5). This council or core team could start the year with a prayer retreat and conclude the year with a time of praise, evaluation, and fun.

The entire ministry team including all committee leaders could begin the year with an orientation day which includes some training (perhaps from an outside resource person), ministry orientation, prayer, and bonding. They could end the ministry year with a day of praise and thanksgiving to God. All ministries and programs should be evaluated with suggested changes for the coming year made in writing.

During the year this large group should meet quarterly for times of training, sharing about the ministry, and prayer. These should be designed more as "events" than "business meetings."

Programs

Bible Study

You may want to add a third or fourth Bible study to the curriculum so women can choose according to their needs. Or design a two-part program in which all women first meet together for study, then break into small groups for interaction and discussion.

Provide ongoing training for teachers and leaders of the Bible studies, small groups, and children's programs.

Consider having a separate time for small group prayer rather than trying to fit it into this midweek program.

Child care should be expanded to include a program for preschoolers.

Offer a study/support group designed to the needs of your working women, meeting perhaps in the early morning, the evening, or on weekends.

Encouragement

In addition to the things already mentioned under small and midsize churches, establish prayer groups and prayer partners. Start a peer counseling ministry. Develop support groups as needed. Possibilities include groups for: single parents, dieters, divorce recovery, grief recovery, alcoholics, spouses of alcoholics, women with unbelieving husbands, women caring for aging parents, etc.

Use the women's retreat as a special time for drawing new women into the fellowship and for building up those involved in ministry.

Evangelism

Use seasonal special events and small group evangelistic and neighborhood Bible studies. Depending on your community's needs you might want to sponsor programs like:

- a church Welcome Wagon for new move-ins
- M.O.P.S. (Mothers of Preschoolers, see bibliography for address), or C.O.P.S. (Carers of Preschoolers)

- Mom's Morning Out (a free church-run child care program)
- aerobics classes at the church
- Working Women's Luncheon, Supper, or Tea
- girl's 4-H club, Pioneer Girls, AWANA, etc.
- day care — with evangelistic emphasis — for children or senior citizens

Service

Service opportunities for a church this size could include programs to meet the needs of special groups such as:

- international students
- the elderly and shut-ins
- refugees and immigrants
- the homeless
- latch-key kids
- the unemployed

What you do will depend on your resources and the needs around you.

Missions

In a large church, missions often comes under the Minister of Evangelism or else is the responsibility of a mission board. If so, women's ministry can still help sponsor and support missions activities.

The Size Factor — Ministry in the Mega Church (over 350 women)

Mega churches have over 750 at worship and comprise only 1 percent of American churches. Administration becomes more important and at the same time more difficult. The ratio of staff to attenders often increases as church size increases. This will also be true within women's ministry.

At this level of complexity the women's ministry is often administrated by a full-time staff person. Since all mega churches face similar problems, it's important that they network with each other. Some mega church women's ministries publish their own handbook, including job descriptions and ministry suggestions and are usually glad to share what they've developed.

Most of us will never attend a mega church. However, they are a rich source of helpful information to use in our own situations. This chapter concludes with a look at two mega churches, one on the east coast and one on the west, followed by a generalized structure and list of possible programs.

Church of the Saviour in Wayne, Pennsylvania, an interdenominational church of 1,500 plus, began in 1972 as an outgrowth of women's evangelistic Bible studies.

The leadership of these studies formed the core team for the fledging women's ministry. Within two years, six women were meeting together monthly, facilitating programs in outreach, Bible studies, follow-up of new believers, evangelistic luncheons, and other special events. This structure served them well for a number of years. Then growth triggered changes.

Decentralization of the ministry began. For example, one kitchen chairman handled everything until the church grew to 700, then each event organized its own kitchen crew. As Church of the Saviour grew to over a thousand, decision-making within a centralized women's ministry became unwieldy. The board felt out of touch with the needs of businesswomen, single parents, and other special interest groups. They released each ministry to make its own decisions.

A communication group comprised of key women's ministry leaders and the pastor now meet quarterly. They oversee scheduling, assist with staffing, and pray for the needs of the ministries, but they have no decision-making authority — that is left to the autonomous ministries.

The primary thrust of the women's ministry has remained the Bible studies and associated personal discipling program. A modified Design for Discipleship series (published by Navpress) is the basis for this successful ministry which now oversees nine daytime classes, seven evening studies, an early bird special for working women plus many small discipling groups. All the Bible studies are directed by an overseer who trains new leadership. She places coaches in charge of four Bible study leaders who visit the classes, encourage the leaders, and assist them in problem-solving.

This Bible study ministry has reached beyond the walls of Church of the Saviour. Both in-house and on-location seminars train women in the successful techniques used in this ministry.

Prayer and missions round out the ministry of women in Wayne, Pennsylvania. There are women's prayer teams meeting in homes as well as at church throughout the week; a careers team meets in various work places. Women in Missions schedules four luncheons featuring furloughed missionaries each year. In addition, they stock a closet containing linens and other households items for use by the missionary families.

In contrast to Church of the Saviour, Saddleback Valley Community Church, located in Mission Viejo, California, has maintained a centralized Women's Board. Saddleback began in 1980 and grew in ten years to a church of 4,000 — all the while meeting in schools.

The Women's Council is composed of five or more women who are members of SVCC. The Women's Fellowship Director and secretary, both full-time staff positions, are also members of the Women's Council. Together they oversee a ministry composed of four large branches.

Education
- Heart to Heart Bible Studies offered mornings, evenings, and before work
- Heart to Heart Children's Care and Education
- Heart to Heart Support Ministries (name tags, registration/welcome table, room arrangements, refreshments)
- Growth Groups which emphasize teaching and stress accountability
- Community Groups designed for building relationships in the context of Bible study
- Nurture Groups emphasize evangelism and follow-up for the non-Christian or nonbeliever

Support
- First We Pray establishes a network of prayer warriors to cover the Women's Program with prayer
- Prayer Chain Ministry: emergency prayer requests of the women of the church and their immediate families
- Caring Heart connects a women in trauma with someone who can offer empathy
- Caring Enough to Comfort Seminar is held yearly to equip women to skillfully reach out to those in need

Service
- Hostess Ministry assists various women's fellowship and church events with decorations, food preparation and service, taking reservations, and phoning
- Wedding Service offers practical assistance for wedding planning
- Golden Angels assures that every hospitalized woman is visited
- Community ministry focuses on a Crisis Pregnancy Center and the Eli Home for Abused Children
- Bake Sales are held periodically to raise money for Mission Projects

Special Events
- Ladies Night Out held three or four times a year
- Craft Workshops
- Celebrate the Season — a pre-Christmas event held on a Friday or Saturday in mid-November

- Women's Annual Conference
- Study Retreat designed to provide an opportunity for in-depth study of God's Word.
- Prayer Retreat
- Mother-Daughter event
- Mother-Son Breakfast
- Golden Belles Ministry provides an outreach focus to senior women through a monthly Sunday brunch

Structure

Women's Ministry Director and Assistant
They oversee all women's ministries. (The Director is often a staff person who will be attending regular church-wide staff meetings.)

Bible Study Coordinator and Assistant
They oversee a committee comprised of the leaders in charge of:
- teachers/discussion leaders, recruitment, and training
- follow-up of first time attenders and new believers
- greeters/hostesses
- special features
- children's programming
- prayer
- refreshments
- setup and cleanup
- ministries to working women

The number of women needed to handle each of these ministries will vary, depending on the size and structure of the Bible study program of the church.

Encouragement Coordinator and Assistant
They oversee a committee comprised of the leaders in charge of:
- discipleship/mentoring
- prayer ministries
- pastoral visitation
- support groups
- peer counseling
- retreats
- special events

Evangelism Coordinator and Assistant
They oversee a committee comprised of the leaders in charge of:
- Sunday greeters/hospitality

- women-visiting-women program
- monthly Ladies Night Out events
- seasonal special events
- evangelistic Bible studies

Other outreaches should be developed according to the resources of
the church and the needs of the community. See the program section
under "evangelism" for some ideas.

Service Coordinator and Assistant

The service ministries in a mega church will vary according to the organization, staffing, and philosophy of ministry of each church. The Service Coordinator and Assistant oversee the committee comprised of the
Leaders of whatever ministries fall under the service area.

A *Missions Coordinator* is probably unnecessary since missions is usually a separate and distinct ministry in a church this large.

The Director and the four major Coordinators should meet weekly, if
possible, for prayer, visionary planning, brainstorming, evaluation, and
ongoing training. They could start the ministry year with a prayer retreat and conclude it with a time of praise, evaluation, and thanksgiving
for what has occurred that year.

The entire women's ministry team, including all committee leaders,
should meet with the Director and Coordinators quarterly for times of
training, inspiration, encouragement, and prayer. All ministries and
programs should be evaluated annually, with suggested changes for the
coming year made in writing.

Programs

Bible Study

Midweek study should be organized around a central teaching session
followed by small group interaction. This small group interaction is essential. It gives the women opportunities to develop relationships.
There should be various levels of study — each requiring different
amounts of biblical knowledge and homework.

Children's programming needs to be well planned and well run, with
special activities for each age-group.

Other Bible studies should be available, in the early mornings, evenings, or on weekends, for working women and those who can't attend a
daytime study. If attenders come from a wide geographical area, hold
Bible studies in homes as well as at the church.

Provide ongoing training for teachers, small group leaders, and children's workers.

Encouragement

This area will expand according to the needs and resources of each particular church. In addition to the ideas mentioned in the previous sections under *Encouragement,* programming could include:

- prayer seminars and retreats
- one-on-one discipling and weekly accountability groups
- Moms-in-Touch (mothers of students in the same school meet weekly for one hour of prayer for their students, faculty, etc.)
- Fall kick-off dinner for all women's activities for the year.

Evangelism

Assess your community's needs to determine your evangelistic activities. Seasonal special events and small group evangelistic and neighborhood Bible studies are always appropriate. To the *Evangelism* suggestions already made (see previous sections) you may want to add:

- Christmas tea
- Easter musical
- fashion show
- yearly bazaar
- craft classes
- Release time education (available in some public schools)
- Saturday seminars on issues affecting the community

Service and Missions

In a mega church these areas are often administrated, in whole or in part, by groups other than women's ministry. Whatever responsibilities women's ministry does have here will be unique to each church.

Bibliography

Dahlman, Dorothy. *A Designer's Guide for Creative Women's Ministries.* Arlington Heights, Ill.: Harvest Publications, 1988.

Exman, Gary W. *Get Ready . . . Church Growth for Town and Country Congregations.* Lima, Ohio: CSS Publishing Co., 1987.

George, Carl F. *Prepare Your Church for the Future.* Old Tappan, N.J.: Fleming H. Revell, 1991.

Hassinger, Edward, edited by Lyle Schaller. *The Rural Church.* Nashville, Tenn.: Abingdon Press, 1988.

Hepburn, Daisy. *A Resource Manual to Be Used with How to Grow a Women's Mins-tree.* Ventura, Calif.: Regal Books, 1986.

Hepburn, Daisy. *How to Grow a Women's Minis-tree.* Ventura, Calif.: Regal Books, 1986.

McGinn, Linda R. *Resource Guide for Women's Ministries.* Nashville, Tenn.: Broadman Press, 1990.

Mothers of Preschoolers (M.O.P.S.), International, 4175 Harlan Street, Suite 105, Wheatridge, CO 80033. (303) 420-6100.

Pittman, Mabel, ed. *How to . . . A Packet of Involvement Skills.* Wheaton, Ill., Conservative Baptist Association, 1984.

Reeves, R. Daniel and Ronald Jenson. *Always Advancing: Modern Strategies for Church Growth.* San Bernardino, Calif.: Here's Life Publishers, 1984.

Schaller, Lyle E. *Growing Plans, Strategies to Increase Your Church's Membership.* Nashville, Tenn.: Abingdon Press, 1984.

Schaller, Lyle E. *The Small Church Is Different.* Nashville, Tenn.: Abingdon Press, 1982.

Wagner, C. Peter. *Your Church Can Grow: Seven Vital Signs of a Healthy Church.* Ventura, Calif.: Regal Books, 1976.

CHAPTER NINE

Organizing Great Bible Study Groups

Major contributors to this chapter were
Bev Hislip and Pat Smith.

A women's Bible study is often the first specific ministry women organize. In a small church (under seventy-five in attendance), it may come
before a recognized women's ministry gets started. Indeed, the study itself may be the springboard from which a full-fledged ministry is
launched.

Here are six reasons for having women's Bible study groups:

Bible study groups provide nurture and care. A "place to belong" is desperately needed in today's fragmented society. High mobility and the
breakdown of the family have caused many women to lose their moor-
ings and be set adrift. A Bible study group can be the only anchor in
their otherwise tumultuous life.

Bible study groups get women into the Word of God. The axis around
which these groups turn is the Word of God, not the word of women.
Women can comfort, encourage, and share life's secrets, but the Word
of God can go to the root of human need. "For the Word of God is living
and active. Sharper than any double-edged sword, it penetrates even to
dividing soul and spirit, joints and marrow; it judges the thoughts and
attitudes of the heart" (Heb. 4:12).

Bible study groups can help bring women to Christ. They provide a nonthreatening environment in which a woman can check out the rele-
vance of the Bible. In such a context, many women eventually commit
their lives to Christ.

Bible study groups provide a point of entry into the church. Often a woman who can't or won't attend church on Sunday morning will become a regular member of a women's Bible study group. The informal study is less threatening to some than a Sunday service. Church growth specialists suggest for every 100 people attending a church there should be seven small groups. A Bible study can be a group that incorporates the shy newcomer.

Bible study groups are effective in encouraging life change. It's possible to sit under great preaching Sunday after Sunday without coming into vital contact with God because the preacher is in the pulpit and we are in the pew. In a study women can hold one another accountable for applying God's Word in specific life situations.

Bible study groups provide a place for women to use their spiritual gifts. Gifts are discovered and developed through use. A well-run Bible study needs administrators, teachers, encouragers, evangelists, servers, givers, and plenty of women with the valuable gift of mercy. Workshops can also be taught to help women improve ministry skills in the areas of their giftedness.

Starting a Bible Study

Begin with at least two women who are committed to the leadership of the Bible study. Pray for others to join you on the leadership team. Five regular attenders is adequate to start a study group. Remember that an attendance of five women means seven or eight on the roster.

Meet for planning and prayer

Determine whether the primary goal is to nurture believers or to reach the lost. If the goal is evangelism, chapter 15 has details on evangelistic Bible studies.

Select a primary leader/organizer

If your group will be larger than twelve, plan to divide into discussion groups of eight to twelve women. Select discussion leaders and assistants for the small groups. Train them in leadership skills before the study begins.

Plan your schedule

Although Bible studies traditionally begin in the fall, with adequate publicity, you can start successfully at other times of the year. Take the local school schedule into account.

Don't plan activities during Christmas, spring, or summer breaks or during other school holidays when mothers need to be with their children.

Determine time and place

An informal telephone survey will help you choose the best time and day for the study. The best place to meet is usually at the church itself. This makes assimilation into the church fellowship a natural step for newcomers. If your church serves a large geographical area, consider holding several studies in strategically located homes.

Decide on a format

Here are some possibilities:

One-hour meeting options:

A. Bible discussion or lecture — thirty minutes
    fellowship/snacks — thirty minutes
B. fellowship/snacks — ten minutes
    Bible discussion or lecture — forty minutes
    prayer — ten minutes

Two-hour meeting options:

A. Bible discussion or lecture — forty-five minutes
    sharing/testimonies — fifteen minutes
    crafts, missionary projects, aerobics — forty-five minutes
    fellowship/snacks — fifteen minutes
B. fellowship/snacks — ten minutes
    specified feature (e.g., crafts) — thirty minutes
    Bible discussion or lecture — fifty minutes
    prayer-and-share time in small groups — thirty minutes
C. fellowship/snacks — fifteen minutes
    singing and announcements — ten minutes
    Bible teaching/lecture — fifty minutes
    break — ten minutes
    discussion of lecture in small groups — thirty-five minutes

Choose topics and appropriate study guides

Here's how.

1. Decide what the felt needs of your group are and choose materials that address those needs. If you have a large group, diverse in age and need, have several different studies. They can all meet at the same time, if the facility is large enough, or at different, more convenient hours, during the week.

2. Determine the best type of study for your group: book study, topical study, or doctrinal study. Today's women are very selective about where they spend their time. They respond best to a short commitment with a specific, relevant focus. In light of this you may want to do two or three shorter studies in a year rather than one long one.

3. Before ordering any material, the leader should complete several lessons in the proposed study guide to see whether it's the right level for the group. She should also note how long it takes to complete and how much prior Bible knowledge it presumes.

Always include questions in the study
This helps women to personally apply what's being taught. Ten to twelve questions in a one-hour discussion allows time for each member to participate.

Arrange for adequate child care
Use volunteers or hire sitters. To cover costs charge each mother a set fee or put an offering basket on the refreshment table. (If a set fee is charged, make arrangements for any who can't afford to pay.)

Publicize the study and recruit new members
For women to attend they must know about the study. Use Sunday morning announcements, church bulletins, posters, flyers, and phone calls. Divide the prospective attendees among the study leaders or committee members, and have them personally invite every woman on their list. Get the names of visitors to the church and invite them to the study. Don't be too pushy; newcomers may need time to look things over before getting involved. In any case they will appreciate an invitation. It tells them this is a friendly church.

Get the approval of the church leaders for your plan
Get their advice and incorporate their suggestions. Keep them informed of progress and give them specific things to pray for.

Keys to an Effective Bible Study

A committed leader
Her commitment is first to Christ as Lord of her life and then to others. Bible study leadership should be her only major-level commitment. It will take as many hours a week as she can put into it. She is responsible for training discussion leaders, teachers, and any other women helping with the study. Depending on her gifts, she may also be the primary lecturer.

Clear goals
Know why the group exists. Set and state clear goals based on the group's felt needs and level of maturity. Be realistic. Take into account

the amount of time women have to prepare for the study. Ask yourself, "What does God want to accomplish in the lives of these women?" Keep your primary focus on spiritual nurturing. Even though your program may benefit from including crafts or other activities, these aren't your main reasons for getting together.

Warm atmosphere
Provide time and activities which will allow the women to get acquainted with one another. Use name tags; it makes your group visitor-friendly.

Sing together (if the group is large enough for it to sound good). It will be a unifying factor. Provide musical accompaniment and the words to each song. Keep the discussion focused on personal applications. Encourage women to share testimonies of God's work in their lives, to share their struggles and to pray for one another.

If you meet in a church building:
- assign hostesses to greet women as they arrive
- use a smaller, warmer room rather than the sanctuary
- arrange groups in small circles or around a table — use comfortable chairs
- have a refreshment table

If you meet in a home:
- use the same location for each meeting
- use an informal, casual room with adequate lighting
- eliminate distractions from the room; magazines, pets, television
- have telephone calls handled by an answering machine
- prepare light, healthy refreshments

Group loyalty
Commitment to one another can be established and expressed in many ways:
- encourage regular attendance and lesson preparation
- choose an identifying name for the group
- build group traditions together
- publish an address/phone list and encourage people to phone or write encouraging notes to others in the group
- be alert for practical ways to minister to one another
- agree to maintain confidentiality

Leading the Bible Study
If you are leading the Bible study you have an important responsibility. To a large degree the group's effectiveness depends on you.

Prepare ahead of time

The first thing you must do is to thoroughly complete your own lesson. Plan to get it done early in the week to allow time to think about the best way to lead it. Look up extra cross-references to enhance the lesson material.

Calculate the estimated discussion time for each question; write that time in the margin near the question. Note which questions to skim, which to develop, and which to omit completely.

Arrive early

That way you won't be flustered at the beginning of the study. Warmly greet as many members as possible. Pay special attention to the newcomers.

Start and end on time

Some women will have to leave promptly to pick up children or go to work. Do not cheat them with a late finish caused by a late start.

Set the tone for the study

- Dress appropriately. Wear clothing that looks good but not over-powering. Know your best colors and stick to them. You are the least threatening when wearing a blouse/sweater that matches your eye color.
- Use positive body language. Smile, turn your body toward the person talking. Maintain an open posture without crossing your arms.
- Use a warm voice. Be interesting, enthusiastic, and conversational. Avoid a monotonous and flat sound.
- Establish eye contact. Look at the person you're addressing. When listening, look around the group; don't concentrate only on one side. Don't neglect those sitting right next to you.

Direct the discussion

- Vary your questioning approach. Go in a circle, open the question to everyone, call on people by name. "Did anyone approach it different-ly?" is a helpful question when a first answer is incomplete or slightly off target. Before moving on to another question ask if anyone noticed any-thing not yet mentioned.
- Draw out each group member. Directly address someone who hasn't shared. If you see by body language a person has a contribution to make, ask, "Jane, what else did you notice?" But remember, people re-spond in differing degrees within a group. Give plenty of freedom for each woman to be herself. Forcing participation can lead to alienation.
- Keep the discussion on track. Avoid digressions by saying some-

thing like, "That's a valid question; let's talk about it later." Then be sure you do talk about it later.

● Always express affirmation and appreciation in your responses. "That was a great insight!" will encourage further sharing.

● Don't let anyone monopolize the group. Seat the monopolizer beside you at the next meeting. Reduced eye contact might diminish her tendency to dominate. If not, you need to talk with her alone. Gently explain how she is negatively impacting the group. Don't make her feel unwanted or guilty. Tell her you value her insight, but not on each question. Your goal is to get her help in pursuing the goals of the group.

● Draw out the quiet person. Sit across from her so you can make eye contact. Never embarrass her by mentioning her shyness in front of the group. Instead, phone her at home and ask her what she enjoyed about the study material. Then ask if she would share that at the next meeting. Prayer, enthusiasm, and encouragement will draw her out.

● When someone shares deep, personal issues be sensitive to her pain, but also realize that not everyone present wants to know the details. Nor should they. Step in and offer to talk privately with her after the meeting.

Make newcomers welcome

As the leader it's up to you to make the new woman feel accepted and at home in the group. She's probably asking herself some basic questions: Who's in charge here? How much control do I want from the leader? What will be my place in this group? How much are others participating? How much do I want to participate? How much openness do these people expect from me? Will they accept me if they really know me? Can I disagree with what's being discussed and still be welcomed? Will they laugh at me if I say something that sounds dumb?

Deal with these apprehensions by setting a positive, genuinely warm and open tone in the study group. Get the new person involved. As she interacts with the group, she will feel a part of it. Commend her strengths and don't dwell on any weaknesses such as shyness, tardiness, or lack of preparation. Introduce her to others who might share her interests. Warmly encourage her to return the next time.

Depend on the Lord

Despite your best intentions things will go wrong sometimes. But God is still in control and can cause all things to work together for good. One time I arrived late and flustered to the study. My first mistake had been to take my basset hound, Samantha, in for surgery on the way to study. She was sicker than I had thought and the doctor advised me she might not survive the surgery. I immediately burst into tears.

It was late by the time I left the vet's so I shot into the fast lane. I was almost to church before I noticed the flashing lights. An emotionally wrung-out, ticketed teacher, I sat in the church parking lot trying to regain my composure. With carefully replaced makeup, I smiled and entered our Bible study room. But when an older friend who knew me well asked what was wrong, I immediately dissolved into tears again.

Somehow we got through an abbreviated form of the lesson. When we were finished, Anita, a woman I'd been praying for and trying to get to know all fall, came over and asked if we could talk. Much to my surprise she said I had appreared perfect to her and unapproachable until today. But my halo had fallen off, I had become real.

God's strength worked through my weakness. Within a week we met together outside the group and began a discipling relationship that lasted for months.

Follow-up after the Study

Evaluate yourself
Use these questions to evaluate how well you're doing at discussion leading. Think them through yourself and have someone you trust critique you as well. Work on those areas that need strengthening.

1. Did I begin and end the meeting on time?
2. Was I familiar enough with the material to interact and lead?
3. Did everyone participate, or did I dominate?
4. Did group members listen to and interact with each other?
5. Did I keep the discussion focused on the subject at hand?
6. Did I frequently summarize the key ideas discussed?
7. Did the discussion increase personal understanding of the material studied?
8. Did I truly listen to each person? Did I express sensitivity through my responses, tone of voice, and eye contact?
9. Did the group discuss how to apply the lesson to their own lives?
10. Were there any areas I didn't handle well? How can I improve next time?

Are you a good listener? The quality of your discussion leading is dramatically affected by your ability to listen. Evaluate yourself in this crucial area as well.

1. Does my mind wander when someone is talking to me?
2. Does my face show my response to what is being said?
3. Do I mentally argue with or contradict someone who is talking to me?

4. Do I state my opinion before I've expressed my understanding of what a person is saying?

5. Can I sit or stand still or do I have to be doing something while I'm listening?

6. If I miss something, do I ask the person to repeat it or do I let it drop?

7. Do I have to ask people to repeat what they've said because I've forgotten it?

8. Do I look at the person talking to me, or do I look around and avoid eye contact?

9. Do I listen and try to put myself in the person's shoes before I respond?

10. Do I let whether I like a person affect my response to her?

Keep in touch by phone

If the study is large, the primary leader/teacher should phone the small group discussion leaders. The discussion leaders should call the women in their own groups.

The purpose of these calls is to stay in touch pastorally. Phoning the Bible study members weekly deepens your relationship with each of them. These calls will help you recognize any struggles a woman is having in studying the Bible or in her personal life. They can also open the door for you to share the Gospel with someone who is not yet a believer.

Ask each group member what's the best time for you to call and then honor their schedule. Pray before you call. Expect God to significantly use you. Be ready to pray at the end of the call if it seems appropriate. The first time you do this it may feel awkward, but God will bless it. I have learned this from personal experience.

I can still remember hearing the tears of my friend, Jennifer, over the phone as she explained a crisis to me. She said she knew I would suggest we pray over the telephone — and the thought terrified her. She had barely gotten past the problem of praying out loud at all. But her need was so great she was willing to pray. We were both blessed through praying together and we had the joy of seeing God work in that urgent situation.

Pray for those in the group

Years ago, Shirley, one of my God-given mentors, said, "Carol, never be involved with more people than you can pray for." She said this in the context of discipling, which has been my primary ministry, but it holds true for leading Bible studies as well.

Tell your group members that *you* will pray regularly for them. Encourage *everyone* to pray for each other at home. When requests are shared write them in your prayer notebook. At the following session, ask people to share any answers to prayer and note these as well. (See chap. 2 for practical suggestions on prayer.)

So Many Things

A women's Bible study group can be many things — a family where new believers can be born, where older sisters and spiritual mothers can nurture new believers and model for them what a growing Christian looks like. It can be a refuge for those who have been deeply hurt, a safe place to hear and to learn new ways of responding to life.

To the woman in the marketplace the study provides a counterbalance to the dehumanizing work environment. To the woman at home with preschoolers, it provides adult contact and the stimulus to broaden her horizons. To the woman whose husband won't allow her to go to church on Sunday it provides a spiritual lifeline. To the struggling or stagnant believer it provides an impetus that pushes her to renewed commitment.

This is one of the most effective ministries a women's committee can encourage. The group can be simple, a handful of women around a kitchen table. Or it can be complex with many different discussion groups and a dynamic lecturer. Whatever the size, God will bless the time and energy you invest and lives will be changed for eternity.

Bibliography

There are many excellent Bible study books available; visit your local Christian bookstore for ideas. Some are specifically designed for women, others are equally suitable for both genders. The list below contains the major publishers of Bible studies.

Churches Alive, Box 3800, San Bernadino, CA 92413
The Love One Another Bible Study Series

Navpress: Colorado Springs, Colo.
Ashker, Helene, *Jesus Cares about Women*
God's Design for the Family Series
Heald, Cynthia, *Becoming a Woman of Excellence*
The Creator, My Confidant
Eve out of Eden

Hendricks, Jeanne, *A Mother's Legacy*

Karssen, Gien, *Her Name Is Woman, Books 1 and 2*

Mayhall, Carol, *Filled to Overflowing*
       Lord of My Rocking Boat

Neighborhood Bible Studies, Box 222, Dobbs Ferry, New York, NY 10522

Regal Books, Ventura, Calif.
  Hepburn, Daisy, *Life with Spice Series*

Victor Books, Wheaton, Ill.
  Christensen, Evelyn, *Gaining through Losing*
         "Lord, Change Me!"
         What Happens When Women Pray

Zondervan Publishing House, Grand Rapids, Mich.
  Women's Workshop Series (many titles and authors available)

CHAPTER TEN

Preparing and Delivering
Life-Changing Messages

Major contributors to this chapter were
Peg Burdick and Pat Smith.

Facing Your Fear

Do your knees knock at the thought of preparing and delivering a message? Does any public speaking, even giving an announcement, make you want to hide? If you have *lallophobia,* the fear of speaking in front of people, you're in good company. It's the number one fear for most Americans.

Even Moses, to whom God gave the task of leading the Israelites to the Promised Land, was afraid to speak. His encounter with God at the burning bush has elements that remind us of ourselves.

Moses was thankful God knew the plight of the Israelites. His plan to bring them out of Egypt was good news. However, when Moses heard he was to be God's spokesman it ceased to be good news. God revealed Himself to Moses as the "I AM" — the eternal present-tense God. The God who would meet the need of the hour. Yet Moses continued to hesitate.

He protested, "O Lord, I have never been eloquent, neither in the past nor since You have spoken to Your servant. I am slow of speech and tongue" (Ex. 4:10).

God's response to Moses should also be an encouragement to us. "Who gave man his mouth? Who makes him deaf or dumb? Who gives him sight or makes him blind? Is it not I, the Lord? Now go; I will help you speak and will teach you what to say" (vv. 11-12).

God more than fulfilled His promise. The Book of Deuteronomy begins, "These are the words Moses spoke to all Israel in the desert east of the Jordan." Moses' words in this book are quoted over eighty times in the New Testament. In the forty years since the burning bush, Moses had become eloquent through practice and divine enablement.

Age isn't a valid excuse to avoid speaking. Paul challenged Timothy, "Don't let anyone look down on you because you are young . . . devote yourself to the public reading of Scripture, to preaching and to teaching" (1 Tim. 4:12-13). Timothy wasn't special because he was male or because he lived when he did. God can just as clearly call you. You may be young and timid like Timothy. Or you may be older. Either way, God can prepare you to speak effectively.

Be prepared
Someone may ask *you* to speak in one of the following contexts:
- announcements at church
- public prayer
- Scripture reading
- master of ceremonies for a special event
- devotional at a bridal or baby shower
- leading a Bible study group discussion
- speaker at an evangelistic outreach event
- conference speaker

Make yourself available and if God gives you the opportunity, take it. Look to Him to help you. His strength can only be made perfect in weakness, so be grateful for circumstances that make you dependent on Him. Whenever we respond in obedience, He is there with His strength.

Be vulnerable, open, and honest in your speaking. Your audience wants a real person, not someone hiding behind a mask. At the end of a series of messages I gave in New Zealand, a lady commented to those in charge of the workshops, "When we heard an American was coming, we expected a 'Marilyn Monroe,' instead we just got Carol." She meant someone who wasn't plastic, someone to whom they could relate.

Keep yourself spiritually clean; identify and confess your sins. Keep short accounts with your family and with God. Otherwise Satan will whisper in your ear, "You have no right to be ministering to others." "How can you say to your brother, 'Let me take the speck out of your eye,' when all the time there is a plank in your own eye?" (Matt. 7:4) Take the beam out of your own life before you try to take the splinter out of theirs.

Overcoming the fear of public speaking
In her helpful handbook, *"Who, Me, Give a Speech?"* (Grand Rapids: Baker Book House, 1987, 23–33) Nancy Alford, speech instructor at

Kirtland Community College, suggests ten ways to counteract the public speaking jitters.

1. *Start small.* Begin by making announcements, volunteer to read the Scripture in a Bible study, or make a short presentation to a group.

2. *Choose the right topic.* Depth of subject information will impart confidence.

3. *Get off to a good start.* Begin with humor. Tell or read an attention-getting anecdote.

4. *Be prepared.* Collect the necessary information. Make good notes. Practice your delivery.

5. *Visual aids.* Where possible support your message with overheads, posters, displays, or illustrative objects. Good visual aids can raise retention approximately 50 percent.

6. *Physical condition.* Get lots of sleep, plenty of exercise, and watch what you eat. Brisk walking just prior to speaking will help decrease excess adrenalin. Several deep breaths immediately prior to speaking will also reduce tension.

7. *Mind control.* Don't worry yourself sick. Jehovah God is your Lord. Let Him pour Himself out through you. You have done the preparation, deliver your speech with confidence. "Be strong and courageous. Do not be afraid or terrified because of them, for the Lord your God goes with you; He will never leave you nor forsake you" (Deut. 31:6).

8. *Be audience-centered.* Pray for them. You have something they need to hear. Even an announcement can have life-changing potential.

9. *Visit the scene before you speak.* If distance prevents a prior visit, get there early. Locate the rest room. Check the height of the podium and microphone. Check the lighting and air flow. People are most attentive if the temperature is cool. Ask to have the podium moved as close to the front row as possible. In addition, ask that the seats be arranged in a semicircle. People respond best when they can see one another and feel part of a group.

10. *Be yourself.* Don't copy the speaking style of another person. My husband is a wonderful speaker. His style is appropriate for him; I fall flat on my face when I copy him.

Selecting Your Topic and Collecting Information

Begin this step at least three weeks prior to speaking.

If you're speaking weekly at a Bible study, you may have several messages in various stages of preparation.

Pray for your message for at least as long as you will speak. A thirty-minute message can be prayed for in six, five-minute segments.

Your topic or Scripture passage may be predetermined. However, you will still need to select a specific theme for your talk. The following list will give you ideas of subjects appropriate for different audiences. Whenever possible speak from a topic that excites you.

Topics relevant to all: adversity, ambition, beauty from God's perspective, gaining wisdom, becoming Christlike, criticism, commitment or complacency, compassion, discipline, encouragement, forgiveness, grief, gossip, healing past hurts, pride, priorities, taking risks and resting in God, self-control, self-love, temperaments, thankfulness, controlling the tongue, triumphing in trials, wealth.

Topics for young mothers: aspects of mothering, attitudes toward husbands, building self-esteem, building communication skills, controlling emotions, handling finances, dealing with conflict, building friendships, growing spiritually, managing time.

Topics for mothers of teens: developing through discipline, equipping teens for life, adjusting to mid-life, preparing for the empty nest and retirement, strengthening your self-image, strengthening your marriage, coping with stress.

Topics for older women: adjusting to change, godly grandparenting, reaching out to others with love, rejoicing in retirement, roots in rough times.

A journal can be a rich source of inspiration. Recently I pulled ten years of journals from the top shelf of my closet. There was my life. As I read, I sat in awe of what God had done. Life is so "daily" that we're unable to see God at work gently molding us unless we take time to reflect. It's easier to encourage an audience after seeing God at work in your own life.

Keep a file folder for interesting message starters. Magazine articles, outlines from good sermons, and newspaper clippings can be helpful. After you select your general topic, tightly define it. Move from the general to the specific. Choose your primary points/applications after you complete most of your research.

Meditate on your topic or passage. Expect the Holy Spirit to enlighten you with ideas, remind you of resources, and help you recall practical illustrations. Look for insight during your regular devotional time. Be sensitive throughout the day. Many key points I've used in messages came to me while walking, showering, or playing ball with my dog.

Record the thoughts that come to you, even if they seem peripheral, and place them in the appropriate folder. Try to keep notepaper with you, but don't lose something for lack of paper. Make notes on anything available — I've used check deposit slips and even small receipts when no other paper was handy.

Be flexible. At this point your topic may require adjusting. Keep in mind the needs of your audience. Ask yourself whether your planned approach speaks to their needs, hurts, or interests. You must be relevant to be heard.

Researching Your Message

Two to three weeks prior to speaking start researching additional information.

Select a key Scripture if you haven't already done so. Whether your starting point is a Scripture passage or a topic, consider hanging your message on one key text. It will be easier for the listeners to follow and recall later.

Study that passage thoroughly. Look for what it has to say about those needs, hurts, and interests you identified earlier.

1. *Look for key words,* words that are repeated, words with theological significance, and words that seem important to the passage.

2. *Note contrasting words, phrases, ideas, or lists.* They're often indicated by words such as "but" or "rather than." Examples: flesh/Spirit; light/dark; put on/put off.

3. *Look for lists,* e.g., the fruit of the Spirit listed in Galatians 5:22-23.

4. *Note any commands.*

5. *Find conclusion or purpose words.* These include: "therefore," "so," "so that," "in order that," "for this reason."

6. *Hunt for key principles in the passage.* A principle is an abiding truth relevant at all times. Here are some suggestions to help develop principles:

• State them in present tense. "Older women should encourage younger women" (see Titus 2:3-4).

• Make the statement personal. "I should learn from older women and be available to teach younger women."

• Evaluate yourself in light of the principle. "Am I willing to accept teaching from older women and spend my time training younger women?"

• Determine to make necessary changes. "I will focus on encouraging three younger women this month." "I will make time to regularly see Elizabeth, who can help me through this phase of my life."

• Plan specific, immediate action. "Today, to apply this truth, I will write a note to encourage Karen. I will ask Elizabeth how to be a good mother-in-law."

• When you give a message, restate the main principles by asking questions: "Do you. . . ? Do I. . . ?"

7. *Look up key words in reference works like* Vine's Expository Dictionary of New Testament Words.

8. *Read good commentaries.* Get suggestions from teachers and students of the Word whose judgment you trust. If you live near a Bible school or seminary get a nonstudent card so you can use the library. Take notes documenting the sources of materials you use.

9. *Read books and listen to tapes dealing with the passage.* Check your church's tape library for messages which might contain relevant material. There are numerous mail-order tape services which can supply you with helpful tapes.

10. *Keep meditating on your topic.*

Outlining Your Message
Begin this step four to seven days prior to speaking.

Review all your notes. Notice those areas in which you have limited material. Do further research to clarify or further develop your key thoughts.

A message has three main sections: an introduction, a body, and a conclusion.

Introduction
Use a story, illustration, or news item to grab attention. Anecdotes involve your listener. Be sure your introduction introduces the message instead of being filler. A humorous incident must relate to what will follow.

Never open with an excuse. Don't say, "This is my first time," "I'm nervous," or "I had to work late every night this week and had little time to prepare." Use an introduction that sets you and the audience at ease, yet gives the impression what you're about to say is important.

The introduction may be the last thing you write. Watch for events in your own life immediately prior to speaking which could serve as an opening.

Body
The primary content is usually divided into three key points. Each of the points will flow logically if you:
- *explain* the content
- *expand* on background information, customs, terms, and concepts
- *expound* and clarify the principles, truths, or promises

Use illustrations from Scripture, nature, common experience, and your own life. Personal illustrations are often the most powerful. Be transparent, let the audience identify with your struggles.

Be specific in your application. Tell what action your listeners should take and give specific directions for follow-through.

Conclusion

Review each of your key points. If possible use an illustration to involve your audience emotionally. Remember to call them to specific action.

Keep the conclusion brief; use simple, positive, yet forceful words. When you are through, quit. Landing a plane is an apt analogy. A pilot lands smoothly and comes to a stop.

Rick Warren, senior pastor of Saddleback Valley Community Church, Mission Viejo, California, suggests the following questions to help you shape your message so your audience will hear and take action.

1. What is the most *practical* way to say it? Tell them the benefits. Show them the steps to achieve it. Keep your audience from saying, "Yes, but how?"

2. What is the most *positive* and encouraging way to say it? Negative teaching results in negative people. Teach to reinforce faith, renew hope, and restore love. Tell your hearers *they can do it!*

3. What is the *simplest* way to say it? Avoid using religious jargon. If it's necessary to use a theological term explain it fully.

4. What it the *most personal* way to say it? Involve yourself. Share your struggles; where you're currently making progress and how you're growing in that area.

In addition Rick suggests you make the main applications the principle points of your outline. These two outlines of Jonah illustrate the concept.

Content Outline

Chapter 1 — See Jonah Running
Chapter 2 — See Jonah Repenting
Chapter 3 — See Jonah Returning
Chapter 4 — See Jonah Raving

Application Outline

Chapter 1 — You can run but you can't hide
Chapter 2 — When you hit bottom look up
Chapter 3 — God gives a second chance
Chapter 4 — God cares about everyone

Writing and Rehearsing Your Message

Three to four days prior to speaking expand the outline into your complete message.

By now you will have your outline and a pile of notes. Arrange each note according to its position in the outline. Occasionally this involves cutting a page into several parts to get information into the appropriate stack. You may discover you need more information in some areas. Fill in where needed.

Add illustrations. *Reader's Digest* and *National Geographic* are great sources. Keep 3x5 cards handy to take down illustrations you hear on the radio or during a good talk. File illustrations according to subject for easy recall.

Use whatever note method works best for you. Some speakers like note cards, others an outline on sheets of paper. If you prefer well-developed notes, try using several different pen colors for ease in speaking (green for illustrations, red for Scripture, and so on.) Several pastors write out their sermon word for word. They pay attention to the sound and content of each phrase. The key thing is do what works for you.

One hundred and seventy words on a typed page (standard double-spaced page) equals one minute's talking time. A fifteen- to twenty-minute talk adds up to ten to twelve typed, double-spaced, pages. Dog ear the lower right hand corner of your notes to facilitate page turning.

Dorothy Sarnoff, founder of Speech Dynamics, Inc., has developed a note-making process called "Phrase-A-Line" (*Never Be Nervous Again* [New York: Crown Publishers, Inc. 1987], 52ff). It is fast-food for the eyes. The notes are typed in upper case, one phrase to a line. This enables the eyes to sweep through the notes, pick up a few lines, and then look at the audience during delivery.

Two to three days prior to "message day" rehearse your talk. Use a tape recorder for practice. You'll be less distracted by the sound of your own voice if you listen with your back to the recorder. Listen for content, note what's missing, or what there is too much of. Listening will trigger new ideas. Reedit your talk and record it again until you're satisfied.

If you practice four times you will remember your talk and be almost free of the need to read your notes.

Check your wardrobe. It's best to wear an outfit you feel comfortable in. My college roommate coined the term "understated elegance" — a good goal for a speaker. Dorothy Sarnoff suggests dresses or blouses that have higher necks. In addition she says, "Add an interesting pin or a couple of chains. Sometimes a chunky necklace with large beads or stones will do the trick. Avoid round Peter Pan collars or stiff man-tailored shirt collars. They look collegiate or little-girlish" (*Never Be Nervous Again* [New York: Crown Publishers, Inc. 1987], 89).

Color is important. Bright ones give you as well as your audience an emotional lift. Red, yellow, bright blues, and kelly greens are good colors. Stay away from brown and black even if they are your colors.

Plan ahead to get a good night's sleep before delivery day.

Delivering Your Message

By this point you should be "prayed up." Ask friends to support you in prayer as well. You have done the work. Ask the Lord to fill your thoughts and words with power to change lives. A verse I learned as a child often comes to mind before I speak, "Let the words of my mouth, and the meditation of my heart, be acceptable in Thy sight, O Lord, my strength, and my Redeemer" (Ps. 19:14, KJV).

Arrive early. Get clear directions from your hostess. Take a map. I courted disaster once by leaving late and forgetting the directions. As a result I was still breathless when I began my message.

Give a typed introduction to your hostess. This is the best way to assure you'll be correctly presented to the audience. Your introducer will be grateful.

Step quickly and confidently to the microphone. Begin immediately with your talk. You will lose the crowd if you fiddle with your notes before beginning. Stand with your weight equally distributed on the balls of both feet. Tighten your stomach muscles and flex your knees slightly.

Delivery do's
- maintain eye contact by sweeping the audience
- vary your pitch and delivery speed
- pause before and after important ideas
- repeat key points
- stress important words
- be yourself
- smile!

and don'ts
- read your notes
- use fillers such as "uh" and "um"
- tug nervously at your hair or clothing
- chew gum
- go over your alloted time

Follow-through

Be available to talk to people after the message. Seek out anyone who seemed especially responsive, particularly anyone who seemed teary or tense during the message. Time with you may trigger a life-changing decision.

Graciously accept compliments if they are given. Don't brush them aside. Give God the credit for using you, but accept thanks for your personal effort.

Evaluating Your Message

Critiquing yourself will help you be more professional and effective each time you speak. These questions can help you evaluate how you did.

1. Did the message begin with people's needs, hurts, or interests? Did I get and keep their attention?

2. Did the message have impact from personal conviction? Did it include what I am currently learning? Was it honest?

3. Did the message offer practical help? Were there sufficient "how-to's"?

4. Was the outline clearly stated?

5. Were there sufficient illustrations to add interest?

6. Was the conclusion powerful, with desired action stated?

7. Was the delivery good? Did I maintain eye contact? Were my gestures appropriate? Was I tied to my notes?

8. Were my grammar and word choices accurate and sharp?

9. Was the message one that I would have wanted to hear?

10. Was I aware of the enabling power of the Holy Spirit as I spoke?

You may think of things you wish you had said and recall words you wish you hadn't. But don't let Satan attack you over it (1 Peter 5:8-9).

Be prepared for a letdown after you speak. Your adrenalin has been flowing. You were being prayed for by many people. Now, only those who regularly pray for you are praying and your adrenalin high is over.

The letdown can be countered by anticipating it, having a lighter schedule for a short period after a major effort, and by starting immediately to plan for the next ministry opportunity.

It's God's Word

Message preparation need not scare us if we prepare well. It's God's Word we are proclaiming not our own. "So is My word that goes out from My mouth: It will not return to Me empty, but will accomplish what I desire and achieve the purpose for which I sent it. You will go out in joy and be led forth in peace" (Isa. 55:11-12).

Depend on the Holy Spirit to take all you are and fill it with all He is for Christ's glory.

Start wherever you are and go on from there. If you're giving announcements in your Sunday School class, take the principles from this chapter that apply and do your announcing well. Maybe someday you will be the plenary speaker at a women's conference.

Bibliography

Alford, Nancy I. *Who, Me, Give a Speech?* Handbook for Christian Women. Grand Rapids: Baker Book House, 1987.

Carnegie, Dale. *How to Develop Self-Confidence and Influence People by Public Speaking.* New York: Pocket Books, 1956.

Davis, Ken. *How to Speak to Youth.* Loveland, Colo.: Group Books, 1968.

Gregory, John Milton. *The Seven Laws of Teaching.* Grand Rapids: Baker Book House, Twenty-eighth printing, 1986.

Hybels, Bill, *Stuart Briscoe, and Haddon Robinson. Mastering Contemporary Preaching.* Portland, Ore.: Multnomah Press, 1989.

Jackson, Edgar N. *How to Preach to People's Needs.* Grand Rapids: Baker Book House, 1970.

Lloyd-Jones, D. Martyn. *Preaching and Preachers.* Grand Rapids: Zondervan Publishing House, 1971.

Pippert, Rebecca M. *Out of the Salt-Shaker and Into the World.* Downers Grove, Ill.: InterVarsity, 1979.

Robinson, Haddon W. *Biblical Preaching — The Development and Delivery of Expository Messages.* Grand Rapids: Baker Book House, 1980.

Sarnoff, Dorothy. *Never Be Nervous Again.* New York: Crown Publishers, Inc., 1987.

Whitesell, Faris D. *Power in Expository Preaching.* Old Tappan, N.J.: Fleming H. Revell, 1963.

Wallace, Joanne. *Dress with Style.* Old Tappan, N.J.: Revell, 1983.

Willingham, Ronald, L. *How to Speak So People Will Listen.* Waco Texas: Word Book Publishers, 1968.

CHAPTER ELEVEN
Helping Women Grow

When God touches a woman's life, His goal is for her to grow into spiritual maturity. Paul explains this in Romans 8:29: "For those God foreknew He also predestined to be conformed to the likeness of His Son." At the moment of salvation, He forgives all her sins; she is pure in His eyes. God is ready to begin the molding process, taking the past and weaving it into a present that will give Him glory. He begins where she is and builds her into a choice vessel.

That molding process can be long and tortuous for some individuals. Mary Magdalene might have been such a person. We know little of her past, only that she had seven demons cast out. We are left in the dark as to how and why they got there. But, under Jesus' care she became a leader among women and the trusted bearer of the Resurrection news. He is still at work in miraculous ways today.

This chapter is about how to help women grow through new believer follow-up and discipling, mentoring friendships, and visitation.

Following Up New Believers

Lynn is one of God's modern-day miracles. Just five years ago Lynn was sitting stiffly on my living room couch. Two days before she had asked Christ into her life. Her decision was not impulsive. A coworker had challenged her to read through the Bible. In addition his life was an open book to her through seven years of contact. She knew what it meant to become a believer — life change. And she wanted it.

She made the decision that started the process. Now what? Though she had read the Bible, Lynn had no idea how to live like a Christian. Nothing in her background prepared her for that. After spending some time getting to know her, I gently suggested that she might like someone to meet with her and help her grow. She just sat there, then a tear started to roll down her face. I set up an appointment for the next Wednesday. Since her husband was not a believer, we would meet at her workplace during lunch.

Today Lynn is a coworker in God's kingdom. She is using her gifts of mercy and encouragement to follow-up other new believers.

All new believers, even the most disciplined, need follow-up and can benefit from regularly meeting with an established Christian. The unmotivated and those with lifestyle problems desperately need help in establishing their new lives in Christ.

Spiritual pediatrics

First Peter 2:2 suggests that the new believer is similar to a newborn baby who will grow best on milk. Concentrate on the basics. Use a simple, basic study guide. Your denomination may publish one or you may want to use some of the materials developed by the Navigators and published by NavPress.

You want the new believer to understand:
- the character and nature of God
- the Lord's authority in her life
- assurance of salvation
- victory over sin
- the importance of studying the Bible and applying it to life
- the necessity of a consistent quiet time
- the need to be involved in a local church and to be ministering to other believers
- the importance of witnessing to non-Christians

There is no single right method for communicating all this. I have found it best to start with a structured series of six to eight sessions. Some new believers come from a chaotic lifestyle. Meeting regularly at a set time can begin to provide order in their lives.

You may meet one-on-one with someone, or, if circumstances allow, you may follow-up several new believers at the same time. A group of three is less intense and may be more comfortable for some women. If you meet with several new believers together they will learn from each other as well as form valuable friendships. If you meet as a group, schedule some individual time with each new believer to assure life application.

A follow-up session should contain the following elements:

Introductory casual conversation. Review the week's events. Be a friend. Ask how different areas of her life are progressing. Be transparent with her as well.

Praying together. Keep your prayers short and to the point. Don't overwhelm her with your ability to pray. Encourage her to pray a short prayer. For the first several sessions, she may not be comfortable praying out loud. Don't push.

Sharing insights from your quiet times. Begin a new believer with the Book of John. Instruct her to read part of a chapter daily and note what God says to her. Encourage, but do not force, note-taking. Writing insights and applications facilitates sharing and encourages accountability.

Reviewing memory work. Most new believer follow-up material includes basic verses like: 1 John 5:11-12 — assurance of salvation; 1 John 1:9 — assurance of forgiveness; John 16:24 — assurance of answered prayer; 1 Corinthians 10:13 — assurance of help in temptation; Proverbs 3:5-6 — assurance of guidance. Be sure you share with her the verses you are memorizing as well.

Discussing the material studied. Assign as much material in the study book you're using as you can cover in one session. Undisciplined, new believers who are not used to reading for information may need help with lesson preparation. Be understanding and do it with them. I have spent over a year working with a young woman for whom reading is difficult. She has more than made up for her lack of reading comprehension by her excitement at being a Christian. Your goal is life change and growing love for the Lord and His Word, not head knowledge.

Making a clear assignment for the next session. Make contact during the week to check on progress and answer any questions. If her schedule is busy, check immediately prior to the appointment to confirm if she can make it.

Closing prayer together. Both of you should pray for practical application of the material covered in the session. Include specific requests from your life and hers.

Who can help new believers grow?
You can. Any woman who is "older" in the faith can help those who are "younger" in the areas of practical Christian living. You don't have to be fully grown yourself, just growing. If you can answer yes to most of the following questions, you're ready to encourage a new believer.

1. Am I following Jesus and seeking to obey Him?
2. Do I have consistent devotional times?
3. Am I studying God's Word, memorizing it, and seeking to apply it to my life daily?
4. Do I have a consistent, systematic prayer life?
5. Am I sharing my faith with others?
6. Is God changing my character to conform me to Jesus?

Finding Someone to Follow-Up

Lifestyle evangelism will lead naturally into follow-up when your friends accept the Lord. I shared Christ, as opportunities developed, over a period of fifteen years with a neighbor. Several years ago she became a believer. Follow-up lessons were the next logical step. Now she is incorporated in a midweek Bible study and attends church regularly.

There are other ways to get started in follow-up. Someone may become a believer at church. Offer to do the follow-up. You can introduce the concept by saying, "When I was a new believer, I was helped by someone meeting with me to show me how to grow as a Christian. Would you like to try getting together for several weeks?" or, "I wish someone had been available to help me get started in the Christian life. Does that sound like a good idea to you?" If the answer is positive, then set the date and place.

There are times when the approach needs to be even more low key. Extend an invitation for coffee at a local restaurant. During the evening introduce the idea. Make it clear that in any case that you are interested in her as a friend, not as a project.

Paula and I got started from a contact initiated at church. Early one Sunday morning she woke with a burning desire to get to a church. She recalled an invitation given to her by a lady to visit our church. After the sermon, Paula was desperate to know God and receive forgiveness for her sins.

I was there to help her commit her life to Christ, after which I made an appointment to meet with her. In Paula's case, her knowledge of what was involved in salvation was marginal. Without the follow-up sessions which lasted over a year, I doubt that her salvation would have been real. Many times the point of salvation will actually occur during the follow-up.

Your church may have a New Believers Class to help young Christians get established. This is wonderful, but a baby believer will still benefit greatly from having a big sister help her on an individual basis. There is never enough time in a class to ask questions. Many new believers would be too intimidated to ask questions. Ask the class leader to suggest someone for you to assist.

You are not alone in the task of follow-up.

We must remember that God has taken up residence in the life of every Christian, and that it is *His* consuming desire to make that person like Christ. You and I have simply been given the privilege of working with Him in this task. The life of Christ becomes ours through what the Holy Spirit does in making us new! But what can this mean to us as we follow up growing Christians?

Most of all it can help motivate us. There is no future in trying to breathe life into a corpse. We can't follow up a dead man. But here is a live one! Surely this person in whom the Spirit of God dwells is worthy of the best efforts we can put forth to help guide him toward maturity (Hugh Harris, *Discipleship Journal*, Issue 16, July 1, 1983, 28).

Discipling Develops Spiritual Reproducers

Discipling is a continuation of the process begun in follow-up. Follow-up and discipling have much in common. Both involve the more mature assisting the less mature. Both can occur in small groups or one-on-one relationships. The outline of a typical session is even similar. But the goals are different.

The goal of follow-up is to get a new baby on her feet. The focus is on the basics. The goal of discipling is to assist someone in developing a lifestyle that is Christlike.

Christian discipleship runs against the tide of contemporary American culture. Freedom and individuality are praised. Self-knowledge and self-actualization have high market value. But Jesus proclaimed self-renunciation, self-surrender, and self-sacrifice. The way of the cross was not popular then and it isn't popular now.

When we disciple someone, we help press the claims of Christ on every area of her life. This is delicate work. A discipler must be humble. We all need someone to sharpen us at one time or another. Each has her own blind spot; a beam lurks in the corner of every eye. But though we need this sharpening, we resist it. Our fragile self-esteem cringes from needed correction. Therefore, discipling must be done within an atmosphere of caring for one another.

Beth Mainhood has written an excellent book on discipling, *Reaching Your World: Disciplemaking for Women* (Colorado Springs: NavPress, 1986). In it she suggests the following three principles for discipling:

The major source of our ministry is Jesus Christ. "For we do not preach ourselves, but Jesus Christ as Lord, and ourselves as your servants for Jesus' sake" (2 Cor. 4:5). Discipling is mentoring. Your life will be an open book and it will be copied. Paul said, "Follow my example, as I follow the example of Christ" (1 Cor. 11:1). Do not proclaim yourself, your life is there for them to see anyway. Actively proclaim the lordship of Jesus Christ. Your teaching is never, "Do as I do," but, "Do as Christ did."

The major content of our ministry is the Word of God. Make study of the Word central in your discipling sessions. If basic doctrine is not coherently presented in your church, follow a specified course of study. Navpress has published a series of studies entitled Design for Discipleship for this purpose. Teach a believer to go to the Word for her answers. It is the Word of God which will perform the work in her life, not the discipler. You are there to model for the believer and to help her stay in touch with the Word (1 Thes. 2:13).

A discipler must be available for the sake of the one she is ministering to. We are in another person's life to consistently model Christ's love. This will mean times of self-sacrifice. You will be tired when she needs you. It will not always be convenient to listen patiently on the phone.

For me it often means setting aside my hobbies of bird-watching or sewing. Jigsaw puzzles had to drop out of my life entirely; they were consumers of time that I needed for ministry. You will need to make your own decisions on what will go. I can assure you that something will. But the returns will be far greater.

Paul spoke of the Thessalonians as his hope, joy, and crown of exultation (1 Thes. 2:19). If you will be poured out as a drink offering for others in a discipling ministry, you too will know the joy Paul spoke of.

Mentoring Friendships Encourage Growth

(This section was adapted from material by Ruth Barton, who is also the author of *Women Like Us, Wisdom for Today's Issues* [Wheaton Ill.: Harold Shaw Publishers, 1989].)

Follow-up and discipling are exciting for those involved. But for most of our adult lives, we aren't new or young believers, yet we often need personal help from those who are more mature. What then?

That's where mentoring comes in. The dictionary defines a mentor as a tutor, coach, or counselor. The key idea is that the more experienced person helps the less experienced. Every one of us can use help from those who are further along the road of life. For some women the need is even more acute. In her wonderful book, *Women Encouraging Women* (Portland, Ore.: Multnomah Press, 1987, 18–19) Lucibel Van Atta describes five categories of women who need the special nurture and care mentoring can provide:

- women from non-Christian homes
- women with emotional hurts
- women without mothers
- widow and single parents
- single women

These women may not need specific discipling, nor professional counseling, they just need somebody who cares and is available.

Mentoring relationships are less structured, more practical, and open-ended. They are as diverse as individual personalities. Though some women may choose to center these helping relationships around Bible study and prayer time, most choose to base them more on friendship, teaching by example, and spontaneous instruction. These friendships focus on sharing experience and expertise in things like marriage, child-rearing, homemaking, hospitality, crafts and hobbies, ministry, spiritual growth, and personal development.

Scripture suggests that mentoring should be going on in the church. Listen to the words of Titus 2:3-5; "Likewise, teach the older women to be reverent in the way they live, not to be slanderers or addicted to much wine, but to teach what is good. Then they can train the younger women to love their husbands and children, to be self-controlled and pure, to be busy at home, to be kind, and to be subject to their husbands so that no one will malign the Word of God." But today's culture mitigates against this happening automatically.

For one thing, older women are busy. Many are back in the work force and don't think they have time to help younger women. Another problem is the perception of a gulf created by experience and perhaps education level between the younger and older generations. This makes even the forty-year-old think she has little to give the younger woman. If the older woman is sixty-five or more, connecting with the younger women may seem a formidable task. A third problem originates in the attitude of the younger woman. Either she doesn't see her need for a mentor or she's waiting for the *perfect* older woman to reach out to her.

Women's ministries leaders can encourage and nourish mentoring relationships in many ways. They can sponsor activities which encourage women from different age-groups to work and share together. Intergenerational Bible study groups and kitchen and nursery service provide natural opportunities for friendships to develop. I have fond memories of several hours spent quilting in a Bucks County, Pennsylvania church. Being right in the middle of "quilting country" the church has an entire room set aside for quilting. During designated hours of the week women of all ages sit and quilt together. It might as well be called the "mentoring room," instead of the "quilting room."

Women's ministry can build older women's confidence by assuring them they don't need formal training in order to be effective mentors of young women. The issue is not having lived perfectly, but having responded biblically to the problems of life. Younger women need realistic role models. They will learn more from the rough spots than from life's pleasant, level paths.

Here are some practical steps you can take to encourage mentoring. Let's start with the young woman. First, she must desire mentoring. The next step is to locate a mentor within her church, perhaps someone she already knows or else someone suggested by the women's council. Then the young woman should just ask to spend some time with the older woman at her convenience. The younger woman can be specific about her needs or just feel her way along. If the first session goes well, she can arrange to spend more time with the prospective mentor. She should ask God to use this older woman in her life.

For the last few months I've been casually mentoring a young single woman. About once a month she reminds me it's time we did something together. We've hiked in the hills, gone to the beach, walked the dog, attended a conference, and seen a movie together. Each time the activity merely formed a backdrop for some mentoring.

Now let's approach the relationship from the position of the mentor-to-be. She should ask God to lead her to that special younger daughter in the Lord, and think about the women in the congregation as she prays.

Next she should select someone and invite her over for lunch or out for coffee in the evening. She should pray that God will guide the conversation and observe what He does with the evening. If the time went well and was profitable then they can mutually agree on another meeting. They can keep the commitment casual and open-ended or agree to explore a topic together for a specified length of time.

Let's not forget the value of peer relationships. I have a special friend who, over the last several years, has mentored me as a peer. We've challenged one another to Scripture memorization in prayer together and shared our treasured Bible verses. My life would be impoverished without her presence in it. In a peer relationship no one is the designated mentor. Both are on an equal plane with each other — near the same age and stage in spiritual growth. God can do mighty things in your life through a peer.

Visitation Encourages Growth

I wish appointments with people were unnecessary. It seems wrong when good friends must call to set up a time together. But that is a reality for most of us, especially those of us who work outside the home.

Deliberate, planned visits with women can be an effective ministry to encourage growth. Newcomers to your church should be visited. Those absent for three consecutive Sundays benefit from a visit. Anyone going through a particularly tough time appreciates a loving chat with another woman.

Some churches have a structured visitation program, which includes a training session and submission of written visitation reports. The church leadership team might suggest an appropriate woman to visit, or the choice might be left to the visitor. An important aspect of such a program is the training of a novice visitor by one experienced in the ministry.

You will be better prepared for evangelistic visits if you know how to give a brief testimony and feel comfortable using one of the many "four-step" tracts to explain the Gospel.

Here are some tips for making visits as effective as possible, adapted from the *Visitation Training Manual* of Fairhaven Bible Chapel in San Leandro, California.

Always show concern for the individual. Listen carefully to what is going on in her life (refer to the self-evaluation at the end of chap. 9). Empathize. Don't be quick to judge or offer solutions. Be a vehicle of God's love and forgiveness.

Ask questions to determine needs. A woman's most important need may be for salvation (see chap. 14 on personal evangelism for ideas on sharing the Gospel). She may need help with her marriage, career choices, parenting, coping with a dysfunctional background, etc. Listen until you discern her primary needs.

Define needed action. After listening to her you may discover areas in which she needs to take action. The action may vary from initiating a Bible reading program, to getting out of an unhealthy relationship. Support her in her decisions. Be patient if she isn't ready to change.

Assist with problems. The one you visit may be a senior citizen who needs help raking leaves or putting on storm windows. Make arrangements for this help.

Encourage in ministry. One of the best ways to solve personal problems is by investing in the lives of others. Help people find a place of ministry within the church body.

The visit doesn't have to take place in a formal environment. Several days ago I conducted a "visit" while sitting on the ground in a field taking turns with a woman throwing a ball for my springer spaniel, Dutchess. An informal atmosphere is often more conducive to sharing on a deeper level. Try meeting in a coffee shop or a nearby park. Your goal is to make her comfortable and relaxed so she will hear God speak through you.

Before concluding the visit inquire if there's anything else she would like to discuss. Beware though, you may be opening a Pandora's box at this point. She may now trust you enough to reveal some deep needs. You can choose to deal with them at this point, schedule another session, or perhaps, if appropriate, refer her to someone else.

Follow-up after the visit by praying for her and watching for her at church. Keep in touch to gauge her progress. Encourage her. She will appreciate the time you took to help her down the road of spiritual growth.

Find Us Faithful

When you and I became believers, we joined a family. Being bought with the price of Christ's blood, we now belong to Him and through Him to every other believer. "For none of us lives to himself [herself] alone" (Rom. 14:7) and because of this we are indeed our sisters' keeper.

Live your life in such a way as to make a positive difference in the lives of others. Your impact may be through casual mentoring, through following-up new believers, or through discipling mature believers into ministry. You may be the peer counselor who gives frightened women hope for the future. Abandon your life to God and His service and He will use you for His glory in the lives of others.

The heartbeat of this chapter is expressed in the words of the song, "Find Us Faithful." May they also express your heartbeat and mine.

Find Us Faithful

We are pilgrims on a journey of a narrow road,
and those who've gone before line the way,
cheering on the faithful, encouraging the weary,
their lives a stirring testament to God's sustaining grace.

Surrounded by so great a cloud of witnesses,
let us run the race not only for the prize.
But as those who've gone before us,
let us leave to those behind us,
the heritage of faithfulness as taught by godly lives.

Oh, may all who come behind us find us faithful,
may the fire of our devotion light their way.
May the footprints that we leave lead them to believe,
and the life we live inspire them to obey.

Oh, may all who come behind us find us faithful,
after all our hopes and dreams have come and gone,
and our children sift through all we've left behind.
May the clues that they discover and the memories that they uncover
become the light that we've been, to the road that we each must find.

Oh, may all who come behind us find us faithful.

CHAPTER TWELVE

Ministering to Women in Pain

I first met Janice at a summer Bible study. About a dozen of us were scattered on brightly colored quilts in a neighborhood park. She usually arrived late and sat on the outside edge of the group. For the first several sessions Janice was quiet. Too quiet. Then bit by bit she began to trust us with who she was. Life had been cruel to her. She was raised by alcoholic, abusive parents and now her husband continued the abusive pattern.

The group accepted and encircled Janice with the warmth of Christ's love. By the end of the summer she began her journey toward wholeness by accepting His death for her sins. But her ability to experience Christ's love and intimate presence was blocked by a past in which she had both sinned and had been sinned against. The trip would be a long and difficult one for Janice, one she could not make without the love and support of a caring Christian community.

Our churches are full of women like Janice. This chapter is about ministering to them. Their stories are different but their pain is similar. Their hurts may be emotional, physical, or a combination of both. Women's ministry can work together with the other ministries of your church to create an environment in which the healing of women in pain can occur. We are not the healers — the Holy Spirit is. But we have the privilege and responsibility to be the human instruments through which He works.

Here are some basic suggestions on ways to minister to sexually abused women and to battered wives. This material isn't exhaustive by any means. But it does give you a foundation on which you can build. (Material dealing with alcohol related abuse can be found in chap. 17.) The chapter concludes with guidelines on developing a counseling ministry in a variety of church settings.

Ministering to the Sexually Abused

(This section was adapted from material by Felecia Thompson.)
Thousands of women in our churches need to be restored spiritually,
emotionally, and socially because of being sexually abused by fathers,
brothers, uncles, cousins, or even by female relatives. They have hidden
within their hearts the agony caused by abuse, molestation, or rape
which they experienced as a child or adolescent.

Statistics indicate that fathers or stepfathers are the offenders in the
majority of reported sexual abuse cases involving young girls. And hun-
dreds of thousands of childhood sexual abuse cases never get reported
because of the victim's fear, shame, or lack of self-esteem. Many abuse
victims have never been able to tell anyone their painful secret. With
love and caring, women's ministries can reach out to these wounded
women. They need love and most of them need Christ as well.

Characteristics of women who were victims of childhood sexual trauma can include:

● Recurrent and intrusive recollections, dreams, or "reliving" of
experiences

● Generalized anxiety, mistrust, and/or isolation

● Difficulty forming or maintaining nonexploitive intimate
relationships

● Sexual dysfunction

● Chronic depression, self-blame, and poor self-esteem — identity focused on a sense of "badness"

● Inappropriate guilt: underlying resentment

● Diminished self-protection, masochistic strivings, and repeated
victimization

● Impulsive or self-injurious behavior (suicide attempts, self-mutila-
tion, substance abuse)

● Contempt for women, including themselves

● Tendency to fear men, yet overvalue and idealize them as well

● Tumultuous adolescence (early pregnancy, running away, substance abuse)

● Passivity and unassertiveness

● History of promiscuity or prostitution

● Intergenerational transmission (abusing own children or marrying
a man who does)

● Defection from family's religion

● History of childhood learning problems

(Taken from "Long Term Effects of Unresolved Sexual Trauma,"
Steven L. Shearer, Ph.D., Carol A. Herbert, M.M., Vol. 36, p. 170, AFB,
October 1987.)

How you can help

1. If you are working with younger children and adolescents, when the sexual abuser has been identified, he must be reported to the proper authorities. If the abuser is a father or stepfather he must be separated from the home until he has been declared "safe" by those able to discern.

2. Attempt to meet the girl in her pain and betrayal. She will be feeling an inability to trust, complete loneliness, and abandonment. In order to bring about healing and restoration she must be ministered to by someone who can understand her intense confusion.

3. The victim of sexual abuse may have a root fear and inability to trust authority figures, work around that — not against it.

4. Learn to intercede in prayer effectively for the abused in areas of healing and protection (Isa. 30:18; Eph. 1:18-19; 3:16).

5. Be aware of vulnerable areas:
- desperate need to be loved and proneness to wrong choices in romantic relationships
- fear of pregnancy
- deep-down fatigue; weakness
- suicidal gesture, desire to die
- vulnerability to drugs and alcohol
- promiscuity
- frigidity
- anorexia/bulimia

6. Help her seek professional counseling with a trained therapist who works with sexual abuse victims.

7. Start a support group at your church with a trained therapist for women victims of sexual abuse.

8. Be there for the victims in a ministry of love and trust-building.

Helpful resources

Allender, Dr. Dan B. *The Wounded Heart, Hope for Adult Victims of Childhood Sexual Abuse.* Colorado Springs, Colo.: NavPress, 1990.

Hancock, Maxine, and Karen Burton Mains. *Child Sexual Abuse: A Hope for Healing.* Wheaton, Ill.: Harold Shaw Publishers, 1987.

Morrison, Jan. *A Safe Place beyond Sexual Abuse.* Wheaton, Ill.: Harold Shaw Publishers, 1990.

Peters, David. *A Betrayal of Innocence: What Everyone Should Know about Child Sexual Abuse.* Waco, Texas: Word Books, 1986.

Tanner, Vicki, and Lynda Elliott. *My Father's Child: Help and Healing for the Victims of Emotional, Sexual, and Physical Abuse.* Brentwood, Tenn.: Wolgemuth and Hyatt, Publishers, Inc., 1988.

Ministering to Battered Wives

Husbands, love your wives, just as Christ loved the church and gave Himself up for her. . . . In this same way, husbands ought to love their wives as their own bodies. He who loves his wife loves himself. . . . However, each one of you also must love his wife as he loves himself, and the wife must respect her husband" (Eph. 5:25, 28, 33).

Sadly, many Christian women are physically abused by their husbands. Strong emotional dependence, coupled with wrong theology, often leaves these women defenseless and confused.

Women leaders in the church should keep their eyes open for women who are bruised or battered in any way. These leaders should work at developing a climate in which women will feel comfortable sharing their deepest needs. They should learn to recognize family situations which can create and foster the cycle of abuse (poor communication between spouses combined with outside stresses). Abuse is cyclical in nature.

1. The abuse occurs.

2. A honeymoon period consisting of forgiveness and easing of the tension follows. This honeymoon often convinces the wife to stay in the abusive situation.

3. Pressure builds through unresolved circumstances and the inability to appropriately express emotions.

4. Abuse recurs. Sometimes the victim deliberately triggers the abuse in order to return to the honeymoon period.

5. Time does not improve the situation. The abuse periods grow closer together and the honeymoon period grows shorter.

6. The wife must be encouraged to take action immediately after an abusive episode before the honeymoon period returns.

God's view of physical abuse in marriage

A battered wife must be told that abuse is not God's will for her. Never is it biblical for a woman to endure beatings: not to save her marriage, not for the sake of the children, and not as a punishment for her sins.

No matter what a wife might do, absolutely no sin warrants being beaten. Jesus forgave the adulterous woman (John 8:1-11). Though a woman may view her sin as beyond forgiveness, God promises that "if we confess our sins, He is faithful and just and will forgive us our sins and purify us from all unrighteousness" (1 John 1:9).

Wife abuse is a sin. A man who beats a woman violates God's law. Wife abuse is illegal, immoral, and ungodly. God hates violence (Ps. 11:5; Isa. 60:18). Both the Old and New Testaments present God as a God of peace (Num. 6:26; Ps. 29:11; Eph. 2:14; Phil. 4:7). As Christians, we are commanded to live in peace with one another (Eph. 4:2-3; 1 Thes. 5:13).

Christians are called to serve God, but a Christian wife oppressed by physical abuse may find it difficult to serve the Lord. God doesn't desire that a woman be demoralized, enslaved, and prevented from serving Him.

Satan's lies about wife abuse

- Your husband's abuse is punishment for your sins and God's way of developing your character
- God wants you to sacrifice yourself and be a martyr
- The beatings are God's way of testing you and drawing you closer to Himself
- Battering is the chastisement of the Lord
- If you suffer enough, your husband will change
- All you have to do is bind Satan effectively and the abuse will stop
- If only you would pray "right," your prayers would be answered

What the battered wife can do

- Pray for your abuser
- Pray for yourself and your children
- Find a prayer partner or prayer group for support
- Surround yourself with love from friends, family, and God
- Stay spiritually fit
- Maintain your purity. Don't imitate your abuser by returning evil for evil (1 Peter 3:8-12)
- Trust in God's promises (Isa. 41:10-13; Joel 2:25-26; Matt. 11:28-30; Rom. 8:15-16, 38-39)
- Practice forgiveness and "tough love"
- Take action. Seek help from Christian friends, pastoral leaders, and professionals experienced with wife abuse
- Know when enough is enough. Only you and God can answer that question

(This material was adapted from *Help for the Battered Woman,* by Lydia Savina, published by Bridge Publishing, 2500 Hamilton Blvd., South Plainfield, NJ 07080, 1987.)

Helpful resources
Alsdurf, James and Phyllis. *Battered into Submission: The Tragedy of Wife Abuse in the Christian Home.* Downers Grove, Ill.: InterVarsity Press, 1989.

Berry, Jo. *Beloved Unbeliever.* Grand Rapids: Zondervan Publishing House, 1981.

Dobson, Dr. James, C. *Love Must Be Tough.* Waco, Texas: Word, 1983.

Foster, Richard. *Money, Sex & Power.* San Francisco: Harper & Row, 1983.

Meier, Paul and Frank Minirth. *Happiness Is a Choice.* Grand Rapids: Baker Book House, 1978.

Walker, Lenore. *The Battered Woman.* New York: Harper & Row, 1979.

National Coalition Against Domestic Violence
2401 Virginia Ave. N.W. Suite 305
Washington, D.C. 20037
1-202-293-8860

Many of us don't have problems as severe as the ones we've just looked at. But all of us at one time or another need encouragement and help with situations that threaten to overwhelm us. That's where a counseling ministry comes in.

Developing a Counseling Ministry
In addition to whatever counseling services a church might have as part of its overall ministry it should also encourage the development of a women's peer counseling ministry.

The purpose of a women's peer counseling ministry is to develop within the church a group of women who are able to encourage, shepherd, and counsel other women. Such a group will provide a safeguard and support for the church pastors (most of us know of situations where a pastor has fallen into sexual sin as a result of a counseling relationship). Trained peer counselors can also be significant loadlifters for the pastoral staff. This ministry also provides a place for women with the gifts of encouragement and mercy to exercise their gifts.

Christian women are best suited to help one another with the struggles of life just by:

- *being good listeners.* "Everyone should be quick to listen, slow to speak and slow to become angry" (James 1:19).
- *praying with and for one another.* "Therefore confess your sins to each other and pray for each other so that you may be healed" (James 5:16).
- *encouraging one another.* "Therefore encourage one another and build each other up" (1 Thes. 5:11).

This "peer" level counseling can be a great help with the everyday business of life. It can't help with everything, though. There are some situations which should be referred to a professional Christian counselor:
- any life-threatening situation in the home
- homosexuality
- incest
- infidelity and other severe marital problems
- physical, emotional, or sexual abuse of a spouse or child
- a seriously defiant teen
- suicidal behavior
- substance abuse
- severe depression
- psychotic behavior
- multiple personalities

The combination of peer and professional counseling ministries that's best for your church will depend on many factors, including size.

Small to medium churches
In churches with less than 200 adults, the leadership should encourage at least one woman to become skilled in counseling and to head up the peer counseling ministry. This woman must be a mature believer and have a committed biblical lifestyle. Whether she is already trained or develops her skills gradually on the job, her effectiveness will be evidenced by life-change in her clients. She must understand her goal is to encourage obedience to Christ and not always to help the client find personal happiness.

Her training could involve:
- formal education
- reading current literature in the field of biblical counseling
- studying videos such as Dr. Larry Crabb's series on encouragement
- attending workshops or training seminars

As her counseling skills improve she should begin training other women through a structured class setting or personal mentoring. Those trained by her to work in the peer counseling ministry should:

• be biblically literate with a hands-on knowledge of how to apply God's principles in daily living

• be gifted in counseling, problem-solving, and communication

• have read several of the recommended books on counseling (see the annotated bibliography at the end of this chapter)

• have received additional training through counseling seminars, video and audio tapes, and observation of actual professional counseling sessions

Larger churches

In larger churches, a pastor or women's leader with some training and experience in counseling can begin teaching people-helping skills to women who already hold leadership positions, including women department heads and Bible study group leaders.

These women should complete a training program, perhaps initially four to eight weeks long. The program could cover basic counseling vocabulary and skills. Training videos made by professional counselors like Dr. Crabb could be used. Resource people from the community such as professional counselors and social workers could be brought in to teach in their areas of expertise. Additional sessions could be scheduled as the needs arose.

These trained women and those they work with could also serve as an Encouragement Team which could minister to people via prayer and counsel after the Sunday worship service.

Mega churches

Option One — A person with a problem goes to a pastoral leader for help. After the initial visit the leader determines if the situation requires a professional counselor. If so, the person is referred to a professional counseling office which works with, but is separate from, the church. This licensed counseling group could have its offices in or near the church.

A sliding-scale fee is used for people from the church which makes help affordable to all. The church underwrites the ministry. Due to the cost involved, this option is not feasible for most churches with fewer than 1,500 in attendance.

Option Two — The church hires a committed Christian woman with a counseling license or degree to serve in a dual capacity. As the need arises, she counsels women in the congregation. In addition she fulfills another role, such as Director of Women's Ministry or Christian Education Director. This option is feasible for a church with at least 750 people in attendance.

Strengthening your people-helping ministry

Whatever your church size your ability to help women with life's problems will be improved if you do three things.

1. *Develop a system for referring people.* Typically, the pastor sees the counselee for the first session. Then he directs her to an appropriate woman counselor or a professional counselor. He should ask a woman counselor to sit in on all of his counseling sessions with women as a safeguard for himself, the church, and the counselee. Another alternative is for him to leave his door ajar with his secretary in the adjoining office during the session.

Or, the counselee could meet first with a woman peer counselor. After the initial session the peer counselor can continue the counseling herself, refer the woman to a professional counselor, or refer her to a discipler/mentor.

Peer counseling should be viewed as a short-term process of four to six weeks before either referral to a professional or termination of counseling.

2. *Maintain a file of community resources* such as women's emergency shelters, social services, government-assisted housing, low-cost medical care, Christian attorneys, and professional Christian counselors for referral needs. You should also be aware of your community's guidelines on reporting sexual abuse, child abuse, or suicide threats.

3. *Have your counseling cases regularly reviewed* by a professional counselor, a well-experienced peer counselor, or an experienced pastor. A regular review with all counselors present is helpful and can also serve as a skill-building time.

Helpful resources

Institute of Biblical Counseling offers an M.A. program in Biblical Counseling at Colorado Christian College. They also offer one-week intensive seminar programs. Contact IBC, 16075 West Belleview Avenue, Morrison, CO 84065 (303-697-5425).

Minirth-Meier Clinic, 2100 N. Collins Blvd., Richardson, TX 75080 (214-669-1733). Minirth and Meier have written several books on counseling and also teach at seminars throughout the country.

Luis Palau Evangelistic Association, P.O. Box 1173, Portland, OR 97207 (503-643-0777). They offer audio/video taped biblical counseling instruction by Dr. James Williams, LPEA Vice President of Counseling Ministries. Dr. Williams has taught biblical counseling to lay men and women around the world for over twenty years.

Annotated Bibliography

Backus, William and Marie Chapian. *Telling Yourself the Truth*. Minneapolis: Bethany House Publishers, 1980. A helpful discussion on eating disorders.

Bradshaw, John. *Bradshaw on: The Family: A Revolutionary Way to Self-Discovery*. Deerfield Beach, Fla: Health Communications, Inc. 1988. Bradshaw studied for the Roman Catholic priesthood and in recent years has developed a television series dealing with the dynamics of dysfunctional families. While not a biblically based book, it is thought-provoking.

Collins, Gary R. *Christian Counseling: A Comprehensive Guide*. Waco, Texas: Word Books, 1980. A full spectrum of problems individuals encounter is covered in understandable form for both professional and lay readers. Each chapter contains what the Bible says about the problem, counseling techniques, and how to prevent the particular difficulty.

Collins, Gary R.. *How to Be a People Helper*. Santa Ana, Calif.: Vision House Publishers, 1976. This work stresses the need for all people to become more sensitive to the feelings, needs, and pains of others. It is basic, but practical. Covers when and to whom to refer those with special needs.

Collins, Gary R. *The People Helper Growth Book*. A manual to accompany *How to Be a People Helper*. Santa Ana, Calif.: Vision House Publishers, 1976.

Crabb, Lawrence, Jr. and Dan Allender. *Encouragement: The Key to Caring*. Grand Rapids: Zondervan Publishing House, 1984. This book helps the reader go beyond "surface community" to meet the emotional needs of others. Anyone who desires to counsel through encouragement can learn from this book. Also available in video form.

Crabb, Lawrence, Jr. *The Marriage Builder.* Grand Rapids: Zondervan, 1982. Dr. Crabb discusses soul oneness, spirit oneness, and body oneness and the biblical route to experiencing these. This book contains many practical tools for building better marriages.

Crabb, Lawrence, Jr. *Inside Out*. Colorado Springs: NavPress, 1988. The author challenges the reader to face life with its pain and disappointments and then to cling fiercely to Christ.

Frank, Jan. *A Door of Hope: Recognizing and Resolving the Pains of Your Past*. San Bernardino, Calif.: Here's Life Publishers, Inc., 1987. Jan was a victim of abuse at age ten. From this background and her professional training, she details ten proven steps toward recovery.

Minirth, Frank B. and Paul D. Meier. *Happiness Is a Choice*. Richardson, Texas: Today Publishers, Inc., 1978. This book discusses the symptoms, causes, and cures of depression.

Rowland, Cynthia. *The Monster Within: Overcoming Bulimia*. Grand Rapids: Baker Book House, 1984. This autobiography chronicles a woman's battle with bulimia. A helpful resource in understanding a bulimic person.

Solomon, Charles R. *The Ins and Outs of Rejection*. Denver, Colo.: Heritage House Publications, 1976. Dr. Solomon demonstrates the role rejection plays in the development of mental and emotional symptoms. He focuses on an understanding of the place of the cross in the life of the believer.

Stoop, David. *Self-talk: The Key to Personal Growth*. Old Tappan, N.J.: Fleming Revell, 1982. Learn how to use self-talk positively to change the way you talk and behave. Using biblical truth, the author demonstrates how to tap this God-given resource to change out-of-control to in-control.

Vath, Raymond, M.D. *Counseling Those with Eating Disorders*, Vol. 4. Waco, Texas.: Word Books, 1986.

Ward, Ruth McRoberts. *Self-Esteem: Gift from God*. Grand Rapids: Baker Book House, 1984. This biblically based book addresses the difference between egotism and self-esteem. It challenges the reader to discover her uniqueness and to accept herself and others.

White, Jerry and Mary. *The Christian in Mid-Life*. Colorado Springs: NavPress, 1980.

W., Claire. *God, Help Me Stop*. San Diego, Calif.: Books West, 1983. Though this book doesn't address counseling, this twelve-step Bible study workbook is a helpful resource for working with those from dysfunctional families.

W., Claire. *God, I'm Still Hurting: Break Free from the Legacy of Family Dysfunction.*. This book is a Bible-based approach to emotion healing for anyone who has grown up in a dysfunctional family. Personal questions for reflection and scriptural references guide the reader through understanding the problem and living in the solution.

CHAPTER THIRTEEN

Planning a Successful Women's Retreat

Major contributors to this chapter were
Peg Burdick and Marilyn Hoekstra.

Do you recall the first retreat you attended? I'll never forget the first one
I went to. I was a young mother with a sick toddler who kept me from
getting there until it was halfway over. The speaker was well known, but
it wasn't her words I remember now. It was what that weekend meant to
a frustrated young mom. My eyes were lifted off myself and on to God; I
discovered my God was bigger than my situation.

Retreats can be magical weekends when lives are transformed. Those
who already know the Savior deepen their commitments, ripe fruit is
harvested for the Lord, and green fruit is exposed to the ripening
process.

The noise from the world and our own lives fade when we are at a retreat so God can be heard. As I write this material, this year's retreat is
fresh in my memory. In the midst of worshiping God through singing,
"Change My Heart, Oh God," by Eddie Espinosa, I heard God speak directly to my heart. "You are the potter, I am the clay," flashed across my
inner being. The concept was not new to me, but the way I heard it was
fresh. At this point in my life I'm aware of being on the potter's wheel;
it's spinning and I'm being molded into a new vessel.

So many times I've said to the Lord, "Stop, I don't like some of the
things You're doing in my life." This is the same thought recorded in Isa-
iah 45:9. "Woe to him who quarrels with his Maker. . . . Does the clay
say to the potter, 'What are you making?' " It wasn't until the closing
session of the retreat that I was prepared for the Spirit to take me a step
farther in my growth.

Why Have a Women's Retreat?

Here are four good reasons:

- To relieve women of the routine and pressures of daily life so they can focus wholly on seeking God
- To strengthen women spiritually through concentrated teaching
- To provide uninterrupted fellowship with other Christians
- To provide an environment in which unbelievers can see Christ in the lives of believers and respond to the Gospel

Several things need to happen if this last purpose is to be a reality. First, the speaker needs to know that unbelievers will be in attendance. She should not speak unfavorably about any denomination or cult. In addition, she should carefully explain any terms that might not be familiar to the unbeliever, such as justification or sanctification. If Bible characters are mentioned, enough should be said to fully identify them.

An unhurried schedule provides time for the unbeliever to talk with other women or just think things through. Resist the temptation to pack the schedule full of meetings. We incorrectly think since the attenders paid for a weekend, the only way to give them full measure is to fill every moment with crafts, seminars, and messages. A packed schedule may steal from them the very thing they need most.

You will also need some women who are prepared to let God use them to lead others to Christ. Those with the gift of soul-winning should go with their antennas fully extended. Most of the time, the registrar will recognize the names of those known to be on the way to Christ and can alert the evangelists in attendance.

Prior to the retreat Janet had been in a support group for hurting women. A friend who loved her had often told her about the Lord, but the world was shouting so loud in her ears she couldn't hear. At the retreat she was simultaneously exposed to the love of the believers for her and the truth of the Word of God. By lunchtime on Saturday morning she was ready to get things settled with God. A group gathered around her and two hours, and lots of tears later, we all had a new sister in the Lord.

Janet's new birth was clear-cut. She went from spiritual death into spiritual life. Susan was a slightly different situation. Many years ago she had made a decision to follow Christ, but a difficult life and little church attendance had almost snuffed out the flame. In addition, a relative for whom she had little respect often preached at her. During the months of church attendance prior to the retreat, Susan's flame had begun to flicker a little brighter. She was opening up to spiritual things once more and was one of the first registrants for the weekend.

Very early on Saturday morning, she had renewed her commitment to

Christ. This time, there was a brightly burning fire within her. She attended the morning prayer meeting and immediately shared what had happened in her life the night before.

Prayer releases God's power to save souls. Pray for the unbelievers by name in your planning session. Schedule a prayer meeting early in the morning at the retreat itself. Make it clear the prayer meeting is not just for the retreat committee but is open to everyone.

At your retreat you may also have unripe fruit. These are the women who will sit back and observe. Much of what the speaker says may go right over their heads. That's fine. They're still being exposed to the love and care of the believers. They will see that Christians can have as much fun as unbelievers. At this year's retreat, one lady who has seen much of the rotten side of life, shared at the campfire what it had meant to her to have so much fun with believers, "And we aren't even drunk."

Don't pressure the unripe fruit. Allow the Holy Spirit to move people along at His, and their, own pace.

Working with the Church Leaders

If this is your church's first women's retreat, pray for a group of women who share your vision. Meet to pray and plan. Be willing to start small. You can either combine with another church for a retreat, or plan one with just your women.

Combining allows you to draw on the resources of a wider group of women and to present a more polished event. However, a small, one-church retreat can provide a unique opportunity for bonding.

When you are presenting your vision to your church leaders for their approval emphasize the following points:

- Retreats provide an opportunity for women to exercise their spiritual gifts.
- Retreats allow time to meet women's specific needs not addressed in the usual church program. Seminars can cover such issues as: husband/wife relationships, dealing with singleness, handling a mid-life crisis (yours or your husband's), time management for the working mom, etc.
- If the male church leadership is skeptical of the value of a retreat, make it clear you are working with and not against them. Retreats are a time when T.L.C. (Tender Loving Care) can be administered in large doses so it becomes a load-lifter for the pastoral staff.

Solicit their suggestions in selecting topics for the plenary sessions. If you do a good job on the first retreat, the renewed enthusiasm for the Lord among the women will convince the leadership that retreats are a wonderful opportunity for the women to grow spiritually.

Leadership

As soon as you decide to have a retreat, *select your leadership.* The two key people are the Retreat Director and the Program Coordinator. If your group is small — under fifty women — these two jobs could be done by the same woman.

Though your key women need to be able to handle details, spiritual maturity is the primary prerequisite for choosing them. Are they women of the Word and women of prayer? Is their character such that they will be able to make the right decisions? Can they keep confidences? Do they have the discernment to select speakers, seminar topics, and oversee programming?

For years my husband has had a sign on his desk that reads, "Keep Prayer Frontal." *Pray, pray, pray.* Pray before selecting the plenary speaker and prior to phoning each committee member. Get personal prayer lists from the women involved in the retreat. Type them up and pass them out at a retreat prayer meeting. My own particular church has seen a dramatic increase in the work of the Holy Spirit at retreats since we incorporated more prayer into the events. We bathe the speaker and other aspects of the retreat in prayer both before and during the actual weekend.

Use the following ministry descriptions as starting points for developing your own.

Retreat director

● meets regularly with Program Coordinator to discuss plans and to pray for the retreat
  ● selects speakers, corresponds with them, arranges transportation.
  ● determines retreat schedule
  ● chooses person to give book reviews during the sessions
  ● appoints seminar leaders
  ● oversees retreat prayer room volunteers
  ● selects music chairwoman; determines when music is needed
  ● chairs retreat sessions by welcoming, leading in prayer, and introducing keynote speaker

Program coordinator

● assists Retreat Director
  ● responsible for brochure content, design, printing, and distribution
  ● contacts retreat site management regarding meeting rooms, sound system, food service, and informational signs
  ● supervises the taping of sessions by checking recording equipment, providing blank tapes, and providing tape order blanks at the book table

- appoints retreat hostesses
- makes all announcements during the retreat

Planning

A successful retreat begins far in advance. How far ahead you plan will depend on several factors. The smaller the group the less advance planning is needed. There are more facilities available for a small group. In addition, since a small group operates as a family, it's more tolerant of imperfections than is a larger group. In general the larger the group the more professional every aspect of the women's ministry must become, so the more advance planning is needed.

Speaker selection will also determine how far in advance you plan. If you intend to get someone who is well known, her schedule is planned months and perhaps years in advance. Usually two years ahead is adequate to get most speakers. If you plan farther ahead than that, by the time you have the retreat the needs of the hearers may have changed and the preselected speaker might not be the best person after all.

Stage one planning

For a larger church this should begin one to two years ahead of the date. Six to nine months is sufficient for a smaller church.

1. *Choose retreat dates.* Avoid dates near the beginning or end of school, school holidays, or special church events. Also avoid the last six weeks of the year. As soon as you select the date, place it on your church calendar.

2. *Choose an accessible location* with comfortable beds. The accessibility of facilities may be the deciding factor in selecting a date. Possible facilities include colleges, universities, high schools, parochial schools, hotels, conference grounds, and church camps.

It's an advantage to hold the retreat away from home. A drive of one to two hours can provide emotional separation from the problems faced at home. The return trip can aid in assimilating the material presented.

3. *Select a keynote speaker.* Never choose a speaker before you or someone you trust has heard her. Some speakers have excellent content, but relate poorly to people. You may be willing to forego high-quality interpersonal time, but be sure you know that in advance. It's often the informal interaction with the speaker that impacts lives at a retreat.

- Contact the speaker and let her know how much time she has to make a decision about coming
- Discuss with her the theme and/or topic for her messages. If you're working a year or two in advance, you can wait until nine to twelve months prior to the date to finalize message topics. It's important that

she speak on a topic God is speaking to her about. Be sure she understands the number of times she will speak and the length of each message

- Clarify fees and transportation costs
- Confirm in writing the dates, format, and other details
- Plan travel arrangements and reimburse in advance
- Ask her to send a photo and a biographical sketch for advertising
- Return the photo as soon as you can

4. *Choose a theme* that complements the speaker's messages.

5. Determine who will prepare and serve the *meals*. They are often provided by the conference grounds staff. If this is the case, check with them about the menu. Today's woman is an informed consumer. Strive for meals low in fats and sugars, high in vegetables and fruit.

Stage two planning

The following should be done six to eight months before the retreat:

1. *Plan the schedule.*

- Plenary sessions. The keynote speaker(s) should present three to five plenary sessions.
- Short, informal workshops. Several simultaneous sessions covering a wide range of topics can be presented by local women. Use women from your own fellowship if possible.
- Planned activities. Include light-to-moderate physical activities, skits, question and answer time, and free time to be alone to digest and pray about what's being learned. Keep the women busy, but don't plan too much activity. The retreat should be fun and relaxing too.

2. *Choose committee chairwomen.* Write specific descriptions. A written ministry description will clarify expectations and allow accountability. Committee leadership is a great place to train young women in handling administrative details for your women's ministry.

3. *Choose workshop leaders.* A good place to begin this selection is with any recommendations made on the previous year's evaluation form. Workshop leaders will need varying degrees of supervision according to their level of experience. Plan a well-balanced selection of topics, so that women of all ages and interests will want to attend at least one seminar.

4. *Choose a music coordinator.* If it's well done, music can have as large an impact as the speaker because it touches the spirit in a way words never can.

5. *Establish a budget.*

- Project total cost including speaker travel and honorarium, promotion, facility rental, food, and decorations or favors.

- Project attendance.
- Ask the church leaders to underwrite some of the costs.
- Determine how much scholarship money is available from women's ministries or individuals.
- Decide whether the committee members will pay their own way or attend free as part of the benefits from planning the retreat. (Unless there is a generous budget, most churches assume committee members will pay their own way.)
- Determine cost per person by dividing uncovered retreat expenses by the estimated number of women who will attend.

Stage three planning

This includes delegating specific tasks and should be initiated about three months prior to the event.

1. *Provide the workshop leaders with the following information:* a list of detailed responsibilities, deadlines for turning in any material to be printed, budget restrictions, location of and directions to the facility. In addition, assign hostesses to assist them at the retreat itself.

2. *Begin aggressively promoting the retreat.* Announce the retreat in the church bulletin every week beginning ten to twelve weeks in advance. Gradually build excitement. Promote via posters, flyers, skits, and by displaying photos from last year's retreat in a prominent place. Be creative! Strive for excellence in your publicity. Color coordinate it and carefully proofread all material.

3. *Registration must be handled carefully.* A good Registrar is important for a smoothly operating event. She needs to handle money and details well. If she works outside the home, it's helpful if she has an answering machine. Establish procedures for handling monies.

4. *Design and print your brochure.* Include a registration form, directions to the facility, transportation needs, list of what to bring, and a place to request either a quiet or not-so-quiet sleeping area. Note to whom checks should be payable. Indicate whether there is wheelchair access.

After the Retreat Coordinator approves it, the brochure should be printed. If you're working with a retreat of 200 or more women, get this done three to four months in advance. Proofread it carefully!

5. *Room assignments.* Assign all mothers with infants to the same area. Then either pre-assign remaining women, or let them choose their rooms when they arrive (for smaller retreats only). If pre-assigning rooms, do this prayerfully; the Holy Spirit will use roommates in one another's lives.

6. *Transportation.* Arrange for group transportation (vans, church

bus) if needed. Coordinate with Registrar to ensure everyone has a ride.

7. *Music.* A month before the retreat, give the committee printing the program a copy of lyrics to all songs to be used.

8. *Skits.* Choose skits and cast. Schedule dress rehearsals.

9. *Recreation.* In case of rain have alternate plans. Board games and a relaxing movie are good choices.

10. *Printed materials.* Write the program including rules, schedule of sessions, speakers' biographical sketches, outlines of workshops, lyrics to songs, thanks to all committees, blank pages for taking notes, and re-treat evaluation form. At least three people should proofread the type-set program before it's printed. It should be printed at least two weeks before the retreat.

Some of the printed materials will be used year after year with only slight modification. If things are done on a word processor they can be easily adapted in succeeding years.

11. *Food.* Unless food is being catered or the retreat facility is provid-ing it, plan menus and purchase all food. Plan healthy, not heavy, foods. Provide milk, decaf coffee, herbal tea, fruit juice, and diet and decaf soft drinks. Remember pregnant women, nursing mothers, and others on special diets. Keep the noon meals light to avoid a sleepy afternoon.

12. *Facilities.* Contact site director to be sure all details are covered. Give site director a copy of the schedule.

13. *Clean up.* Unless the retreat facility provides this service, assign a clean-up crew.

Stage four planning

This involves continuing to oversee the work of the retreat committees. Remember, what isn't inspected can't be expected. I've had a personal struggle through the years learning to delegate authority and monitor progress. I had considered checking up on the progress of committees under my authority as being pushy. I thought to myself, "It's their prob-lem now, not mine. I just need to pray and trust them to do their tasks well." This is faulty thinking because good administration includes eval-uating the work of others. But it must be done in a way that encourages instead of accuses.

1. *Write to the keynote speaker* to confirm final details including pro-gram schedule, transportation, (including special arrangements if com-ing early or staying late). Three days later follow up by phoning the speaker to make sure she received your letter. It's a nice extra touch to send a small portion of the honorarium in advance to cover any special purchases she might want to make.

2. *Check the progress* of all committees. This is not a one-time occur-

rence. Helpful monitoring of progress should go on continuously.

3. *Promote the retreat* through the bulletin, announcements, and skits.

4. *Provide partial or full scholarships* for those in need.

5. *Schedule a prayer meeting for the retreat staff.* Check with the speaker and others involved for their personal prayer needs. Pray specifically for those nonbelievers planning to attend. Prepare a written list of these prayer needs.

6. *Pamper the keynote speaker.* Provide a fruit basket in her room and a note saying you're praying for her. Give the speaker her honorarium before she leaves.

7. *Collect the evaluation forms.* Immediately after the retreat complete the Retreat Record Form (see sample at the end of this chapter) and file it for reference next year.

8. *Plan a post-retreat celebration party* for everyone involved in the planning. This is a great way to cap off the work and to praise God. Allow time for sharing how the Lord worked in their lives and the lives of the attendees. Share comments from the evaluation forms and discuss briefly any changes to be made as a result.

Give a small gift to each committee member, just to say thanks. Close with a time of praise.

Larger Retreats

Though both small and large retreats can share the same structure, large retreats require much more planning, cooperation, and striving for excellence in every detail. An option for a larger retreat site could be a motel or hotel. These may need to be reserved two or more years in advance.

Ministry descriptions for large retreats

Though these are written with the larger retreat in mind, many of the recommendations may be scaled down and applied to a smaller retreat. A large group requires a degree of excellence in preparation, but even for a small group that same excellence should be the goal.

Executive committee
- responsible for decisions
- formulates statement of purpose for the retreat
- determines size of the retreat
- selects site
- selects speaker(s)
- determines honorarium for each speaker. Also decides who receives monetary gifts and free registration

- evaluates progress reports from each committee member

This committee consists of the Retreat Director, the Program Coordinator, the Facilities Coordinator and the Business Coordinator. (If this retreat is being held by a group of churches from the same denomination or geographic area, then these key people can represent different churches.) The Retreat Director makes all final decisions.

It's easy for the Executive Committee to become overwhelmed with the number of tasks and overlook the primary purpose for holding a retreat: the spiritual growth of the women. So be sure each planning meeting begins with a time of prayer of sufficient length to allow each woman to pray. Maintain a focus on God's work through you.

Retreat director (This description is different from the one given earlier.)
- chairs and works closely with Executive Committee
- regularly schedules Executive Committee meetings and at least one meeting of all committee heads
- chooses an assistant
- writes a welcome letter included in the registration packet
- coordinates general announcements at meals and meetings
- writes a detailed written report for those directing the next retreat

Program coordinator (This description is different from the one given earlier.)
- chooses retreat theme with the help and approval of Retreat Director and with input from keynote speaker
- chooses assistants to help with details
- appoints the Music, Special Feature, and Graphics Coordinators
- recommends potential speakers to the Executive Committee and contacts the chosen speakers
- works with the Retreat Director in planning the complete program and time schedule for the retreat
- plans all workshops/seminars; contacts workshop speakers
- obtains outlines of all seminars before retreat
- determines content of registration brochure and packet. Approves all graphics material before it is printed

Facilities coordinator
- chooses assistants to help with details, but all correspondence with the retreat site is approved and signed by Facilities Coordinator
- appoints Book Sales and Decorations Coordinators and Ushers/Hostesses from participating churches

• contacts retreat site to reserve dates, ascertain meal and room rates, and requests a list of available facilities. Makes all arrangements with retreat site by letter or phone

• assigns meetings rooms and arranges for set-up

Business coordinator (not needed unless the retreat is extremely large)

• appoints the Registration and Finance Coordinators. Works closely with and assists all the leaders

• makes sure all deadlines are met

Registration coordinator

• receives the number of rooms and prices from the Facilities Coordinator. Takes written (no verbal) registrations and assigns rooms

• handles all registration monies and gives to Finance Coordinator

• assembles the program packets to be distributed when the women register

• appoints women to register all participants. Arranges registration location and set-up of tables with the Facilities Coordinator

Finance coordinator

• opens bank account with money from prior retreat

• receives and pays all bills

• receives all monies paid to the retreat including the offerings and registration monies

• keeps account of all receipts and expenditures and files a written report after the retreat. (See the Retreat Record Form at the end of this chapter.)

Music coordinator

• arranges for special music

• chooses and contacts the pianist for all meetings

• chooses a worship leader

• produces a song booklet and submits it to Graphics Coordinator

• asks the Facilities Coordinator to check on the sound system and condition of piano

Book sales coordinator

• contacts a bookseller to provide a book table. Recommends books, tapes, and other items to be sold. Include books that address the retreat theme and any books to be reviewed in the plenary sessions

• works with Facilities Coordinator regarding room location and table set-up

- provides bookseller with directions to the site, a schedule of events, location of book table, and probable times women will purchase books
- assigns women to be sales assistants if the bookseller needs help unloading books and working the book table
- arranges for overnight accommodations for the bookseller
- arranges with bookseller the percentage of sales profits the retreat will receive

Graphics coordinator
- chooses a logo depicting the retreat's theme. This logo should appear on all printed material including the name tag
- arranges for design and printing of all retreat material (flyers, posters, registration brochures, maps to the site as well as maps of the facilities, program booklets, etc.). All materials must be approved by the Program Coordinator and Retreat Director before being printed

Decorations coordinator
- provides decorations for speaking platforms
- provides dining room decorations including one centerpiece per table
- works within the budget guidelines established by the Finance Coordinator. (Note: It takes special effort for this committee to stay within budget guidelines.)
- sells any appropriate items at a price determined by estimated expenditures

Special feature coordinator
- plans special-interest workshops and events (crafts, films, nature hikes). Coordinates with Facilities Coordinator for needed rooms, equipment, and hostesses
- contacts and assists special-interest workshop leaders

Hostesses (one for each seminar and meals as needed)
- assist with seating
- introduce speaker
- assist speaker with any needs

Ushers
- help women find a seat, especially those who arrive after the meeting begins
- collect and help count offerings

ORGANIZATIONAL CHART FOR LARGE RETREATS

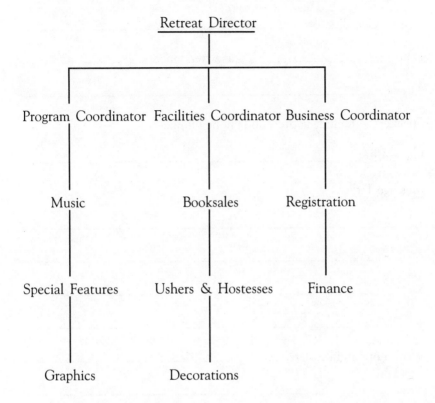

RETREAT RECORD FORM

Retreat Coordinator: _____

Date: _____ Total Attendance: _____

Theme: _____

Speaker(s) (include address and phone number):

Location: _____

Message Titles:

1. _____

2. _____

3. _____

4. _____

Workshops and Leaders: _____

_____

Special Events and Skits: _____

_____

Recreational Activities: _____

_____

_____

Additional Comments: _____

_____

_____

(Attach a copy of the budget, food usage, printed program, registration list, and evaluation summary.)

SAMPLE EVALUATION FORM

1. Is this your first women's retreat? How did you hear about it?

2. What was the highlight of the retreat for you?

3. What would you suggest as a theme for future retreats?

4. Please suggest any speakers you have heard and would appreciate hearing again.

5. Are there any particular subjects you would like addressed in workshops?

6. Have you any suggestions for the program schedule?

7. Would you be willing to help with future retreats? In what capacity?

Thank you for taking the time to fill this out.
Name Address Telephone (Optional)

CHAPTER FOURTEEN
Personal Evangelism

A Personal Call to Evangelism

There was a time when I didn't want to hear the word "evangelism." I don't understand all the reasons why this was so, but I know it involved guilt for not witnessing, fear of rejection by my peers, and perhaps, at its root, a concern that if someone did "receive Christ," it wouldn't take. All these reasons grew out of placing my faith in myself and not in God.

I still have a lot to learn about evangelism, but at least I'm now willing to be taught. The change began in the summer of 1986 when my husband, Mark, and I attended the Billy Graham Itinerant Evangelism Conference in Amsterdam. Before we went to that conference I had us labeled as nonevangelists. He is a teacher/preacher; while I usually function as an encourager/discipler. I had us pigeonholed, with no room for "evangelist." Not now, nor ever in the future.

At the conference, I gladly participated in all the seminars on follow-up and discipling—the joy of my life. I also continued my monologue with God about my gifts. My "conversation" with Him consisted of thanking Him for the gifts He'd given me and reaffirming that I was not called to evangelize.

God, however, was not willing to let me stay in that frame of mind. I can remember the exact place where I was standing in the enormous arena when the Lord of the Harvest demanded my attention.

"Carol, what about your neighbors? Who will tell them about Me?"

My stock reply came out, "I don't have the gift of evangelism."

His reply startled me, "Who on your street does?"

Since we were the only born-again believers I was aware of in our neighborhood at the time, I quickly answered in my mind, "No one."

"Who will reach them?" He asked.

It was immediately obvious that, "Nobody" was an unacceptable reply. I was backed into a corner. As millions have answered through the centuries, I replied, "With Your Spirit's power I will go."

This chapter will give you some of the tools to "go" with. Choose the ones that fit you best and "Go!"

This material was developed by Olive Liefeld and Marie Little. Olive is the widow of Pete Fleming who was killed by the Auca Indians in Ecuador in 1954. She is the author of *Unfolding Destinies* (Grand Rapids: Zondervan Publishing House, 1990). Marie is the widow of Paul Little, author of *How to Give Away Your Faith* (a classic on evangelism which has been revised by Marie and reprinted). She's been a role model to many in evangelism. Hers is a learned as well as Spirit-taught skill. Some people she reaches through her own personal witness, others she contacts as part of the evangelism committee in her church. The rest of this chapter is narrated by Marie.

When newlyweds moved in next door, I wondered how I could tell whether the wind of the Holy Spirit was blowing in their lives. Though we were very different, we soon became friends. Karen, the bride, visited me often. One day she mentioned her parochial school upbringing and her strict religious background but added, "It doesn't mean the same to me as your religion means to you."

At times my mentioning God, faith, or the Bible had caused Karen to become reserved and aloof. I concluded that the wind wasn't blowing. Still, I decided to take a chance. When I asked Karen to go with me to a home Bible study with some young couples from our church, she agreed so quickly that it surprised me. How little had I known her true heart.

The fifth time Karen attended the Bible study, the leader asked for prayer requests before we closed. Karen, who was wringing her hands nervously, blurted out, "I have to ask you to pray for me, but I don't know what to ask God about."

She related that before they were married, she and her husband had a baby which they gave up for adoption. Her heart was broken that she didn't have that child now. To make matters worse, her mother continued to blame and dislike Karen's husband. Overcome with guilt and anguish, Karen asked us if God could accept her.

The study leader suggested that we kneel and each of us talk to the Lord on Karen's behalf. He reminded us that God wants to forgive us and for that reason, He had sent His Son to die for us. He also encouraged Karen to pray for forgiveness.

On the way home, Karen didn't say much. I thought it best to keep silent and let the Holy Spirit work. Later that week Karen asked, "Tell me what happened to me that night. God seems real to me now." I told her about the wind of the Holy Spirit, the new birth, and all that the Lord Jesus wants to do for her as she trusts Him and becomes His child. The following week she sent me a note which read, "Thank you for helping me find Jesus. I didn't even know who I was looking for."

Relating to Unbelievers

Perhaps you have shared your faith with a friend and have seen that friend receive Jesus Christ. Hearing the wind of the Holy Spirit bringing new birth to another person is one of life's most exhilarating experiences. Here are some key principles I've found helpful for effective one-on-one witnessing:

Be open and honest about yourself. Don't present yourself as a saintly, perfect person free of inner struggles and problems. Candidly relate your own problems to your unbelieving friends. Every person — including you and me — needs forgiveness through faith in Christ. Simply put, evangelism is one beggar telling another beggar where to find food.

Relate to the seeker as a friend. You aren't the "Church Lady" so grossly satirized on "Saturday Night Live." Friendship always involves a warm relationship, time spent with the other person, and mutual sharing of dreams, hopes, and burdens. Make specific plans to find mutual interests. A friendship develops when two people meet over coffee to talk about children or gardening, walk together every morning, go to craft classes, or attend PTA meetings together. Take the initiative by inviting an unchurched neighbor over for coffee or to do something you both enjoy.

Express genuine appreciation for the person as an individual. Even the most rebellious or unlikable person has supreme worth in God's eyes. So much so that He gave His Son for them.

Be alert for a person's point of vulnerability. God often begins working at the point of a person's need. Career changes, academic failure, divorce, emotional turmoil, financial problems, loneliness, or illness can make people aware of their need for God.

Find appropriate tools to whet the seeker's spiritual appetite. Here are some ideas:

- films featuring Dr. James Dobson or Gary Smalley
- books such as *Dr. Dobson Answers Your Questions* (Wheaton, Ill.: Tyndale Publishing House, 1982), *Born Again* (Old Tappan, N.J.: Fleming H. Revell Co., 1976) or *Mere Christianity* (New York: Collier Books, MacMillan Publishing Co., 1943)
- Christian magazines like *Decision, Focus on the Family,* or *Today's Christian Woman* can provide good conversation starters

Be gentle, not pushy in offering these to people. Obnoxious witnessing tactics can hinder the Lord's gentle, winsome work.

Small, caring groups can open the seeker's heart. This was true in Karen's case. She saw our weekly church group with its love as well as its tatters, and she felt welcome. She helped us too by livening up our group with her fresh questions and transparency.

Explaining the Gospel
Jesus didn't give His disciples a crash course on the content of the Gospel message and how to explain it to others. Instead, the disciples learned by watching the Lord interact with other people. In the Book of Acts their message focused on the Lord Jesus Himself, His life, death, and resurrection.

The simplest Gospel message I ever heard was given by an athlete being interviewed on TV. When asked about his religion, he turned to the camera and said, "Weeell, I met Jesus." Simple, but right to the point.

What do we say about Jesus Christ when telling another person how to have a relationship with Him? There are four facts to communicate:

- Who Jesus Christ is (John 5:18; Heb. 4:15)
- His diagnosis of human nature (Mark 7:1-23)
- The meaning of His crucifixion (Matt. 26:28; 1 Peter 3:18) and His resurrection (1 Cor. 18:25)
- Becoming a Christian is repenting of our self-centeredness and making His will the center of our lives (John 1:12; Acts 20:26).

These are weighty facts, but they can be shared in your own words, or in one of the easy-to-understand formats outlined below.

Four spiritual laws
Originally developed by Campus Crusade for Christ (other organizations publish their own versions), this booklet helps you maintain continuity and progress in a logical fashion through the primary points of the Gospel. It also provides a clear explanation to leave with the person.

- God loves you, and has a wonderful plan for your life (John 3:16; 10:10)
- Man is sinful and separated from God (Rom. 3:23; 6:23)
- Jesus Christ is God's only provision for man's sin (John 14:6; Rom. 5:8)
- Each person must receive Jesus Christ as Savior and Lord (John 1:12; Rev. 3:20)

Four steps to God
- God: Twin facts — He is holy; He is the loving Creator (Ps. 100:3; 1 John 1:5)

- People: Twin tragedies — we have rebelled; we have broken God's law (Ps. 14:2-3; James 2:10)
- Jesus Christ: He reconciled people to God by His death (Rom. 5:9-11)
- Required response: repent, believe, receive (John 1:12; Acts 17:30)

Three-phase pattern

- Jesus' definition of mankind's problem — We are separated from our Maker (Isa. 53:6; Rom. 2:11-12)
- Jesus' diagnosis — Our disease of sin causes this separation
- Jesus' solution — Through His death and resurrection Christ restores our relationship with God (Rom. 5:8; 1 Peter 2:24)

The Romans' road

- All have sinned (Rom. 3:23)
- The gift of God is eternal life (Rom. 6:23)
- Believe in your heart and confess with your mouth (Rom. 10:9-10)

Use one verse to explain the Gospel (Take each phrase one by one and discuss its meaning.)
John 3:16

- God: Describe what God is like (Isa. 43:3; 1 Peter 1:16)
- So loved: Talk about God's love (Jer. 31:3; John 13:1)
- The world: This includes everyone (Isa. 53:6; Rom. 3:23)
- That He gave His one and only Son: Tell how this shows His love (1 Peter 2:24; 1 John 3:16)
- That whoever believes in Him: To believe is to receive (John 1:12)
- Shall not perish but have eternal life: If I believe, what then? (Eph. 2:8-9; 2 Peter 3:18)

Romans 6:23 (based on the article, "One-Verse Evangelism" by Randy Raysbrook)

- Wages: Wages is the reward we receive for work done
- Sin: Sin is thinking or behaving below God's standard revealed in Jesus Christ
- Death: Death means separation from God now and eternally
- But: This word indicates hope
- Gift: A gift is bought by the giver and given free to the receiver
- Of God: God wants to give the gift because He loves us so much
- Eternal life: Eternal life contrasts with death. Nothing ends eternal life

- Christ Jesus: Jesus can offer eternal life because He bought it with His life
- Lord: The gift is offered to everyone who is willing to surrender his or her life to the control of Jesus Christ

Any presentation of the Gospel can be finished with the ABCs of salvation.

A = Admit you are a sinner and need to receive salvation.

B = Believe Christ paid for your sins on the cross.

C = Commit your life to Christ as Lord.

Starting a Conversation about God

Turning a conversation to spiritual matters is an art. Each woman must develop her own style. Don't try to imitate someone you admire. What you say must be authentic in your own experience. Choose your words carefully, and speak from your heart.

When introducing a seeker to Christ, your goal is twofold: First, the seeker should be overcome by God's everlasting love and complete involvement in her life. Second, she should understand that she is special in God's eyes.

Three phrases Jesus said to the Samaritan woman at the well (John 4) demonstrate guidelines for starting a conversation about God. He said:

"Will you give Me a drink?" (v. 7) He started the conversation with a neutral subject.

"If you knew the gift of God" (v. 10). He controlled the conversation by mentioning God, but He didn't smother the woman with too many details or a three-point sermon.

"I who speak to you am He" (v. 26). He knew the core truth — the truth she needed to know. But He persisted, waited, and discussed until He knew the time was right to introduce the core truth. The core truth involves, "Who is Jesus Christ?"

Here are some openers that may help you start a conversation about God with your friend.

Introducing spirituality into the conversation

"I brought the Sunday School material to show you what I'm teaching your children on Sunday."

"It's important to me to attend a church where my family grows in their character and learns about God."

"Do you have a church background?"

"Are you interested in spiritual matters?"

"Are you interested in reading the Bible?"

Introducing God into the conversation

"I've found out that God loves me and cares about what happens to me."

"Do you know that you matter to God? He genuinely cares about what is happening with you."

"Have you thought much about God? I've found that I need His help."

"Would you like me to pray for you about this [a problem someone is having]? God has helped me through many problems. I don't know how I could have made it without Him."

Introducing Jesus into the conversation

"I found Jesus helped me when I got into tough situations."

"When I'm lonely, I pray to Jesus Christ. I know He's alive and cares that I'm alone. I can feel His presence."

"I used to feel that way too [scared, hopeless], but when I prayed to Jesus Christ, those feelings disappeared. If you like, I could tell you about it."

"I haven't experienced this same difficulty as you have, but in my own life, prayer has helped me know that Jesus is with me. Would it be OK if I prayed for you?"

"I'm mightily impressed with Jesus. The whole world was changed by His life."

"It makes sense to think that if God truly sent Jesus, He wouldn't need Buddha or any other so-called god."

Introducing salvation into the conversation

"Have you ever trusted Jesus Christ personally? Would you like to know how to become a real Christian?"

"Have you considered how a person becomes a real Christian?"

"I believed all the facts about Jesus, and thought that was enough to make me a Christian. But Jesus never made a difference in my life. It amazed me that after discovering the facts about Him, I still needed to commit my life to Him."

"I thought I had to be perfect before God would accept me. Then I learned that He gave His Son to offer me the kind of forgiveness I needed. After He forgives me, He helps me daily to live a clean life. But no Christian is perfect until he or she reaches heaven."

"Would you be interested in this book? It reminded me of the conversation we had yesterday. I'd like to know what you think of it."

"What do you think is wrong with the world? I believe what the Bible says about everyone needing forgiveness. Our natural tendency is toward evil. A child has to be taught to be good; he doesn't have to be taught to behave badly."

"What do you think will happen when you die? Do you think God will accept you? Jesus answered that question for me."

Responding to Erroneous Thinking
Most seekers believe one of the two following views of God, but neither view is biblical. Determine into which of the following schools of thought a seeker falls:

- she views God as a scrooge, interested only in punishing her, inhibiting her, and spoiling her fun
- she views God as a benign grandfather, benevolent, generous, and surely not capable of sending anyone to hell

You can begin to expose and clarify this wrong thinking by saying something like, "I used to think . . .

. . . that God was like an old scrooge interested only in rules. *But* I discovered He's far from being an ogre. In fact, He gave us His Son, Jesus Christ, who died in order to help us."

. . . that because my parents were religious, I was born a Christian. *Then* I learned that no one is born a Christian."

. . . that any road would lead to God. *Then* I read Christ's words that He alone was the way to God, and He backed His claim in many ways."

. . . that attending church regularly made me a Christian. *But* going to church couldn't be all there is to becoming a Christian."

. . . that if my good deeds outweighed my bad deeds, I was a Christian. *Then* I wondered how to know the number of good deeds God wanted me to do. I learned I needed Jesus' death to forgive my wrongs, and God's help so I could live like a Christian."

. . . that God was too kind to turn away anyone from heaven. *Then* I realized that a holy God must judge sin."

. . . that Christianity consisted of negative prohibitions, rules, and restrictions. I had heard Christians say that they didn't believe in smoking, drinking, or gambling. *Then* someone told me that these restrictions didn't explain Christianity."

. . . that there was no one truth or one absolute God. *But* then I read the Bible and realized otherwise."

. . . that each person had his own truth. *Then* I discovered that God's truth is as exact as mathematical truth. Two plus two always makes four. And God's truth is just as exact."

. . . that because some evangelist's immoral scandals are reported on the evening news, that all Christians were fakes. *But* I realized that true Christians do exist. I also learned that a Christian is not perfect. Jesus

Christ is perfect, but Christians are imperfect until they reach heaven."

To the person who is *self-satisfied* I ask, "Do you ever feel you haven't lived up to what God intended for you?"

To the *atheist* I ask, "Don't you think it's possible that God might exist outside of all you think and know?"

To the *uninterested* I say, "I think if you knew God's great concern and love for you, you'd be astounded."

To the person *who doesn't believe the Bible* I ask, "Have you considered reading the Bible to investigate the life and history of Jesus Christ?"

Be Ready
Marie Little has found the best way for *her* to present the truths concerning Jesus Christ. You will need to experiment and find out what is best for you personally. Let God play you, His instrument, so others hear the special music He wants to sound through your life. Be ready always to give an answer to anyone who asks you for the hope that lies in you (1 Peter 3:15).

Bibliography
See bibliography at the end of chapter 15 for books on evangelism.

CHAPTER FIFTEEN
Event Evangelism

Do you not say, "Four months more and then the harvest"? I tell you, open your eyes and look at the fields! They are ripe for harvest. Even now the reaper draws his wages, even now he harvests the crop for eternal life, so that the sower and the reaper may be glad together. Thus the saying "One sows and another reaps" is true. I sent you to reap what you have not worked for. Others have done the hard work, and you have reaped the benefits of their labor (John 4:35-38).

John 4:35-38 expresses a clear principle of evangelism: the harvest is ready and can be reaped by many people working together. Those "many people" can be the women in your church, energized and directed by your women's ministry.

The Harvest

Seeing the harvest
Did you ever stop to think that in the incident recorded in John 4:1-42, the disciples may have passed the "woman at the well" on her way back into the village to tell her friends about the Messiah. But they had only one thing on their minds — getting food to satisfy their *physical hunger*. They didn't see the *spiritual hunger* of the people around them.

Like many of you, I have gone through years of not seeing the spiritual hunger around me. But in the last few years, the Lord has been opening my eyes to the field right in my own neighborhood. I've had to make the Lord of the harvest the Lord of my days so I could sow, cultivate, or reap as opportunities arose.

Help the women in your church develop evangelistic eyes. Highlight evangelism through your ministries. Recognize and affirm those who are effective at lifestyle evangelism.

Include on your women's council at least one woman whose focus is evangelism. Send some of your key women to seminars on evangelism and encourage the reading of books on outreach (see the bibliography at the end of this chapter).

Praying for the harvest

James wrote that the prayer of a righteous person is powerful and effective (James 5:16). He also taught the simple truth, "You do not have, because you do not ask God" (4:2). If you want a women's ministry that is evangelistically effective, you must pray.

Identify your prayer warriors. Each church has a few — and they are usually women. Keep them informed about upcoming evangelistic events. Provide them with the names of unbelievers who attend church and women's events. Let them know how their prayers are being answered.

Set aside extra time to pray when planning evangelistic events. Include a time of praise and thanksgiving when you review the effectiveness of your outreach. If your women's ministry has weekly, monthly, or yearly special days of prayer, use them to undergird your evangelism efforts.

Training the harvesters

In order to teach women how to share their faith, sponsor a witnessing workshop. Publicize it well (don't leave attendance to chance), and specifically invite those you know are interested in evangelism. Don't worry if only a few come to the first one. You'll have accomplished more than if you didn't hold the workshop. Incorporate some of the following ideas:

● Interview women who are effective in lifestyle evangelism. Learn all you can from them.

● Give each attendee a witnessing packet which includes good tracts and presentations of the Gospel such as the "Bridge to Life" published by NavPress.

● With a partner, practice turning a conversation toward Jesus Christ (see the last chapter for ideas).

● Write the Gospel message in letter form to a hypothetical friend who has asked you how she can become a Christian.

● Encourage attendees to tell a seeker about their project of learning how to explain basic Christianity. Have them ask her if she will listen while they practice explaining the Gospel. They could also ask for suggestions to make their explanation clearer.

Understanding the crop

The crop you're seeking to harvest will affect your approach and choice of tools. The largest segment of today's potential harvest is the baby boomers — those people born between 1946 and 1964. Programs designed to reach them should take into account their unique traits.

- They are suspicious of organized religion. (Make them feel comfortable and wanted. Give them "space." "Button-holing" is likely to scare them off.)
- They want quality. (Put your best detail women to work on outreach events.)
- They like music with a beat. (At your events use upbeat, contemporary music.)
- They like participation instead of watching. (Involve them in the event through applause, games, "getting-to-know-you" questionnaires.)
- They respond best to fast-paced programs. (Design one segment of the event to move swiftly into the next.)
- They are hungry for relationships. (In your events allow significant time for casual conversation designed to build friendships.)
- They are concerned about their children. (Develop seminars dealing with topics of interest to young mothers.)
- They are interested in physical fitness. (Use aerobics, outdoor activities, and sports as bridge events.)

Outreach Programs

In addition to training and encouraging women in lifestyle evangelism, here are three types of programs women's ministries can use to move people toward salvation:

- bridge events
- evangelistic events
- evangelistic Bible studies

This order matches the sequence of events in the lives of many women who come to Christ. First there is the bridge event, a nonthreatening time when relationships between Christians and non-Christians can be built. Next the woman might be invited to an evangelistic evening featuring good food and an exciting speaker who shares what Christ means in her life. A final step might be to join an evangelistic Bible study.

Ken Engstrom of the Billy Graham Evangelism Association suggests you answer these preliminary questions before scheduling an event.

1. Who are we trying to reach with this event?
2. Is the church building the best place for this event to be held?
3. Which people in our church have a burden for those this event might reach?

4. Should we open the event with prayer?

5. How should we close this event? Ask for commitment? Announce the next such event?

6. What is our follow-up plan should someone become a believer? Is there a class for her? Will someone do specific one-on-one follow-up?

7. Are we being realistic in trying to make this event happen? Is there enough time before the event to plan it well? Do we have enough people to do the work?

Bridge Events

Selecting and scheduling a bridge event
Think of a bridge event as the widest opening of a funnel. It should be something unbelievers will want to attend. Men often enjoy sporting events. Women enjoy things like:
- craft demonstrations
- visits to boutiques — particularly around Christmas
- museum or historical interest tours
- hikes in nearby nature areas
- swim parties or barbecues
- concerts
- speakers well-versed in current women's issues
- all-day workshops (Feminars)

Brainstorm in your leadership group to find appropriate outreach events. Vary your approach to appeal to different age/interest groups. A concert may not appeal to the same group as a swim party. Providing child-care will increase your attendance, though at times it isn't feasible.

The frequency of such events will depend on the size of your church and your available womanpower. A realistic goal for a small or midsize church might be two to four events a year, perhaps alternating with evangelistic events at which the Gospel is presented. Don't schedule so many events that you turn life into a rat race. Don't expect everyone to attend everything.

When a date has been selected, put it on the church calendar. If the event involves travel, a meal on location, or other such details, the person in charge must go there in advance to assure everything goes as planned. You don't want any surprises such as the place being closed for renovation. This will not impress your visiting non-Christians!

Promoting the bridge event
Keep your target group in mind — the church newcomer, who may or may not be a believer, and the contacts of your regular attenders. Your pub-

licity must be informative and attractive to the unchurched. It should be as creatively and expertly done as possible. Include pertinent data in an easy-to-read format. Proofread and re-proofread!

Design posters and place them on the bulletin boards in grocery stores, community centers, laundromats, bookstores, and day-care centers. Highlight the event on the women's ministries bulletin board at church. If you use a women's ministries table, design an attractive sign to place on or above it advertising this event. If weather and space allow, set up outside the primary entrance of your building or choose a high traffic location inside.

Send invitational flyers or letters to all the women who have recently visited any church event. Encourage your regulars to give flyers to neighbors, friends, and relatives.

Managing the bridge event
Keep your goal in mind. It's to make the unbeliever comfortable so she'll want to attend another event. Beforehand, remind the Christians who attend that this isn't the place to discuss missionary friends, refer to the history of the church, or use clichés that will exclude the outsider.

Do everything possible to assure a smoothly run affair. Stick as close to the schedule as feasible, but be relaxed and flexible. You don't want your guests to feel under pressure.

Get the name, address, and phone number of every visitor. If it's awkward to do it at the event, call those who brought guests for the information afterward. Remember, making contact with the visitors is the reason the event was held.

Evangelistic Events
In many churches, people don't expect professionally planned and executed events. If slipups occur they are lovingly overlooked. "After all, it's just family." And that's true, it often is "just family." But what we're talking about here is moving beyond family. Outreach events should be "outreach." The goal is to bring in women who are unreached and unchurched. They aren't "family" and will evaluate the event through the eyes of an outsider. So as not to detract from your message you must aim for excellence!

Planning a great event
Begin planning at least three to six months in advance. The larger the event and the more well-known the speaker, the more lead time is required for planning.

Have a planning meeting. Planning might be done by the entire women's council, the evangelistic committee, or by an event coordinator or committee, depending on the size and structure of your church. However you are structured, remember that the more people involved in planning an event, the higher the attendance will be.

Pray for direction. Don't plunge right in to the planning without stopping to pray. Don't postpone prayer to the end of the meeting. It's easy to run late making it necessary for women to leave before the prayertime.

Decide which individuals or committees will handle things like:
- publicity
- decorations
- program
- clean-up
- visitor follow-up

Choose a theme. The theme can be built around a particular speaker or the speaker can be instructed to speak to the theme. Develop the theme through the decorations, printed programs, food, music, and programming.

Contact the speaker. Phone the proposed speaker to invite her to speak. Tell her the date, place, beginning, and ending times of the event. Discuss the subject and length of her message. Give her time to think and pray about her response, then get back to her.

If she's unable to speak you may want to ask if she could recommend another qualified speaker. If she agrees to come, clarify remuneration. Some speakers have a set fee, others accept a love offering. Don't be stingy. Speaking is hard work deserving of the honor of a financial reward. Follow-up the phone call with a letter confirming everything discussed on the phone. Include a map and directions to the event.

Contact the speaker again prior to the event to be sure everything is clear concerning date and directions. Pre-arrange remuneration so she can be paid at the event. It's a nice touch to insert the check in a personal thank-you note. Assign someone to greet her at the door and help her during the event. It's awkward for the speaker to arrive and wonder what to do next.

Ticket sales should begin three–four weeks prior to the event. A larger congregation needs three weeks just to "hear" an announcement due to the fluid nature of its attendance. A smaller congregation can use sign-up sheets and may not need advance ticket sales to get an approximate head count.

Make it clear that children too small to sit still for the entire program should not be brought.

Be prepared. If possible, set up for the event the day before. Arrange chairs, tables, podium, decorations, and signs. Check the sound system and overhead projector, if one is needed (have a spare bulb handy). Check for good ventilation. A temperature of 65 degrees with air circulating will help keep people alert.

Start final preparations early on the day of the event to avoid last minute crises. Expect the unexpected. Fuses may blow from too many coffeepots. The five-gallon pot of cooking water may take longer than expected to come to a boil. There's always something!

Developing your program
The actual program details will vary according to the type of event. However, the following elements will apply to most events:
- welcome and explanation of the event, including any directions about food service
- prayer of thanks for the food
- food service
- special music can be presented toward the end of the meal
- special feature (occasionally the speaker will handle this time along with her message; they can effectively be woven into one unit)
- a short personal testimony can be given at this point
- more special music
- introduction of the speaker (ask her for information you can use)
- message (be sure the speaker ends on time)
- closing prayer and, if appropriate, an opportunity for personal response to the Gospel

Begin background music fifteen minutes before the event is to start. This can be taped or live. If live, be sure it is well-rehearsed and adequately amplified.

Write out and distribute the schedule. If the food is being prepared on the premises, the person in charge of the preparation/serving should provide a list of each item that must be done in chronological order. This can be posted in the kitchen to help the crew. The M.C., or woman in charge of the entire event, should write out a program including time bench marks. This should be distributed to everyone involved.

Appoint friendly table hostesses to ensure that everyone is included in the conversation. Seat newcomers next to church members.

Follow-up
Follow-up begins before the event starts. Keep the evangelistic nature of the event foremost in the minds of everyone involved. Pray for the lost to attend. Make it easy for this to happen by underwriting the cost of bringing unsaved friends.

Tell the speaker about any known unbelievers who will be there so she can pray specifically for them. Encourage the speaker through her personal testimony or other means to clearly explain how an individual can make Christ her personal Savior and Lord.

Determine how people will indicate any commitment made. You can have everyone fill out a registration card at the close of the program. Include on the card various types of responses such as:

- made a first-time decision to follow Christ
- recommitted my life to Christ
- need more information about what it means to be a Christian

Another effective means is for the speaker to ask anyone who invited Christ to take over her life to give her name-tag to the speaker at the door.

In your printed and verbal communication avoid the phrase "becoming a Christian." This is offensive to Catholics and others, who see themselves as Christian already. You don't want the seeker to stumble over your words.

Follow-up all visitors. Obtain a complete list of visitors including address and telephone. The table hostesses can help compile this list if you choose not to use registration cards. Those who brought visitors can also be contacted for information.

Women who made a decision should be contacted within forty-eight hours. The contact should be low pressure, friendly, and positive. Mention receiving the information about her decision and ask if she would like to talk to someone. Usually the response will be positive.

Within a week after the event, mail each visitor a "nice-to-have-you-visit" letter. Include a list of upcoming events and an invitation to attend any that might interest her.

Pray for those who came. Divide the visitors' names among the ministry team for prayer. If the visitor isn't a believer, pray for her salvation. If she is a believer with no church home, pray for her to become increasingly involved in your church.

For more detailed information on special events, read Carol Treachler's excellent book, *From Start-Up to Clean-Up*, Wheaton, Ill.: Victor Books, 1991.

Evangelistic Bible Studies

(This section on evangelistic Bible studies was adapted from material by Marie Little and Olive Liefeld.)

The next step for those who have attended a special event might be an investigative Bible study. Such a study is planned to allow an individual to take her time examining the claims of Christ. Unchurched women around the country are responding to invitations to study the Bible in small groups. As a result, many have trusted Jesus as Savior and Lord. Your church can also reach women through an evangelistic study/discussion group.

Starting an evangelistic study
Find the women in your fellowship who are interested in reaching the un-churched in your community through evangelistic Bible studies. You might use a survey or make personal contacts, based on the size of your church. Get those who are interested together, explain your vision to them, and ask them to make a commitment to this ministry.

Pray together for God's Spirit to lead you.

Plan the study. Choose the subject to be studied and a corresponding study guide. Plan the physical arrangements; date, time, place, etc. Remember that some unchurched women will feel more comfortable if the study group meets in a home rather than at the church.

Decide on the teaching format.

● *Discussion only.* Make the Bible the authority for all answers, not a designated leader. Encourage everyone to contribute to the discussion. Try dividing the group into small units to encourage each member to participate, especially if the group is large.

● *Group discussion with wrap-up by leader.* Divide large groups into smaller discussion groups of no more than 15 members each.

Choose a strong, capable leader. Divide the time between small-group discussion and a wrap-up led by the leader. If the leader has the gift of evangelism, the lecture format can be evangelistic.

Promote the study to your community. The women in your church can go in pairs to visit neighborhood women, Sunday visitors, and non-attending parents of Sunday School children to invite them to the group. Encourage everyone to use their natural opportunities for making new friends: aerobic classes, college or craft classes, work associates, carpools, neighborhood block parties. Provide attractive literature for them to use in inviting these friends to the study.

Use informal neighborhood get-togethers to introduce the study. Each participating woman can ask her friends and neighbors to her home in order to learn about the discussion group. The hostess explains how the study works. Let them look through the study guide and ask questions. The fact that no biblical knowledge is needed and that everyone who attends will have an opportunity to participate should be stressed.

Don't get discouraged. If you invite twenty women, only two may respond at first. But momentum will build after the study begins as you pray and continue to publicize the study.

Managing an evangelistic study

Review the material on Bible study groups in chapter 9. Most of the same guidelines apply to an evangelistically oriented study. Here are four other things to also take into consideration:

Keep the Bible central. This is a discovery group in which each person is seeking to understand what the Bible really says, and not merely what she's heard about it. Try to answer questions from the biblical passage being studied, if possible, and not from other parts of the Bible. This will keep new attendees from getting discouraged by their lack of Bible knowledge.

Encourage and model an open attitude. Regardless of a person's previous Bible study experience, she should come as a learner. Everyone should share openly and listen closely to each other's answers. Even those who have been Christians for a long time can learn a lot from the study and from those attending.

Avoid Christian jargon and phrases not understood by unchurched people. Explain any terms you do have to use.

Complete one lesson per week. Don't carry over an unfinished lesson to the following week.

Your Most Important Ministry

When a woman first comes to your bridge event, you don't know how God plans to use your women's ministry in her life. She might quickly become a believer, or it might take years. God waits patiently for the harvest, and we must be as patient with others.

However, patience doesn't mean inactivity. There is work between sowing the seed and reaping the harvest. Each spring I plant tomatoes, corn, and beans for a fall harvest. But between the planting and the harvest constant care is necessary. Weeds need to be pulled, the ground cultivated, and fertilizer and water applied. An abundant harvest will come if I work for it.

The same law of the harvest applies spiritually. If your women's ministry will faithfully work toward a harvest by scheduling bridge events, planning outreach dinners, and initiating evangelistic Bible studies, you will reap a harvest. Your crop is not food for a season but people who will live for eternity.

Reaching people for Christ is the number one priority of women's ministry.

Bibliography

Aldrich, Joseph C. *Gentle Persuasion.* Portland, Ore.: Multnomah Press, 1988.

Aldrich, Joseph C. *Life-Style Evangelism*. Portland, Ore.: Multnomah Press, 1981.

King, Marilyn and Catherine Shell. *How to Start a Neighborhood Bible Study*. Dobbs Ferry, N.Y.: Neighborhood Bible Studies, 1966.

Little, Paul. *How to Give Away Your Faith*. Downers Grove, Ill.: InterVarsity Press, 1988.

Little, Paul. *Know Why You Believe*. Downers Grove, Ill.: InterVarsity Press, 1988.

Petersen, Jim. *Evangelism as a Lifestyle*. Colorado Springs: Navpress, 1980.

Pippert, Rebecca Manley. *Out of the Salt-Shaker and into the World*. Downers Grove, Ill.: InterVarsity Press, 1979.

Raysbook, Randy. "One-Verse Evangelism," *Discipleship Journal 61*. 1991.

Bible study guides tailored for seekers

Ashker, Helene. *Jesus Cares for Women*. Colorado Springs: Navpress, 1987.

Design for Discipleship Series, Colorado Springs: Navpress, 1980.
    Book One: *Your Life in Christ*
    Book Two: *The Spirit-filled Christian*
    Book Three: *Walking with Christ*

Ford, Leighton. *Meeting Jesus*. Downers Grove, Ill.: InterVarsity Press, 1988.

Hillis, Don. *Teach Yourself the Bible Series: John, Gospel of Light and Life*. Chicago: Moody Press, 1982, 1986.

Hoover, James. *Book of Mark*. Downers Grove, Ill.: InterVarsity Press, 1985.

Kuhatschek, Jack. *Self-esteem*. Downers Grove, Ill.: InterVarsity Press, 1990.

Morrissey, Kirkie. *A Woman's Workshop Series, Designed by God for Wholeness*. Grand Rapids: Zondervan Publishing House, 1987.

Nystrom, Carol, *A Woman's Workshop Series: Book of John*. Grand Rapids: Zondervan Publishing House, 1990.

Ryan, Dave and Juanita. Life Recovery Guides. Downers Grove, Ill.:

InterVarsity Press, 1990 (8 guides on topics such as Recovery from Abuse, Recovery from Addiction).

York, William. *One to One*. Downers Grove, Ill.: InterVarsity Press.

CHAPTER SIXTEEN
Community Outreach — Part One

Your women's ministry can approach community evangelism in two ways. You can develop programs designed to bring people into the church (like those suggested in the previous chapter), or you can minister to them right where they are. The primary thrust of the next two chapters is on witnessing and working in the community.

The church ministering in the world is what Frank Tillapaugh calls the "church unleashed." In his excellent book, *The Church Unleashed* (Ventura, Calif.: Regal Books, 1982), Tillapaugh challenges the church to get outside her walls and impact the community. Women's ministry can help release and encourage those the Spirit has uniquely prepared to be salt and light to a rotting, dark world.

Home base ministries like Bible studies, personal and group discipling, retreats, special events, and missionary support activities should be done well. However, all too often that is where women's ministries stop. Some churches either deliberately or subtly discourage their members from getting involved in things that could be construed as "social action."

Other churches are involved in social action instead of preaching the Gospel. Salvation is by grace through faith alone. Ours is not a "works salvation." Social action does not pave the highway to heaven. But, the very fact that we are saved by faith should motivate us to reach out into a sin-damaged community with our message of the grace of God.

In the following pages are some ideas on how you can minister to four different kinds of needy people:
- mothers of preschoolers
- latchkey and other children
- single, pregnant women
- working women

These are only four of the many community outreach possibilities. Let these examples jog your thinking and prick your conscience. Look around at your community. What needs do you see that God wants your women's ministry to meet?

Starting a Community Outreach

Whatever community outreach you decide to undertake you should do the following things:

Appoint a coordinator of community outreach programs. The key is to find someone who has a burden for this area, then release and encourage her to do the ministry. In a small church this woman might also have other responsibilities, such as evangelism or missions.

Identify legitimate needs within the community. This could be accomplished through contact with social agencies or with larger churches already involved in community ministry.

Publicize the outreach. Talk it up. Use posters, flyers, and pulpit announcements. Feature reports at your Bible studies about lives that have been impacted. A permanent location for the collection of needed items will help promote the ministry.

Involve other ministries of the church. Although women might spearhead these programs, they need not be the staffed only by women. Draw in the teens, Sunday School classes of all ages, men's fellowship groups, and Bible studies. The more people included, the more will happen.

Celebrate successes. Let the congregation know what's happening in these particular ministries. Use bulletin inserts and public announcements to keep them informed of how the church is helping make a difference in the lives of needy individuals.

C.O.P.S. Program (Carers of Preschoolers)

(This section was adapted from material by Joanne McCoy.)

Laurie was a young mother who knew she needed help in raising her children. They were controlling her instead of her controlling them. Her sister-in-law, a Christian, was concerned about Laurie, but didn't know how to reach her spiritually or how to give her practical help in mothering. However, she did invite Laurie to attend the C.O.P.S. program. There Laurie heard principles based on Scripture, and she began to investigate for herself what the Bible said. Eleven months later as she watched a Billy Graham broadcast she committed her life to Christ. Today her husband has returned to the Lord and together they are serving in the church.

C.O.P.S. began as an outgrowth of a preschool program conducted by a local church. The basic stimulus for its beginning came from the teachers dealing with out-of-control children and the mothers wanting help in parenting. It was originally set up as an outreach program. As a result, the majority of mothers or other care-providers don't attend the church on a regular basis.

This program can start small and build as the interest increases. Initially only one leader is required. The target group for this ministry includes pregnant moms, nannies, and moms (and dads, via evening programs) of infants through kindergarten children.

Purpose
- provide a Christian outreach in the community
- lead members to a personal relationship with Christ
- teach biblical principles to care-givers of preschoolers
- communicate self-esteem and confidence to them in their God-given responsibilities to care for their children
- teach them to be content in their daily lives, and to love and train their children

Suggested morning program schedule
9:30–9:50 — visiting, coffee, and sharing
9:50–10:20 — special speaker
10:20–10:40 — small group discussion led by group leader
10:40–10:50 — regroup to summarize information
If the group is small or just beginning you can combine the lecture and discussion times by asking the speaker to handle questions and discussion following her presentation.

Suggested topics to discuss
- teaching children about Jesus and helping them know Him as personal Savior
- developing self-esteem in children and helping them feel secure
- developing family relationships
- handling sibling rivalry
- planning a family budget
- planning family fun times
- reading to children (ask a local children's librarian to speak on this topic, and to bring a suggested reading list)
- making a home safe for young children; learning first aid
- brushing up on job skills or pursuing a career while raising young children
- maintaining a home

Child care

While the parents are attending the session, their children are divided into three age-groups for care and classes which can include biblical instruction, singing, crafts, and games.

- newborn to seventeen months: care and playtime only
- eighteen months to three years: class
- three to six years: class

Additional services

- exchange center for used maternity, baby, and children's clothes, toys, and equipment (cribs, playpens, high chairs)
- baby-sitting co-op (see section 4 of this book for details)
- weekly play group
- outings with moms and kids (e.g., picnics, the zoo, short hikes, bicycle rides to parks, trips to the library for storytime and for checking out books)

Remember that your primary goals involve evangelism and discipleship. Through personal contact make opportunities to share the Gospel with unbelievers and nurture those who already know Christ to a deeper commitment.

Homework Club

With a Homework Club, you can reach into a largely untapped mission field — the children in your own neighborhood (latch-key kids and those whose parents are home after school).

A neighborhood home or your church can serve as the meeting place. The number of children you work with will depend on the number of volunteers, the space available, and your energy. A Chicago family developed a Homework Club that reaches thirty children each week. Fifteen attend on Mondays and Wednesdays, and another fifteen come on Tuesdays and Thursdays. Use the following information to start your own club.

Purpose

The purpose of a Homework Club is to help children grow academically, physically, spiritually, and socially, and have the kind of balanced life Jesus had as He grew up (see Luke 2:52). This is done by providing:

- tutoring
- a positive place to do homework
- a drop-in center
- homemade snacks
- opportunities to try crafts and games after homework is completed

- financial aid to purchase supplies
- educational, no-cost adult supervision after school
- transportation home if needed
- prayer for the children

Getting started

Invite friends of your children who attend the schools in your neighborhood to the club. Let the school know what you're doing and ask them to refer children to you. Doing volunteer work at the local school will put you in touch with many children who might want to get involved.

Suggested program and schedule

Children arrive after school and are admitted only if they have homework and written permission from a parent or guardian. They pick up their snack — which is an important part of this program because many children today never get homemade treats — and go to a designated work area, with no more than five children per area.

Homework time begins. Older children or adults can assist younger children as needed. When the children complete their homework, they go to the Reading Room until the set time when they're allowed to sign up for activities.

The children choose which activity to do (activities will vary according to the age and interests of the children and the facility's equipment and space). To minimize fighting, only two or three children may sign up for each activity. Everyone must sign up for an activity so that no one is free to wander around bothering others. Half-hour activity periods work well with a child's attention span.

Homework Club ends at 5:30 P.M. Elementary school children must be picked up by a parent or guardian. If parents aren't able to pick up children a volunteer takes them home.

Those who come must obey the club rules:

- no swearing
- no stealing
- no hitting or fighting
- no name calling
- no smoking, drinking, or drugs
- if you play with it, put it away
- have fun!

Supplies needed

- a set of encyclopedias and a new dictionary
- flash cards

- calculators
- Storybooks and books suitable for book reports. Ask a local children's librarian for a list of suggested books, such as those that have received the Caldecott and Newbery awards. Arrange to check out a stack of library books weekly.
  - paper, pencils, erasers, and pencil sharpener
  - typewriter and typing paper (or Apple computer with printer)
  - materials for special projects (these will vary according to age and interests: e.g., puzzles, modeling clay, sewing machine, acrylic paints, construction paper, glue, colored felt pens, rubber stamps and ink pads, etc.)
  - games for children: e.g., Chutes and Ladders, checkers, chess, Pictionary Junior, Monopoly, Clue, dominos, Uno

This is a very difficult ministry if you view your house as your possession and your time as your own. But if you see your home as God's and the club as the very least you can do in light of all He has done for you, you can impact your community for Christ, and have fun with the kids in the process.

Some children may commit their lives to Christ through direct discussion with you during the Homework Club. For others the tangible love you demonstrate will stay with them and the Holy Spirit can use it later in their lives.

Helping Single Pregnant Women
A woman who is single and pregnant stands in great need of the practical love of Christians. She may be the stereotypical sexually active teenager or she may be a more mature woman. Your first contact with her may be through a member of the church (or she may be a member herself).

Women's ministries can help single, pregnant women in many practical ways including:
- providing maternity and baby clothes (new and used)
- providing financial assistance with housing, medical bills, food, and clothing
- finding a nurturing home for her (such as a guest room in the home of a church family) until the baby's birth
- having a baby shower complete with cake, games, and plenty of gifts for the baby (if her family isn't supportive, this may be her only baby shower; make it a wonderful celebration)
- helping to obtain needed furniture (crib, carseat, high chair, diaper bag, stroller, front or backpack baby carrier, playpen, etc.) Mothers of toddlers in the congregation may be ready to pass on some of their baby

gear. Thrift shops also carry used baby equipment. Or, you can pool your money and buy new equipment.

- meals and housekeeping help immediately after the baby's birth, providing baby-sitting and day care if needed

- asking someone to be a "big sister" who can accompany her to doctor's or counseling appointments and help her get ready for the baby's arrival. This special friend can be a positive role model and share her own memorable experiences of birth and child-rearing. She can also be the labor and delivery coach if the woman needs one.

- recognizing that the woman may be struggling with a decision to single parent, get married, make an adoption plan, or abort. She may need to be referred for professional counseling as she works through these crucial choices.

The woman who chooses adoption
(Insight for this section was provided by Rebecca Stahr MacDougall, MSW.)

Women who consider adoption often must deal with society's judgment of this choice. Contrary to well accepted myths, a birthmother who places her child in an adoptive home *does* care about her child, will *never* forget about that child, and can benefit from being involved in the adoption plan, perhaps even meeting the adoptive parents. A woman in this situation needs a great deal of prayer and support. Women's ministries can:

- have a packet of information available for the pregnant woman including general information about adoption and local referrals to agencies which provide choices, counseling (including pre-and post-delivery support), and the names and numbers of other women who have placed a baby for adoption

- direct the woman to a professional agency to help her find an adoptive family. Adoption involves many complicated emotional and legal aspects; "in house" (or "in church") matching can cause undue pressure, anxiety, and heartache for all involved

- provide personal support and a listening ear for the woman who has released her baby. Feelings of numbness, fear, ambivalence, anger, and depression are all normal to the grief process she may experience before and after she releases her child. Listen to the pain, while affirming her choice. This may be a positive decision for her in terms of providing direction for her life

- celebrate the life with her. Send cards, flowers, and talk about the pregnancy and her child, following her lead

- reach out to her mother who may also be struggling with a great deal of guilt and pain. She may be the most influential and affected person involved in her daughter's decision

• pray for and with her. Most women who make an adoption plan are leaning on any faith they have and are very open to spiritual counsel at this time

Dealing with abortion

Many women in this predicament may view abortion as their only solution. They may lack moral and practical support from their family and friends. Statistics indicate that women who have had abortions were encouraged to do so by boyfriends or parents. Often the woman, and those who help her make her decision, aren't aware of the medical and psycho-social ramifications of abortion.

Women's ministries can:

• encourage women in the church to befriend single pregnant women in the church and the community

• conduct seminars to inform church members about the abortion issue and what they can do about it

• encourage political action. As Christians we must address the abortion issue and take a firm stand in our communities. Write letters to your local, state, and federal politicians and legislators voicing your concerns about the abortion issue. Urge them to support prolife legislation. Firmly, but politely, make your views known. Change can start at the grassroots level. It can start with you and your church

• encourage women (and men) in the fellowship to volunteer at the local crisis pregnancy center. Designate a woman to serve as the liaison between women's ministries and the center. If your community doesn't have a center, meet with other concerned individuals and churches and get one started

Through involvement in a crisis pregnancy center, Christian women can provide medical information, supportive counsel, and prayer during pregnancy. Caring support should also be extended to the woman who has been traumatized by abortion. Listening to her is perhaps the most important way to help.

Encouraging preventative training

The majority of teens today face the opportunity to have sexual intercourse before they graduate from high school. Arm your kids with the spiritual and emotional tools they'll need to stand firm against peer and social pressures.

Preventative training about sex should begin at home and in the church. Too many Christian parents make the mistake of avoiding discussing sex with their children. If you don't tell them about it, the kids at school will, and their perception is probably quite different from your own. If you're the parent of middle school, junior, or senior high student, talk to them openly about sex. Give them the facts about teen pregnancy, abortion, AIDS, and venereal disease. Teach them how they can remain sexually pure in a world that challenges them to do otherwise.

Women's ministries can encourage junior and senior high Sunday School teachers and youth workers to discuss with their children the biblical standards for purity, the ramifications of premarital sex, and how to hold onto their virginity when their peers pressure them not to. Kids are curious about sex, but often are too embarrassed to ask their own parents about it. They may be more open with a loving, objective adult such as their Sunday School teacher or youth pastor.

Suggested Reading

Lewis, Gay. *Bittersweet.* South Plainsfield, N.J.: Bridge Publishing, 1984. A poignant telling of her daughter's pregnancy and adoption.

Silber, Kathleen and Phylis Speedlin. *Dear Birthmother: Thank You for Our Baby.* San Antonio, Texas: Corona Publishing Company, 1991. This book explores some of the myths of adoption and details the evolution of open adoption using letters written by birthmothers.

VanDerMolen, Henrietta. *Pregnant and Alone: How You Can Help a Pregnant Friend.* Wheaton, Ill: Shaw Publishers, 1989. A resource exploring crisis pregnancy and equipping the birthmother, her family, and her friends to make important decisions.

Reaching Working Women with the Gospel

(This section was adapted from material by Felecia Thompson and Cheryl Smith.)

The percentage of mothers who work outside of the home has increased to 68 percent of women with children aged six to twelve and 54 percent of mothers with children under six. In order to reach these busy women with the Gospel, we must minister to them in the workplace. The following suggestions include guidelines for three different approaches:

- a lunchtime study
- a light supper with lecture/study
- a Saturday afternoon "High Tea"

Select the approach that's appropriate for the type of women you want to reach and for the contacts you have within the working community.

Lunchtime Bible study

Pray for a woman who will sponsor a lunchtime or after-work Bible study in her office building, school, or other workplace. You're ready to begin when you have three or more women interested in attending. Plan a short-term study of four to eight weeks. (Working women respond best to limited time commitments.)

Develop an attractive flyer with Bible study date, location, subject, and a contact person's name and phone number. Have several people proofread the piece. You will be dead before you start if your publicity isn't attractive and error-free. Post it on all bulletin boards in your target area.

If you are the Bible study leader:

● Eat your lunch before the Bible study (it's difficult to eat and lead a discussion at the same time)

● Wear clothing appropriate to the particular workplace (dresses and heels to an office, slacks to a factory, etc.)

● Begin and end the study on time

● Select a study with chapters/segments that stand alone so people can feel comfortable on their first visit. Choose material that can be completed in forty-five minutes

● Once the initial short-term study is completed, consider continuing for another short-term study. If interest wanes, call a recess for a few weeks, then restart

● Don't meet between Thanksgiving and Christmas or in the summer

Light supper study

A "soup supper and Bible study" concept is attractive to busy working women who can't attend long-term evening Bible studies. The group meets over a light supper (soup and salad) for two hours after work — perhaps from 5:30 to 7:30 P.M. The study could be held in a convenient home, restaurant, or room in an office building. A three-weeks-on, one-week-off pattern works well.

Begin the Bible discussion after most of the women are through with their meal. Stick to the schedule. Women may need to leave to pick up children or have other evening engagements.

Saturday afternoon "High Tea"

Corporate women experience the same stresses as corporate men, but many of them also have the full-time job of managing a household. A Saturday afternoon High Tea is a tasteful and fun way to present the Gospel to these busy women.

A committee of at least three women should organize this event. Each should supervise one of the following areas:
- location (greeters, lighting, sound system, parking)
- food (menu, preparation, presentation, table decorations)
- program (speaker, music/musicians, evangelistic literature)

Don't hold this event in the church basement. Remember your audience: corporate women who are used to quality and excellence. Choose a comfortable, attractive setting, such as a hotel banquet room or a nice home. Set a reasonable ticket price so that both the executive woman and her assistants can afford to attend.

Have the hotel provide the food (for a tea: finger sandwiches, tea cookies, and cakes). If you meet in a home, don't turn this classy event into a potluck. Have it catered or ask the best cooks in the congregation to prepare a delicious light meal and dessert.

The program should feature an executive woman who is both a strong Christian and an experienced and interesting speaker. Have her present a short devotional and a brief invitation to trust Christ as Savior. Provide a card at each place setting for women to indicate if they would like to receive more information about following Christ.

Classical music playing in the background before and after the devotional is an elegant touch, whether it's an audio tape or a live string quartet. Have Bibles, well-written evangelistic tracts, and other Christian literature available on a table after the devotional.

Because these are very busy women, begin and end on time, but keep the atmosphere relaxed and unrushed. Have the Tea on a monthly or quarterly basis according to interest level and availability of women to make the necessary arrangements.

Important things to remember

- Avoid office gossip and deal with personal problems in a confidential setting. Christians who attend are responsible for leading the conversation to Christ-centered topics.
- Choose study/lecture subjects attractive to unbelievers.
- Don't use Christian jargon or terms.
- Use an up-to-date translation of the Bible.
- Use Scripture as your authority, but avoid reference to specific denominations and church doctrines.
- Pray for each person who attends.
- Don't be discouraged by turnover in attendance. Women may be interested, but may have other occasional obligations.

(For more information on how to lead Bible studies and organize special events see chaps. 9 and 15.)

Helpful resources

Women in the Workplace Seminars
c/o Mary Whelchel, Moody Church
LaSalle and North Avenue
Chicago, IL 60610

ETTC (Equal To The Challenge)
c/o Dianne Lewis
P.O. Box 811520
Chicago, IL 60681-1520

Christian Businesswoman's Association
Stonecroft Ministries
U.S. Headquarters
P.O. Box 9609
Kansas City, MO 64134

Canadian Headquarters
P.O. Box 1220 Pos. St.
Willowdale, ONT M2N 5T5

Asker, Helene. *Jesus Cares for Women.* Colorado Springs: NavPress, 1987. The evangelistic lessons in this easy-to-use, five-week series are designed to be photocopied and distributed to study members, who are not required to buy a book.

Lessons on Assurance. Colorado Springs: NavPress, 1980. This five-lesson series addresses assurance regarding salvation, forgiveness, answered prayer, help in overcoming temptation, and guidance.

Thatcher, Martha. *When the Squeeze Is On.* Colorado Springs: NavPress, 1987. This eight-lesson study on dealing with life's pressures contains excellent material. It will take sixteen weeks to cover during a lunch-hour format due to the length of the lessons. Since the chapters are not sequential, choose which topics hold the most interest for your group.

CHAPTER SEVENTEEN
Community Outreach — Part Two

This chapter was adapted from material by
Cheryl Smith and Felecia Thompson.

You are the salt of the earth. But if the salt loses its saltiness, how can it be made salty again? It is no longer good for anything, except to be thrown out and trampled by men. You are the light of the world. A city on a hill cannot be hidden. Neither do people light a lamp and put it under a bowl. Instead they put it on its stand, and it gives light to everyone in the house. In the same way, let your light shine before men, that they may see your good deeds and praise your Father in heaven (Matt. 5:13-16).

Many believers spend much of their leisure time at church-related activities and have little contact with unbelievers. Their salt and light is hidden behind church walls and isn't at work in their communities. The last chapter outlined some ways women's ministries could get involved with the needs around them. Here are some further suggestions on reaching out with the love of Christ to:

- the poor
- adult children of alcoholics
- prisoners
- AIDS patients

Before we get into these ministries, let's not forget volunteerism.

Volunteer Opportunities
Every year millions of people in the United States and Canada impact their neighborhoods by volunteering their time and talents to local com-

munity service organizations. Involvement as community volunteers will enable Christian women to have regular contact with the world and to touch others with Christ's love and forgiveness.

A volunteer committee established under the supervision of women's ministries can help by identifying meaningful service opportunities, encouraging women to serve in them, and supporting those who do. Here are just a few of the many possibilities:

- museum, opera, theater company, or symphony office worker
- helping with political campaigns
- craft teacher at children's art center
- hospital gift shop cashier
- neighborhood or park clean-up crew member
- reading and other services to people in nursing homes, group homes, and hospices
- school playground supervisor or crosswalk monitor
- music teacher at community center
- tutor for children
- day camp counselor
- parent-teacher organization volunteer
- advocate for low-income women
- drug, alcohol, or pregnancy counselor
- board member for local social service agency
- clothing room worker at YWCA
- teaching English as a Second Language (ESL) to internationals
- foreign language interpreter for local court or clinic
- reading tutor for community literacy program
- Big Sister program volunteer
- soup kitchen helper
- Meals-on-Wheels volunteer

Almost every nonprofit organization needs volunteers. Don't worry about a lack of training. Many jobs don't require specialized skills. For those that do there are usually training programs provided.

The harvest is ripe with opportunities for Christians to make a spiritual impact through volunteerism. You can keep the need for volunteers before the congregation through:

- announcements and bulletin inserts
- highlighting volunteer accomplishments at women's events
- encouraging each Bible study to adopt a community project
- selecting a particular ministry each quarter and collecting gifts (monetary or otherwise) for that ministry

One of the best things you could do to get your church involved would be to start a volunteer network.

Designing a volunteer network

Before you recruit even one volunteer, firmly establish the mechanics of the volunteer network by determining:

- what are the network's goals and objectives
- who is responsible for contacting community organizations to ascertain specific needs
- what methods will be used to recruit volunteers in the congregation
- what kind of training and orientation will be needed and how it will be handled
- "if" and "how" a volunteer and her ministry will be evaluated
- who is responsible for keeping the program's records including: volunteer profiles, volunteer hours and activities, and most importantly, records of spiritual fruit resulting from volunteer ministry

Keep the focus of the network on providing Christians with frontline opportunities to be salt and light. Before a volunteer begins any community project she should receive training in evangelism. The trained Christian volunteer, willing to give of herself to help others, can expect to see spiritual fruit as a result of her labors.

Helpful resources

Ellis, Susan and Katherine Noyes. *By the People: A History of Americans as Volunteers.* Philadelphia: Energize Books, 1978.

Gilbert, Sara. *Lend a Hand.* New York: Morrow Junior Books, 1988.

Ilsley, Paul and John A. Niemi. *Recruiting and Training Volunteers.* New York: McGraw Hill, 1981.

McCurley, Steve and Sue Vineyard. *101 Ideas for Volunteer Programs.* Downers Grove, Ill.: Heritage Art Publications, 1986.

Wilson, Mariene. *The Effective Management of Volunteer Programs.* Boulder, Colo.: Volunteer Management Assoc., 1976.

How to Mobilize Church Volunteers. Minneapolis: Augsburg Publishing House, 1983.

Meeting the Needs of the Poor

Despite our national image of affluence almost 40 million Americans live in poverty. Many of them are black or Hispanic. The majority are women and children, living in families without a male head of the household. They can't afford adequate housing, food, clothing, heat, or medical care for themselves. What a hopeless situation!

But Jesus Christ came with a message of hope for the poor. "The Spirit of the Lord is on Me, because He has anointed Me to preach good news to the poor. He has sent Me to proclaim freedom for the prisoners and recovery of sight for the blind, to release the oppressed, to proclaim the year of the Lord's favor" (Luke 4:18-19).

As ambassadors of Christ, our message and ministry should address the needs of impoverished women and children. Beginning in our own cities and neighborhoods we can open our arms and extend our hands with Christian love and concern.

As women we can take the lead in this ministry. Proverbs 31, in describing the ideal woman, says she is one who "opens her arms to the poor and extends her hands to the needy" (v. 20). Start by appointing a small Special Needs committee made up of women who have a heart for helping the less fortunate. They can:

● encourage women to volunteer their time and services at a local shelter or mission which aids the poor

● research the needs in their area and support or start appropriate ministries

● learn about the local and federal welfare policies which need reform and lobby the government agencies to make the necessary changes in the system

Some of the programs mentioned in Section 4 of this book — like the Food Pantry or Clothes Closet — can be expanded to extend into the community. Here are some others things you could do:

● Contact the local United Way and ask for names of those in your area who have run out of food stamps and money. Buy bags of groceries or cook meals for them. When you visit their home to drop off food, invite them to your church or to your home for dinner.

● Make the holidays special for your low-income neighbors. Prepare a feast with all the trimmings, festively decorate the church and invite them to come. Provide child care, inspirational music, and a message of hope.

● Set up a benevolent fund to cover the emergencies of the poor in your neighborhood. Read the local newspaper and note those who may have special needs due to fire, robbery, illness, etc. Call to offer the assistance of your church family.

● Assure that elderly women are receiving adequate health care.

Provide transportation to the doctor's when needed. Use the benevolent fund to get prescriptions for those who can't afford to pay themselves.

- Many mothers can't afford to work because they can't afford day care. Provide low-cost or free day care to low-income and welfare moms.

Through word of mouth, people in your community will learn that your church is serious about helping the poor. The good that you do will open doors to share the love and forgiveness of Jesus Christ. Train your women in evangelism. Encourage them to prepare short, personal testimonies that can be informally shared as they meet and work with people through community outreach. Even if you never hear of anyone coming to Christ through your witness, you are being obedient to God in helping those who can't help themselves.

The good that you do will also be rewarded by Christ.

For I was hungry and you gave Me something to eat, I was thirsty and you gave Me something to drink, I was a stranger and you invited Me in, I needed clothes and you clothed Me, I was sick and you looked after Me, I was in prison and you came to visit Me. . . . I tell you the truth, whatever you did for one of the least of these brothers of Mine, you did for Me (Matt. 25:35-36, 40).

Helpful resources

Sidel, Ruth. *Women and Children Last.* New York: Penguin Books, 1986.

Sider, Ronald. *Rich Christians in an Age of Hunger: A Biblical Study.* Downers Grove, Ill.: InterVarsity Press, 1984.

Helping Adult Children of Alcoholics

Increasingly our society is recognizing the enormous impact an alcoholic parent has on a child — even after the child has become an adult. An alcoholic parent in the home produces a dysfunctional family, often characterized by chaotic behavior patterns. This environment can produce adults who have difficulty dealing with their emotions and with trusting others, including God.

Women's ministries, or your local church, can sponsor an Adult Children of Alcoholics (ACA) group as an evangelistic outreach to your community and a significant help to hurting people within your fellowship.

If the primary thrust of your group is to the community, design your program with that in mind. Secure a meeting room in a public building such as a library, community center, or bank. Advertise the meeting throughout the community by flyers/posters in supermarkets and storefronts. If a member of your church attends AA or Al-Anon, have them invite people from these meetings to visit your ACA meeting. People go to such support groups seven days a week. Many of them are open to new groups that follow the AA rule of confidentiality and can help them in their search for recovery.

Starting an ACA ministry supported by your church

1. Pray for direction and for others to share your burden for this ministry.

2. Present the ministry to the church leaders. Get their support before you start.

3. Attend a secular ACA group to become acquainted with the program. Call or write one of the following organizations to inquire about branches in your community:

Adult Children of Alcoholics
Central Service Board
P.O. Box 35632
Los Angeles, CA 90035
(213) 464-4423

National Association for Children of Alcoholics
31706 Coast Highway, Suite 201
South Laguna, CA 92677
(714) 499-3889

4. Introduce yourself to the facilitator at the secular ACA meeting and explain your church's interest in sponsoring a group. ACA groups sometimes help churches start a similar ministry.

5. Call other churches with ACA ministries and enlist their help in starting your own group. Or work with them and other local churches to sponsor a group together.

ACA group formats

Educational lectures — presented by professionals (medical, legal, family counselors, Alcoholics Anonymous leaders) as well as by knowledgeable Christians. A lecture series could be promoted throughout your community and presented on a weekly basis for eight weeks.

Topic-oriented discussion groups — in which adult children of alcoholics are led to express their thoughts and feelings. Discussion groups move beyond the general information about ACAs presented in educational lectures and focus on the specifics of their own lives. These groups generally meet weekly for six to eighteen weeks.

Support groups — these are similar to discussion groups, but they focus more on current events in the lives of the members rather than on a scheduled course of topics. These groups often are open-ended with no definite stopping date for the group.

Helpful resources
Cermak, Timmen L., M.D. *A Time to Heal: The Road to Recovery for Adult Children of Alcoholics.* New York: Avon Books, 1988.

W., Claudia. *God Help Me Stop.* Books West, Wemberly Square, P.O. Box 27364, San Diego, CA 92128, 1983. A 12-step Bible study workbook for those battling current addictions or for members of a dysfunctional family. An excellent tool for individual Bible study or group discussion.

The 12 Steps — A Way Out: A Working Guide for Adult Children of Alcoholic & Other Dysfunctional Families. Recovery Publications, 1201 Knoxville Street, San Diego, CA 92110, 1987, (619) 275-1350.

Ministering to Prisoners
Christians have a biblical responsibility to visit prisoners and their families (see Matt. 25:35-39). Before beginning an outreach in the local jail or prison, invite a representative from one of the numerous Christian prison ministries to speak to your church or women's council (see the list of ministries at the end of this section).

With direction and help from established prison ministries you can try several things, depending on your burden and available woman power.

• Write letters to prisoners. This gives them written proof of God's love for them through the concern of virtual strangers. As they read and reread the letters from members of your church, they are ministered to by the Scripture verses and the encouragement offered.

• Provide correspondence courses and Christian books to prisoners enabling them to build a basic library, not just for themselves, but also for other prisoners.

• Remember birthdays, holidays, and special occasions with cards and appropriate gifts. This can mean a lot to someone who is cut off from family and friends.

• Help the prisoner's family. Contact them and ask if they have any pressing needs the church can help meet (e.g., financial help with groceries and bills, providing child care while the spouse visits the prison, helping the spouse to receive job training). Invite them to your church and give them a ride if needed.

- Pray daily for the salvation of specific prisoners and their families. Meet regularly for prayer with other Christians who share your burden for this ministry.
- Help reintegrate the released prisoner into society if he or she demonstrates a true behavioral change. Attempt this cautiously and with direct involvement from the pastoral staff. Employment sometimes deters an ex-prisoner's return to jail, but helping him to find employment requires a faithful church ready to walk beside the person every step of the way.

Visitation guidelines
(These do's and don't's are from Allen Hanson.)

Do:
- dress casually; avoid flashy clothing
- arrive early; sometimes prison security officials need extra time to process your visit
- smile and be at ease
- talk about a bright future for the prisoner; be positive and upbeat
- tell the prisoner about Jesus; he or she will be more receptive to your testimony than you might think
- tell the prisoner you care about him or her; this has special meaning to someone shut off from society
- tell the prisoner when you will visit again and make sure you come when you promise
- encourage other Christians to visit prisoners; relate your positive visitation experiences
- contribute your time and money to a prison ministry

Don't:
- be afraid; visiting a prison doesn't put you in danger
- visit without first getting permission from prison authorities; otherwise you may be turned away
- take a camera or tape recorder; they usually aren't allowed inside prisons
- give the prisoner anything unless you first check with prison authorities; contraband may be suspected if you do
- mention family problems; if the prisoner wants to talk about family you can follow the lead
- talk about the prisoner's case
- compliment any part of the prison system
- forget to pray daily for those you visit
- forget to contribute to a prison ministry

Helpful resources
Nettler, Gwynn. *Explaining Crime.* New York: McGraw-Hill, 1974.

Packe, Dale K. *A Christian's Guide to Effective Jail and Prison Ministries.* Old Tappan, N.J.: Fleming H. Revell, 1976.

Smarto, Donald. *Justice and Mercy.* Wheaton, Ill.: Tyndale House, 1987.

Tippit, Sammy. *The Prayer Factor.* Chicago: Moody Press, 1988.

International Prison Ministry
P.O. Box 63
Dallas, TX 75221

Prison Fellowship
P.O. Box 17500
Washington, D.C. 20041
(703) 471-0695

Prison Mission Association, Inc.
P.O. Box N
Alameda, CA 94501
(714) 686-2613

Helping AIDS Patients

Today AIDS is as devastating to our modern era as the Black Plague was to the Middle Ages. The Center for Disease Control reported 83,145 deaths from AIDS by May 1990. By the end of 1992, the death toll is estimated to reach 263,000. AIDS victims and their families need the Gospel message and the compassionate ministry of the church.

When AIDS first surfaced in North America, it was known as a homosexual disease. This is no longer the case. But some Christians still think of it as a "sinner's disease." This attitude must change before we can effectively minister to AIDS patients. Instead of asking why people have AIDS, we need to ask what we can do to help them.

So far Christians have been slow to speak and act. But we can't ignore this vast mission field of dying people any longer. The church should be devoted to giving spiritual, emotional, and physical aid to the weak and vulnerable. She should provide unconditional love to the abandoned and spiritual direction to the lost and suffering.

Your church should find out what community resources are available to assist AIDS patients, then get involved — individually and collectively — in helping them and their families. Learn more about AIDS through books, articles, and conferences, or contact one of the agencies listed below. Encourage your members to serve as volunteers in local AIDS-related programs.

There is so much that can be done. Here are just a few examples:

Practical help
- prepare and deliver meals
- run errands: banking, laundry, groceries, etc.
- help with housecleaning, lawn work, and home repairs
- provide financial help
- provide transportation to the hospital and doctor's appointments

Spiritual help
- share the Gospel and the love of Christ
- read the Bible aloud
- supply tapes of Scripture and praise songs
- pray for and with the person
- read a Christian book together

Emotional help
- spend time listening and sharing
- show a consistent, genuine concern
- make physical contact by hugging and holding hands
- send encouraging notes and cards and make phone calls
- spend time together

Helpful resources
Hoffman, Wendell W. and Stanley J. Grenz. *AIDS: Ministry in the Midst of an Epidemic.* Grand Rapids: Baker Book House, 1989.

Wood, Glenn G., M.D. and John E. Dietrich, M.D. *The AIDS Epidemic: Balancing Compassion and Justice.* Portland, Ore.: Multnomah Press, 1990.

AIDS Information Line 1-800-342-AIDS

AIDS Crisis and Christians Today
P.O. Box 24647
Nashville, TN 37202
(615) 371-1616

National Hospice Organization
1901 N. Moore Street
Arlington, VA 22209
(703) 243-5900

National AIDS Centre
301 Elgin Street
Ottawa, Ontario K1A 1A0
Canada

CHAPTER EIGHTEEN
World Missions — Part One

*The material in the next two chapters on missions
was collected by Mary McCallum.*

Missions used to be the flag around which many women's groups rallied. Dorothy Dahlman in her book, *A Designer's Guide for Creative Women's Ministries* (Arlington Heights, Ill.: Harvest Publications, 1988, 14–15) explains the missions focus of the women in the Baptist General Conference.

> In the early 1940's the BGC took some significant steps to identify ourselves as Baptists who have a strong desire to reach out in home and world missions. Our program of sending missionaries from our churches through our own world missions board brought a high level of commitment to God. . . . For women of the Baptist General Conference, missions was an unbeatable cause. As a result of this strong emphasis on missions, the focus was on women who had come through the church and were committed to missions as the most important cause in their lives. Women that were invited to the circles and to the large meetings knew that missions was our cause.

Women can still play a key role in missions, even though it's no longer the primary focus of most women's ministries. They can be active on the missions committee in a larger church, or be the key individuals in a smaller church that help maintain an appropriate emphasis on missions.

The next two chapters outline the basic functions of a missions committee and offer practical suggestions on how to develop and implement an effective missions program.

Organizing a Missions Committee

The purpose of a missions committee is twofold:

- to serve as an information and resource network between the church and its missionaries
- to promote missions by educating all age-levels in the body

How the missions committee is organized will depend on the size and organizational structure of your church. Some churches have an appointed missions coordinator who oversees missions activities and serves as a liaison between the fellowship and its missionaries.

Other churches have a women's ministries missions committee which works under one or more of the deacons/elders/pastoral staff.

In some instances a group of men and women, committed to missions and led by specific goals and guidelines, is responsible for coordinating the missions program.

However the individual or committee is chosen, the next step is to set clear goals and make specific plans to reach them. As in any ministry area, it's better to start small than to undertake too much too soon.

Here are three things a good missions committee should be devoted to doing:

- increasing prayer for missions
- educating the church about missions. This includes providing adequate, up-to-date information about the church's missionaries and their needs
- sponsoring special missions events, such as luncheons, conferences, or festivals to raise missions awareness (see next chapter)

Increasing Prayer for Missions

Collect prayer requests from missionaries and circulate them regularly via the church bulletin, home Bible studies, prayer chains, and Sunday School classes. Prayer requests can be obtained from the letters of missionaries or from telephone calls, depending on the missionaries' location. The task is simplified by having several people involved in getting the requests. This is especially important if the number of missionaries is large. Keep those who are praying informed about answers to their prayers. This will stimulate increased commitment to prayer.

Here are some guidelines for starting regular missionary prayer meetings or for improving an already existing missions prayer meeting:

- Present requests in an organized fashion. Type them out and duplicate for distribution, or make copies of the original letters and highlight key requests.
- Share a brief devotional on prayer or some aspect of missions work to start the meeting.

- Include group singing and other relevant activities along with prayer.

Don't be discouraged by low attendance. If the prayertime had not been scheduled no praying at all would have been done. If the time goes well, and God is seen at work, more people will come.

What to pray for missionaries

(The material is excerpted from an article by Mark Kieft. He grew up on the mission field and served as a missionary in Ecuador and Bolivia.)

1. Apply prayers of the Bible to missionaries. Paul urged the churches in Colosse and Ephesus to pray for an open door for the message, clarity in presenting it, and courage to proclaim it fearlessly. Pray this same prayer for your missionaries. See also Ephesians 1:17-19; 3:16-19; Philippians 1:9-11; Colossians 1:9-12; 4:3.

2. Pray for their physical needs. Those in underdeveloped countries face serious illnesses, yet available medical care is poor. Pray for their health and daily stamina.

3. Pray for their emotional health. Some missionaries serving in isolated areas don't see relatives or close friends for several years at a time. Pray that they maintain close fellowship with the Lord first of all, and also with coworkers and nationals.

4. Pray for their spiritual needs. Those with far-reaching and effective ministries face harsh satanic attacks. Some cultures tolerate a shocking level of immorality. Ask the Lord to protect missionaries and to give them strength to remain pure in all areas of their lives.

5. Pray for fruitful labor. Satan is ready to snatch away any seed that is sown. Pray for effectiveness in ministry; for the salvation of unbelievers, and the growth and maturity of believers. Pray for wisdom in decision-making, for organizational ability, and for the best use of time.

6. Pray for the difficult cultural pressures they face. Communicating in a foreign language complicates ministry as well as daily life. Pray that they quickly learn the language and adapt to their new culture. Pray that the Lord gives them grace and strength to continue, even when they're discouraged and feel like quitting.

7. Pray for the children of missionaries. Growing up bilingually and biculturally can cause children to struggle with their identity. Pray that they adapt to their new culture and learn to appreciate their unique heritage. Some children of missionaries attend boarding schools far away from their parents. Ask the Lord to protect and deepen family ties. Pray also for the dorm parents and other adults who have an influence on the children. If the children are being home schooled, pray for their mother to have wisdom to deal with resulting pressures.

8. Pray for the ability to handle financial pressures. Often missionaries are unsure of their monthly support. This is especially difficult in areas with a high cost of living. Ask the Lord to meet all of their financial needs and to give them wisdom in knowing how to divide their income among pressing needs. Ask God to stir His people (including us) to be more faithful in giving to missionaries.

9. Pray for the political stability of the country. Learn about the country and city in which the missionaries serve (living conditions, the country's political and economic stability, and its predicted future) so that you can pray more intelligently and effectively.

Educating the Church about Missions
One of the most important functions of a missions committee is education. (Avoid "education" that's only a thinly disguised appeal for money.) The more a church understands about missions, the more they will pray and give both time and money. A church that thinks missions is most likely to become a sending church as well.

Educating people about missions might include:

• encouraging the pastor/teacher to preach a series of missions-oriented sermons

• providing mission-oriented material for Sunday School teachers

• increasing the number of missions books in the church library

• publishing a reading list of missions-related books and distributing it to each family in the fellowship. Publishing book reviews of missionary biographies

• planning summer missions trips for the church youth group or sending a task force of adults to a mission field to help with a project or observe and report on what's happening

• keeping the church abreast of missions activities. One of the best ways to do this is through a Missions Bulletin Board.

Missions bulletin board
Follow these guidelines for an effective missions bulletin board.

Get one person to be responsible for the bulletin board. She may then develop a committee to help if necessary. Clearly identify the board's theme. In this case: *missions*.

Use an *up-to-date* world map. Show where your missionaries are serving. Post *recent* letters in appropriate places. To encourage church members to write to missionaries, make available pre-addressed and stamped aerogrammes or envelopes. One church had an attractive missions bulletin board under which was a series of clear plastic boxes holding copies of the latest letter and pre-addressed envelopes to the appropriate missionaries. As you might expect, they had a large number of families interested in their missionaries.

The missions committee might want to *feature one missionary per month or quarter* highlighting them on the missions bulletin board. You'll need to start accumulating information such as pictures and memorabilia several months in advance, depending on the location of the missionary family. The Sunday School can also be involved in a "Missionary of the Month" project.

Reserve part of the bulletin board for *announcing the next church missions event.*

Be creative!

You can also publicize missions by adding a missions emphasis to already existing programs. Short, appropriate missionary testimonies can become part of church dinners and other functions.

You can also prepare a missionary calendar for your church, including birthdays and other special occasions pertaining to your missionaries like furlough dates, etc.

Practical Care of Missionaries

Missionaries on the field
Stay in touch. Write letters. Make an occasional phone call. If missionaries are an extension of their home church, communication must be a two-way street. Send them the church bulletins to keep them abreast of activities at home.

Remember birthdays and other special occasions. A "Missionary Fact Sheet" like the one at the end of this chapter can help you keep track of important dates.

Send "Request Forms" periodically to those who serve in third and fourth world countries or are far from a source of supply. Keep the forms updated (see sample form at the end of the chapter).

Encourage people within the church to *adopt a missionary family for a specified length of time.* Individual families or committees like women's ministries can adopt a missionary. Help them find out which missionaries need some extra spiritual encouragement or financial help. Once a choice has been made the family or group can introduce themselves through letters, photos, a video or audio tape.

Make clear to the missionary the commitment you're making as a family, group, or class, including length of time and the goals of the adoption. For example: "We have chosen your family as our missions emphasis project for next year. We are committed to pray for you regularly and to provide (amount) toward your children's education."

A ministry committee may want to *sponsor fundraisers* to raise money for their missionaries. Church yard, bake, or craft sales are possibilities. Or perhaps you'll want to cater wedding receptions or dinners and use the profits for the missionaries.

Missionaries on furlough

(These suggestions on ministering to the missionary on furlough are excerpted from an address given at Keswick, New Jersey, by Mary Lou Stam. Mrs. Stam is Director of Furlough Services of the Africa Inland Mission. She served with her family for eighteen years in Zaire and is now working with missionaries on furlough.)

Missionaries in the field adjust in ways we can't imagine. Would you give up your microwave oven, dishwasher, phone, color television, public schools, shopping malls, and safe drinking water for the cause of Christ? Most missionaries have. Especially in underdeveloped countries, missionaries have a much lower standard of living than we do. Many of them must learn to live at a slower pace and to stop letting their actions be dictated by the clock. When they come home they need time to get reoriented.

Cultural adjustment may make the missionary's return home on furlough more difficult than leaving for the mission field. A missionary returning after several years is a changed person who can be misunderstood by his or her church, the very people who want to make him or her feel at home.

Give the missionaries time to adjust. Missionaries on furlough feel pressured to accept speaking engagements, to recruit, and to raise support. But first they may need a few months to get used to American or Canadian life again. This is especially true for families. Don't pressure them to do too much too fast.

Be a friend. Extend invitations to lunch, dinner, a picnic, or a ball game. Share yourself as you would with other friends, eating and relaxing together. Offer to keep the couple's children for a weekend or evening while they enjoy some time alone.

Take initiative in evaluating the missionary's finances. Don't wait for them to mention the delicate subject. Their support base may change when they're not on the field and the church should be aware of and respond to their needs.

Consider the wife's role as missionary. Although the missionary wife has been half of the ministry team on the field, Christians at home do not treat her as a partner in the ministry. Give her opportunities to discuss her role in their mutual calling, either before the church or at a Bible study or women's event. Treat her with honor and respect.

In addition to the above comments by Mrs. Stam, a few other suggestions will contribute to an easy furlough.

Help provide a comfortable "haven" for the family. Don't expect them to spend most of the time on the road, living out of suitcases, unless that's their choice. Furnishing this home for them will require many basic items and a woman's touch. (The same kind of set-up help should be given to retiring missionaries.)

If necessary, *help the family get suitable clothing* for their time in the States. Take the wife on a shopping spree. She should be able to dress at least as well as the rest of the church. Provide the children with up-to-date clothing for school wear. This will ease their transition into local schools.

Tips from Missionaries for Missionaries

The following guidelines were written as tips to missionaries from missionaries. It would be appropriate to share this material with any missionary invited to speak at your church or special missions event.

Speak from your heart

Tell your audience what your own personal burdens are and what is important to you in your ministry. Share with others about your hurts and struggles as well as the victories and blessings. As you are transparent, people will be able to understand your life and ministry situation more completely and therefore be able to pray more intelligently.

Pick a theme and weave it through your message in order to keep continuity.
A theme can be help you tie the various pieces of life and ministry together as you speak.

Be creative

Using national costumes, music, relics, or customs can help people catch a vision of what you do. If possible, act out a specific aspect of your day or work which differs from North American culture. If you work in another language teach a song or a verse to the group. If you can, prepare a national dish and have copies of recipes available for the women to take. Make something that everyone can get a taste of.

Tell people how you do what you do

If you work in translation, demonstrate some of the techniques used. If you have an evangelistic outreach in your neighborhood or elsewhere explain how you do it. It is likely that many of the principles can be transferred to the North American context. Challenge them to be missionaries in their own sphere of influence.

Talk about specific people and their individual needs
People relate to people more than statistics and miscellaneous data. Weave true-life stories and situations throughout your talk.

Interview your spouse
If you and your spouse are speaking, you may want to *interview each other* about your specific ministry and special prayer requests. If you have children, tell about their special needs. Explain about your daily life and routine.

When using slide presentations use only clear photos and a well-rehearsed dialogue
Never read your manuscript as you show your slides; rather, interact more intimately with your audience. Incorporate either praise or national music as you show your audience your surroundings and the people you work with. Introduce as few people as possible. Rarely does an audience remember all the names and faces; it's better to share a few they may pray for. Rehearse your slide show ahead of time to assure your slides are not upside down, backward, or jamming. Make sure that your tape is clear and understandable.

Bring a recent convert
If you are a home missionary, bring along one of your recent contacts who has become a Christian and allow them to share their testimony.

When working with children make it as visual as possible
If your children are bold enough, ask them to speak about their personal experience in a different culture.

Bibliography
See the bibliography at the end of chapter 19 for books on world missions.

MISSIONARY FACT SHEET

Name: _____ Birthday: _____

_____

Spouse's Name: _____ Birthday: _____

_____

Anniversary: _____

_____

Children's Names: _____ Year in School: _____ Birthdays: _____

_____   _____   _____

_____   _____   _____

_____   _____   _____

Mission Board: _____

_____

Home Address: _____

_____

Field Address: _____

_____

General Categories of service: _____

    Husband: _____

_____

    Wife: _____

_____

MISSIONARY REQUEST FORM

Name: _____

Address: _____

_____

Clothing (include sizes and quantity): _____

_____

Food (needs and "treats"): _____

_____

Linens: _____

_____

Medicine chest items: _____

_____

Personal care items: _____

_____

Sewing and craft supplies: _____

_____

Stationery supplies: _____

_____

Tools: _____

_____

Books, games, music, magazines: _____

_____

Other: _____

_____

When completing this sheet, please be specific!

CHAPTER NINETEEN
World Missions — Part Two

Sponsoring Special Missionary Events
Determine how often to sponsor large missions events. These events
might include:
- a ladies luncheon
- a one-day conference
- a missions festival
- a World Hunger Dinner

Missionary Luncheon
The following suggestions will help you have a missionary luncheon
(dinner, brunch, dessert) which is memorable to the attenders and a
pleasure for the speaker.

Plan well in advance. If the meeting is area-wide, start three to six
months before the event.

Use good publicity to reach a maximum number of women. Mail initial
publicity to neighboring churches, and then check by phone to make
sure it's been received and is being promoted.

Use decorations that match the country of the missionary. Contact the
prospective speaker for suggestions. Use a menu that reflects the native
cooking of the country. Place thematic favors at each place with a specific item for prayer attached.

Arrange display space for cultural items. Occasionally, missionaries will
be selling items made by natives. If so, make sure adequate space is
available.

Make sure the slide projector works (have an extra bulb handy) and the
microphone is in order.

Select and rehearse any special music for the program.

If the speaker is known to have trouble staying with a predetermined schedule, consider interviewing her instead of asking her to speak. This technique can also help with missionaries who have much to share but are not accomplished public speakers. Appropriate interview questions might include:

1. When did you start thinking about missions?
2. What areas of Christian work were you involved in before going to the field? What things in your background benefit you now in missionary service?
3. Why did you choose the particular country you did?
4. What is your living situation on the field?
5. What is the greatest cultural barrier in winning people to Christ?
6. Is there a funny or embarrassing cross-cultural error you've made that you can share with us?
7. What is your greatest joy as a missionary?
8. In what ways do you and your husband (fellow missionaries) work together?
9. What can we do to help you in your work?
10. How can we pray for you?

Missionary Conference
A missionary conference can be exciting or routine; it all depends on the committee putting it together. In many instances the missionary conference is planned to meet the needs and interests of the older generation. If you want to interest the younger generation you must involve them in the planning.

Decide on the length and format of the conference (e.g., weeknight meetings with weekend finale, all-day meetings on the weekend). Choose a theme, following through in the publicity, decorations, music. Invite two to four missionaries, depending on your time frame. Include new outgoing missionaries and recently returned short-termers when available. Try to get a mix of ages among the speakers when possible.

Add variety to the program through special music, book tables, and displays. Use skits and demonstrations. Every ninety minutes adults need to stretch and have a break. Build this into the schedule. If your conference lasts all day, leave time for a quick walk after lunch. Keep the afternoon session upbeat. Use your most interesting speakers right after lunch. Avoid long slide shows in the early afternoon — even the best are sleep inducers after a meal. Serving a light, nutritious meal can reduce the tendency to nod during a session.

Plan for group prayer at intervals during the day. If acoustics allow, have spontaneous prayer from the audience, or have people gather in small groups for short sessions of prayer.

Present an interest-catching missionary project. It can be funded by the conference offering (after speakers' gifts and expenses are met). If a conference was held the previous year, give details concerning the use of that year's offering.

Plan a children's conference to coincide with the adult session.

Missions Festival

An exciting missions festival can help the entire church experience through sight, sound, smell, and taste, the conditions of cultures around the world in order to better relate to missionaries and their work. It can also provide opportunities for informal conversation with missionaries.

You can attract the attention of all ages by providing activities of wide appeal oriented to world missions using ethnic costumes, flags, music, games, artifacts, finger food, travel posters, crafts, and hands-on demonstrations. Use anyone with mission experience to demonstrate street evangelism, Gospel pantomime, door-to-door ministry, etc.

Here's an example of what you can do. Invite festival goers to fly with World Mission Airlines and to stop in Africa, Asia, Europe, Latin America, and North America. They purchase airline tickets with non-perishable foods to be donated to a designated world hunger ministry.

Set up the World Mission Travel Agency and airport in a central location. Travel posters, travel agents, security guards, and a passport agent all add to the atmosphere. People dressed in ethnic clothes welcome festival goers and direct them to the airport "terminal."

Attendees enjoy international games and prizes. Some activities should be provided for small children. Invite international students, tentmaker missionaries, and nationals to participate in the activities of their country.

Divide a large area in the church into five continents: Africa, Asia, Europe, Latin America, and North America. Within each area depict a sense of that continent by providing interactive and experiential opportunities such as those below. If you have internationals in your fellowship, focus on their countries using some of these suggestions. Be creative and brainstorm. Add your own ideas to this list.

- learn to sing a hymn or praise song in another language
- sample ethnic food and drink prepared by visiting nationals
- learn to play a game from this part of the world
- listen to the various types of music native to the continent
- do something indigenous to the region like learning to cook in a Chinese wok or making a handcraft
- use multimedia presentations to give background information or highlight important ministries

In an area separate from the continents provide a forum for special events featuring short presentations on things like:

- Good News Clubs
- ministries to international students
- summer evangelism and work teams
- tentmaking opportunities
- puppet ministry

If your church sends missionaries through several missions agencies, invite them to set up booths. Your denomination may be able to supply you with additional literature, displays, or multimedia resources.

World Hunger Dinner

A World Hunger Dinner increases empathy for the world's hungry by helping people visualize the difficulties of survival encountered by millions of people daily. Schedule a World Hunger Dinner during the annual missions conference or on a particular Sunday when world concerns are being addressed. The entire church can be involved, or just the women or teens. If your church doesn't have a large youth group or women's ministry, consider working together with other churches.

Planning the dinner

Select a small planning committee who will keep the "secret" of the dinner.

Plan the menu. The meal's staple must be rice with an all-vegetable stir-fry and a meat-based stir-fry. Additional food is at your discretion. The meal must be served buffet style.

Room decorations should present a world view. Contact libraries, travel agencies, and museums for maps and flags from various countries.

Seat eight to ten people per table. At each table place one white index card (representing the first world), two red cards (representing the second world), six yellow cards (third world), and one blue card (fourth world, nondeveloping). Each place setting should have only one card. Decorate the cards with flags of countries in that category. For example, the United States, Canada, and England (first world); Soviet Union, Yugoslavia (second world); India, Pakistan, Nigeria (third world); and Haiti, Ethiopia, Sudan (fourth world).

Select a master of ceremonies capable of researching the needs of the first, second, third, and fourth worlds. He or she will present a five- to ten-minute world hunger introduction before dinner is served.

Organizing the program

At each place setting, put one of the cards decorated with the name and flag of a particular country. If fewer than ten people are at a table, remove one red card and one yellow card.

After saying grace, the M.C. will introduce the subject of world hunger, clearly distinguishing between first, second, third, and fourth world countries. Then he or she will introduce the meal as a global village reenactment.

People with white cards are served first. They are invited to the buffet table and urged to help themselves to whatever they wish and to return for more if they want.

Next those with red cards are invited to go to the buffet table where they are served a certain amount of certain foods, but none containing meat. They are not permitted to return for seconds. They should be served rather than helping themselves.

Then, one table at a time, people with yellow cards are invited to the buffet table. They are served only one bowl of rice. Don't give them anything on their rice, and tell them they must sit down and eat it. They are not permitted to return for seconds. Get ready for some grumbling.

Then people with blue cards are told that they cannot go to the buffet at all because there is not enough food for them. Be prepared for major grumbling!

The M.C. invites those with white cards to return to the buffet at any time. They don't have to wait in line, but will be served immediately.

After several minutes the guests realize that the first world (people with white cards) can return to the buffet table to get enough food for the rest of the people at their table. But only the white card holders can return, so they must serve the rest of the table one at a time.

Don't rush this process. Let each table discover the method on their own, and let them discuss it independently. Don't let anyone in the committee "leak" this secret or the program is not effective. Be prepared for hurt feelings and some anger.

Concluding the dinner

The M.C. must pull everything together at the end of the evening by addressing global cooperation and the need to carry each other's burdens. Scripture passages about the poor and hungry should be highlighted in the wrap-up.

Invite a speaker from a hunger relief ministry to conclude the evening with a speech or a video presentation.

Take an offering designated exclusively to meet the needs of the world's hungry. Contact missions agencies or your denominational mission headquarters for information on hunger relief resources. *Rich Christians in an Age of Hunger: A Biblical Study* by Ronald Sider (Downers Grove, Ill.: InterVarsity Press, 1984) is a good resource book.

Bibliography

Church Missions Policy Handbook, 2nd edition. Association of Church Missions Committees, P.O. Box ACMC, Wheaton, Ill. 60189 (708-260-1660), 1987.

Cultivating a Missions-Active Church, Association of Church Missions Committees, P.O. Box ACMC, Wheaton, Ill.: 60189 (708-260-1660), 1989.

Engle, James and Jerry Jones. *Baby Boomers and the Future of World Missions.* Management Development Associates, 1744 West Katella, Suite 22, Orange, Calif. 92667, 1989.

Johnstone, P.J. *Operation World: A Handbook for World Intercession.* STL Books, P.O. Box 28, Waynesboro, Ga.

Mobilizers' Resource Manual, Available from the Proclaim Committee, P.O. Box 5574, Portland, Ore. 97228 (503) 249-0151. (This booklet is a complete resource tool for locating, purchasing, or renting anything having to do with missions.)

Parvin, Earl. *Missions USA.* Chicago: Moody Press, 1985.

Sider, Ronald. *Rich Christians in an Age of Hunger: A Biblical Study.* Downers Grove, Ill.: InterVarsity Press, 1984.

Wagner, Peter. *On the Crest of the Wave: Becoming a World Christian.* Ventura, Calif.: Regal Books, 1983.

Introduction

Our primary service is to the Lord Jesus Christ. His service to us is the pattern. "[He came not] to be served, but to serve, and to give His life as a ransom for many" (Matt. 20:28). He modeled practical service when He washed the disciples' feet (John 13:1-17). He humbled Himself to meet the most basic of needs.

The root meaning of the word "serve" is "to be of use." The Bible says we are to:

"Serve Him with wholehearted devotion and with a willing mind, for the Lord searches every heart and understands every motive behind the thoughts" (1 Chron. 28:9).

Serve "in the new way of the Spirit, and not in the old way of the written code" (Rom. 7:6).

"Never be lacking in zeal, but keep your spiritual fervor, serving the Lord" (Rom. 12:11).

"Serve one another in love" (Gal. 5:13).

Acceptable service is wholehearted, full of spiritual intensity, guided by the Holy Spirit, and motivated by love for the one served. Such service never demeans others, but is appropriate and timely. When the server is directed by the Spirit, she will avoid burnout through over involvement.

This section is different from the previous three sections. The material here is in smaller, more specialized sections for easy referencing. While the material is directed to women's ministries, it can also be used by other appropriate service committees within the church.

Prayer Chain

Purpose

This ministry might fit many places in this book, but it seems to go best here in the "serving the body" section since prayer touches and involves the entire church. There are many ways to organize and encourage people to pray:

- prayer groups
- quarterly or yearly Day of Prayer
- setting apart a special room in the church as a prayer room

One of the most effective prayer ministries can be the prayer chain.

Structure

Someone should be selected to be responsible for the prayer chain ministry. This chairwoman then selects coordinators for each of the prayer chains. Each chain should contain no more than ten people. If multiple chains are tied into an emergency chain, the chairwoman starts each chain herself or through her assistants.

The chain operates on specified days each week unless an emergency arises. If an individual is not at home, she is skipped that day. She may call her chain coordinator later if she desires to receive the requests. Each chain makes its phone calls at a specific time of day. Those interested in participating in this ministry select the chain that best suits their own schedule.

Requests are phoned to the chairwoman. She summarizes each request into one clear sentence, then writes it, along with the date, in her prayer notebook. She calls the prayer chain coordinators and dictates the requests word for word. Use the prayer chain for short-term definite requests rather than for long-term, indefinite needs.

Each prayer chain coordinator writes the request in a prayer notebook she keeps by the phone. She then phones the first person on the chain, dictates the requests word for word, hangs up, and prays. No other conversation is allowed during the prayer chain phone call because the requests must pass through all ten people in the chain as rapidly as possible.

Each prayer chain member then calls the next person in the chain, dictates the requests word for word, hangs up, and prays for the requests. The last person in the chain calls the chairwoman to indicate that the calls are completed. Following these guidelines will allow you to complete the chain in about thirty minutes.

People making requests should be encouraged to send praise and thanksgiving for answered prayer through the prayer chain as well.

Bibliography
Christenson, Evelyn. *What Happens When Women Pray*. Wheaton, Ill.: Victor Books, 1975. A leader's guide for small groups is also available. Audio tapes of her prayer seminar and an accompanying leader's workbook are available directly from Evelyn Christenson at 4265 Brigadoon Drive, St. Paul, MN 55126.

Caring for the Church Building

There are many activities women are involved in that don't typically fall under the jurisdiction of women's ministries. Care of the church building is among them. The condition of the building and property is important. It has a direct affect on whether people visit and whether they stay. This in turn will affect how many women can be reached for Christ through your women's ministries. All of the items mentioned below can be delegated to women's committees, which can organize the work and involve others in the body as appropriate.

Take a walk with me through your church facility. See it through the eyes of the first-time visitor. We'll begin outside the church.

Exterior
Is the sign clearly visible from all directions? Is it lit at night? Is the landscaping attractive and weed free? (Bright pots of seasonally appropriate plants at the entrance are an inviting note.) Is there a fresh coat of paint around the entryway? Is there adequate parking with several close-in spaces designated for visitors and the handicapped?

Foyer
Is it bright and inviting? Are there attractive pictures, plants, banners? If there are bulletin boards, are they informative and up-to-date? Are there greeters to welcome everyone and answer visitors' questions? Is the people flow smooth? Are there adequate signs, helping visitors find the sanctuary, rest rooms, nursery, and church offices?

Sanctuary
Is the decor contemporary and cheerful? Are flowers and/or plants well-maintained? Is the carpet kept clean? If there are tables or shelves at the

rear of the sanctuary, are they kept free of clutter and outdated material? Is the lighting and sound system sufficient for the room size?

Rest Rooms
Every person sooner or later will visit your rest rooms. Are they clean and pleasant places? Are there adequate supplies? If space allows is there a sofa in the women's room that can double as a bed for a sick person? Is there a pillow and blanket stored nearby? (The men's rest room is often more run down than the women's. Keep it well maintained.)

Kitchen
The kitchen is an important center for fellowship in a church. Who is designated to maintain it? (Everybody's job is nobody's job.) If an inexperienced person is asked to make coffee for a meeting, can she find what she needs: coffee and the directions on how to make it? Are the drawers and cabinets labeled as to contents? Is the refrigerator kept clean? Are supplies fresh?

Nursery
The nursery should be located as close to the sanctuary and adult classrooms as possible. Is it bright and attractive? Clean and safe? Are all electrical sockets covered? Is the floor carpeted? (If you rent a facility you may have to provide your own carpet.) Is it equipped with age-appropriate toys which are routinely washed? Is there a system (like name tags) for identifying children and their belongings?

Sunday School Rooms
Are directions clear to the Sunday School rooms? Regular attenders may know where the third-graders meet, but for the visitor it can be an embarrassing mystery. Are the rooms attractively decorated and adequate in size?

God does not dwell in buildings made by human hands. He has taken up residence in our Spirits. However, our church buildings reflect what we think about God and about ourselves as His body. We can choose to glorify God through our buildings. Be the catalyst to get these things taken care of in your church.

Food in the Church

Sunday Morning Refreshments

Serving refreshments on Sunday morning accomplishes far more than just relieving hunger pangs. It promotes interaction among members and newcomers alike. Serve refreshments as many times during the morning as possible.

Using this time to incorporate visitors is a good idea. A visitor can figuratively hide behind a coffee cup or a muffin until she or he feels comfortable. Make sure the location is accessible and inviting, drawing visitors in. Use the foyer or a hallway near the sanctuary if possible. Stop serving five minutes prior to the beginning of a meeting.

Always make your fellowship area attractive. Place lighted candles on the serving table (out of the reach of children). Arrange at least one bouquet of fresh flowers in the serving area. If you don't have a budget for flowers, ask various gardeners in the church to bring some from home, or get a nice silk flower arrangement. Display posters of beautiful outdoor scenery or photographs of church members and activities. Decorate appropriately for holidays and other special occasions.

Organizing and training servers

Food service is a great place to involve people, especially newcomers, in ministry. After three months of attendance most newcomers are ready for some type of ministry. Look for those who might enjoy serving in this way. There are many who prefer low-commitment or hands-on ministries that are nonverbal. Not everyone feels comfortable leading a Bible study or teaching children.

The number of servers will depend on the size of your congregation, the facilities, and the number of times refreshments are offered. You will need a minimum of two people with primary responsibility. Other servers can sign up on a rotating basis. This ministry is a natural for pairing an older woman with a younger one. Casual mentoring can take place while cutting up fruit or arranging muffins on a tray. This nonthreatening environment is conducive to working on the knotty problems of life.

Provide two weeks of on-the-job training before a person assumes full responsibility for refreshment time. Post directions for making coffee, tea, and punch in an easy-to-find location in the kitchen. One person should order all supplies and do the weekly shopping. Some churches charge a nominal amount for coffee and food, others absorb it within the budget which is always nicer and more visitor-friendly. Still others ask members to supply pastries and fruit.

Public recognition of the servers, especially from the pulpit, helps keep them motivated. Thank-you notes and hugs are always fitting for people in a ministry, especially those who serve behind-the-scenes.

At the church my husband and I attend, we have coffee, tea, punch, fruit slices, muffins, and sweet rolls at every break on Sunday morning. Several years ago Elaine came to check out the church. Though she had met several of the ladies at a midweek Bible study, this was her first Sunday. It was hard for her to feel comfortable anywhere because of low self-esteem. She was also separated from her husband at the time. But when she saw the coffee and goodies her first reaction was, "They love people here." She took her coffee cup into the service and just held it, feeling a sense of security. It's no wonder Elaine and her husband, Ted, enjoy working in this ministry today.

Supplies

For a church which serves 100 people once per Sunday the following amounts are suggested. Adjust as necessary for your own situation.

- coffee: twenty-five cups decaf, twenty-five cups regular
- tea: a mix of tea bags including herbal, regular, and decaf
- punch: two gallons plus a pint size chunk of ice
- whole milk (1 pint) or creamer
- sugar and artificial sweetener
- fruit/pastry: three pieces per person: e.g., four dozen donut holes; five boxes of pastry cut into fourteen to twenty pieces; seasonal fruit cut up into 100 pieces; several boxes of oatmeal cookies. On special occasions such as Christmas, Easter, Mother's Day, also serve homemade pastries, muffins, etc.
- napkins, paper cups (don't use styrofoam since they're not biodegradable). Avoid using small plates; people will tend to take too much food.

Sunday Buffet

Some churches have a buffet on a regular basis following the morning service. To make this successful, stick to a simple menu (see sample menus). Use servers to limit first-time portions and to help mothers with small children. One hundred people can be served by twenty people — five bringing desserts, five supplying salads, and ten contributing main dishes.

Sample menus

The following meals can be quickly heated and assembled in the church kitchen. Amounts are for 100 people, including children. Select one of your detail-oriented women to keep a list of recipes used including date and amounts needed. The bibliography for this section lists books that give bulk recipes.

Spaghetti Dinner

Item	Amount	People to bring
Ground beef	4 lbs precooked	5
Spaghetti noodles	1 1/2 lbs precooked	5
Green Salad	serving for 15	5
Dessert	15 pieces	5

Servers, or the church, should buy french bread and tomato or spaghetti sauce in bulk.

Tostadas

Item	Amount	People to bring
Ground beef	1 1/2 lbs precooked	5
Shredded lettuce	4 heads	1
Chopped tomatoes	10	2
Sour cream	4 pint-size tubs	1
Grated cheese	3 1/2 lbs	1
Fruit Tray	20 pieces per tray	5
Dessert	20 pieces	5

Servers, or the church, should buy 100 + flour tortillas, six large cans of refried beans and one gallon of salsa (it keeps well).

Chili Dogs and Buns

Item	Amount	People to bring
Grated cheese	1 1/2 lbs	5

Potato salad	serving for 12	7
Dessert	20 pieces	5

Servers, or the church, should purchase hot dogs, buns, and chili sauce. Chili sauce eliminates the need to have other condiments.

Baked Potato Bar

Item	Amount	People to bring
Cheese sauce	1 large can	2
Sour cream	2 pint-size tubs	2
Broccoli (chopped and cooked)	1 bunch	5
Bacon bits	1 large jar	2
Chili	1 large can	2
Dessert	20 pieces	5

Servers, or the church, should purchase large Idaho potatoes and deliver twenty each to four people who will bake them Sunday morning and bring as soon as church is over. (They can be baked at church if you have sufficient oven space.) It only takes eighty large potatoes for 100 people because at least twenty people will only want half a potato. Twenty potatoes take 2 hours at 400°. Keep them hot in a picnic cooler.

Meals on Wheels Ministry

Purpose
Sooner or later most people in a church will need special care. Some will require short-term help, others may require longer-term support. Providing meals is one way we can show practical love and care to:
- mothers of newborn infants
- those with hospitalized loved ones
- those who have had a death in the family
- those just released from a hospital or convalescent center
- those with debilitating illnesses
- the terminally ill and elderly who can't cook for themselves and aren't able to hire help

Several years ago I learned firsthand what a blessing it can be to have meals provided during a stressful time. My husband was in the hospital with a severe lung infection. It never occurred to me I would need help. I had no children at home and could just grab fast food when I got hungry.

Others knew better. Yes, I appreciated the food, but what I needed more was the love and spiritual support given by the women who brought it. They hugged me and, more importantly, prayed with me. I cried when a friend insisted that she would come and clean my house. Pride is such an awful beast. It took an act of my will to admit my house could stand the loving touch of another woman. After several months Mark fully recovered, and we both learned valuable lessons about letting others help us.

Structure

Establish a list of volunteer cooks and drivers to prepare and deliver complete meals to church members in need. Depending on the church's size, one or two women should be designated as coordinators of this ministry. Here are suggested ministry descriptions and guidelines for co-ordinators, cooks, and drivers.

Coordinators

• Compile a list of volunteer cooks and drivers who are willing to prepare and deliver complete meals, sometimes on short notice. (Why not enlist the driving teens in the church to handle deliveries of the meals?)

• Purchase disposable pans and serving dishes so that cooks don't have to worry about retrieving their dishes. An alternative is to purchase at least two dozen casserole dishes and serving dishes, and with a permanent felt pen write your church name and "Meals Ministry" on all pieces including covers.

Distribute dishes to the cooks as needed. Each should have at least two sets of casserole dishes with lids, pans, serving bowls, and platters on hand at all times.

• Receive requests for meals from church members. Get the following information: when and where to deliver the meal; number of people to be served; any special dietary needs (diabetic, salt-free, soft foods, vegetarian).

• Contact a cook and a driver to fill the need.

• The following day phone the meal recipient to see whether the meal was delivered as promised and to ask whether more meals will be needed. See that all dishes are returned to the church.

Cooks

● A complete meal consists of either an entree, salad, vegetable, and dessert, or a casserole, salad, and dessert.

● Choose two or three favorite recipes and keep the necessary ingredients on hand so you won't have to go shopping if asked to prepare a meal on short notice. Use recipes you have had success with in the past. This isn't the time to experiment with new recipes.

● When you cook a favorite recipe for your family, double it and freeze the second portion for the Meals Ministry.

● Carefully follow any dietary guidelines received from the Coordinator. Don't prepare pork chops for a vegetarian or chocolate cake for a diabetic. Choose mild foods, especially for those who have been ill.

● Cover all foods with tight-fitting lids. On a note card write the menu you are sending. Include cooking or warming instructions on the card. Tightly pack all food containers into a cardboard box, basket, or cooler (which the driver will return to you the following day). Use disposable dishes, pans, and bowls or those owned by the church so you don't have to worry about retrieving your dishes.

Drivers

● Get clear directions to the homes of the cook and the meal recipient from the Coordinator.

● Pick up the meal box at the scheduled time. Make sure all foods are covered with tight-fitting lids that won't allow spilling during transport.

● Deliver the meal at the scheduled time. Remove the food containers from the box, basket, or cooler.

● If the person is ill, elderly, or alone and is planning to eat immediately, offer to help by setting the table and heating the food if necessary.

● Return the dishes to the cook by the following day.

Food Pantry

Purpose

The purpose of a food pantry is to collect and distribute nonperishable foods to those in need within the congregation. This ministry fulfills the command to care for the hungry. Both the givers and the receivers will be blessed. Family members and neighbors who observe how Christians care for one another will see the Gospel in action and may be drawn one step closer to Christ.

Needs exist even in highly affluent areas, though they aren't always obvious. Church families experiencing illness or changes in employment will welcome a food pantry.

Structure
The pantry can be administered by a committee of women from the ser-vice branch of the women's ministry. Any member of the congregation may contact them, perhaps through the church office, with the names of those in need. The committee then evaluates the need and distributes food accordingly.

Publicity. At the project's inception, make announcements during church services. Distribute informational flyers requesting donations. (Encourage families and children to be a part of the giving.) Once the project is underway, promote via bulletin inserts.

Collection and storage. One Sunday per month church members bring pantry items to a highly visible area in the church, identified by a large poster and a large hamper-size basket. Monetary contributions are also acceptable. The committee sorts the food and puts it in a locked storage area.

Distribution. In a low-key manner, committee members unobtrusively deliver pantry items at an appropriate time to a person's car or home. All gifts are designated as from the food pantry rather than from a particular individual. Special efforts are made during Thanksgiving and Christmas to provide items for a holiday meal: potatoes, canned vegetables, fruit, dessert mix, and a gift certificate for a turkey from a local grocery store.

Bibliography

Bax, Doris. *The Church Kitchen.* Nashville, Tenn.: Broadman Press, 1977.

Morgen, Sarah. *The Church Supper.* Minneapolis: Bethany House, 1976.

West, Bessie Brooks, Grace Severance Shergart, and Maxine Faye Wilson. *Food for Fifty,* 7th ed. New York: John Wiley and Sons, 1985.

Clothes Closet

(This material on setting up a clothes closet was contributed by Dora Rios. Her church, a Spanish-speaking congregation in Houston, Texas, ministers to people across a wide socioeconomic spectrum.)

Purpose
The purpose of a clothes closet is to provide clothing and other house-hold items like kitchen utensils, linens, blankets, furniture, etc. to

church members. This ministry can be expanded to serve visitors to the church who are in need or people in the community referred by Social Service agencies. Goods can also be collected for a special community service project or to send to the mission field.

If you attend a predominantly middle-class church it's easy to shut your eyes and ears to the needs around you. But the Bible strongly warns against such an attitude.

> What good is it, my brothers, if a man claims to have faith but has no deeds? Can such faith save him? Suppose a brother or sister is without clothes and daily food. If one of you says to him, "Go, I wish you well; keep warm and well fed," but does nothing about his physical needs, what good is it? In the same way, faith by itself, if it is not accompanied by action, is dead (James 2:14-17).

Structure
Maintenance. The clothes closet can be administered by a woman or a committee from the service branch of women's ministries. The maintenance of a well-organized closet is vital to the success of this excellent outreach tool. Depending on the size of the closet, a large room with built-in shelves could be used. Some churches may purchase or build a storage room separate from the main building. Clothing racks are preferable, however, steel shelves can also be used to store items and folded clothing, arranged by sizes.

Only accept used clothing or items that meet the following criteria:

• The person who makes the donation would not mind wearing or using the items him/herself, or allowing the members of his/her family to use it.

• Clothing/items are clean, ironed, and folded as applicable.

• Items are safe to use, particularly toys, baby or children's furniture, and electrical appliances.

Distribution. Priorities should be established. Distribution guidelines will vary with different groups:

• *Church members or visitors in need.* People in this category should be identified as being in need by church workers (elders, pastors, Sunday School teachers, etc.) during home visits or other contacts. The worker or the person in need can make the request to the individual or committee in charge of the closet. It can be verbal or written depending on the type of distribution system the church has adopted.

• *Community people in need.* If the closet is large and well stocked, its services can be made known to one or several Social Service agencies in the community. A referral system covering things like: forms, frequency of assistance, quantity of items, etc., may need to be developed by the church.

● *Special community service project.* Sunday School classes, youth groups, or women's Bible study groups may select a specific Social Service organization and collect clothing and items as a service project for the year. Recipient organizations might include: Women's Shelters, Homeless Shelters, Crisis Pregnancy Centers, Residential or Children's Group Homes, Youth Shelters, etc. There is a great and ever-increasing need for clothing in centers working with runaway youth or the homeless.

● *Mission field.* The need for adequate clothing in countries in Latin America, Asia, and Africa is urgent. A church with a clear missions vision will keep abreast of the needs of their missionaries and send them periodic shipments of clothing and other useful items.

Practical Care Ministry

Purpose

The purpose of this ministry is to facilitate matching people who need things with people who have things to give away. It's a practical application of Acts 4:32, "All the believers were one in heart and mind. No one claimed that any of his possessions was his own, but they shared everything they had."

This isn't suggesting communal living where everyone owns everything in common. But the truth is most of us give away to charity or just toss things out that our brothers and sisters in Christ need. We would be happy to pass along the item if a system existed in the church to facilitate that happening.

In a small, particularly rural church, people might know one another well enough to automatically share as a need arose. In other churches the exchange of items might be handled through a newsletter or a bulletin board. However, people often want to give or receive anonymously. The structure suggested below (used by Willow Creek Community Church, South Barrington, Ill.) will maintain a degree of confidentiality as well as expedite the smooth transfer of items.

Structure

This ministry can be administered by one person. A computer and telephone answering machine are beneficial, but a phone and file card box are sufficient. The calls can come into the church office or be taken by a designated individual in her home. This is an ideal ministry for a home-bound senior, since it only involves the telephone and accurate record-keeping.

At the inception of this ministry advertise it well. Use inserts in the bulletin and public announcements. Once the program is well established, publicize it at set intervals to inform newcomers and jog the memory of regular attenders.

Instruct church members to call the coordinator with items they want to share or things they need to borrow or have. When she receives a call, the person in charge makes an appropriate entry consisting of name, address, phone number, and item. In addition she should inquire whether the item is needed on a short-term, longer term, or permanent basis. (For instance a Rototiller may be needed for one day, a bed over the weekend for visiting relatives, a crib for several years, or a couch permanently.)

Each entry is assigned a letter and number and filed accordingly. "A" can be used for items needed and "B" for items to share/give.

An updated handout listing current needs and resources is distributed monthly to the church family (see sample below). People make contact with each other through the coordinator. Everyone must arrange his or her own transportation. Don't allow items to be dropped off at the church.

This same system can be extended to include physical help needed such as in moving furniture, lawn care, or house cleaning.

It is up to the coordinator to monitor the program so some individuals don't take advantage of it.

Sample Handout

Date _____

ITEMS NEEDED

A101   Maternity clothes
A110   Dinette table and chairs
A118   Extra casserole dishes for Meals Ministry
A121   Folding chairs for church meetings in my home

ITEMS TO SHARE

B88	Children's clothing: boys size 2–6, girls size 6–10
B95	Used skis, poles, and boots (men's size 9)
B100	Kitchen equipment: pots and pans, silverware
B105	Bunk beds without mattresses
B108	Canister vacuum cleaner

Coordinator's phone number and "office" hours

Showers of Blessing

The following information was contributed by
Heather Rausch.

Showers are opportunities to show love to a person at a time of need or special celebration. In a small church a shower can include the entire congregation. In larger churches, fellowship groups can organize showers.

In this, and all other ministries, keep the goals of evangelism and spiritual growth before you. Encourage women to go to showers with their "ministry-colored glasses" on. Encourage shower recipients to invite neighbors and relatives and not just women from the church. If appropriate a brief Gospel message could be woven into the shower devotional.

The love of believers for one another is a great testimony. I recently had the joy of introducing a young woman to Christ whom I first met at a baby shower several years ago. If that contact had not been made she would not have come to me in her time of personal crisis.

Getting Organized
Preparations for a shower should include:
- Clearing the date with the person to be honored and with the church calendar.
- Choosing the shower location.
- Deciding on a theme and arranging for someone to give an appropriate devotional. (If your church has a "Shower Coordinator" she can make suggestions in these areas.)

- Discussing with the shower recipient what types and sizes of gifts would be appropriate.
- Arranging for food, decorations, set up, serving, and cleanup. Make sure there are scissors and paper on hand for last minute wrapping.
- Asking a competent amateur photographer to take pictures during the shower.
- Publicizing the event through the church bulletin and mailing invitations.

Types of Showers

There are traditional showers like bridal showers, baby showers, house-warming showers, and special event showers (celebrating things like a 50th wedding anniversary). But you don't need to do the same old thing every time. Be creative! How about a . . .

"Dew-Drop Inn" shower. If a new mother is too weak to enjoy a full shower, arrange for two or three women at a time to drop in for short, three-to-five minute visits. Place a decorated wicker laundry basket at the door to receive the gifts. Across the top of the basket put a tiny clothes line with doll clothes. Place refreshments on a nearby table.

Casserole shower. If a mother-to-be doesn't need baby clothes, but has a freezer, guests can bring a frozen dinner entree instead of a baby gift.

"Jack and Jill" wedding shower. Invite both men and women. Have guests buy gifts for the prospective husband as well as the wife.

All-church baby shower. For first-time parents. Schedule the shower after an evening church service. Don't open the gifts then. Instead have singing and fellowship time during which others can share what it was like when they had their first child.

You can also have a shower to help out various ministries in the church.

Library shower. Send invitations in the form of a booklet inviting everyone to come and bring their unused Christian books and tapes to the church library. Play games such as Literary Hash with scrambled names of currently popular Christian books.

Kitchen shower. Have it in the church kitchen if space allows. Gifts could be needed utensils and appliances. The devotional could be on various women in the Bible who were involved in food preparation (e.g., Martha, Abagail).

Missionary baby shower (for missionaries on the field). Make a tape of the shower and send it along with the shower gifts to the new mother.

Helping with Weddings

*This section was adapted from materials by
Arlington Countryside Church in Arlington Heights, Illinois.*

Weddings are such important events in people's lives that you want to do everything you can as a church family to make them successful. If your church has a wedding consultant, she can help prevent calamities like the one we experienced a few years ago. A bride at our church completely underestimated the number of people who would be at her reception. After ten minutes the few plates of hors d'oeuvres were consumed, the nuts and mints were gone. So was the punch. Those of us working in the kitchen began to improvise. The leftover packages of lemonade mix were the first to be used; then came the emergency supply of cookies reserved for preschool.

Wedding Consultant

The primary functions of a wedding consultant are to advise the bride concerning preparations prior to the wedding, to direct the rehearsal and to assure that the wedding and reception run smoothly.

The consultant should be someone who pays attention to details and can work tactfully with people. While understanding the importance of tradition, she must be flexible enough to allow the bride to design a wedding that reflects her own taste. The following material provides some guidelines and suggestions for anyone interested or already involved in wedding consulting:

Advanced planning (several months prior to the wedding)
● Decide on the general style of the wedding and reception: elegant, simple, outdoors, indoors.
● Determine a working budget and plan accordingly.
● Assist in planning the overall color scheme if not already done.
● Contact necessary participants.
Minister — Meet with him four to six weeks prior to the wedding to plan the ceremony.
Organist, pianist — Plan music well in advance.
Soloist (optional) — Decide placement in the ceremony.
Candlelighter(s) — This can be done by jr. bridesmaids, ushers, etc.
Bridesmaids, Groomsmen — Discuss clothing for men; whether to buy or make dresses for ladies.

Flower Girl, Ring Bearer — It's best if these children are old enough to behave during the wedding.

Florist — Flower style should be in keeping with the general tone of the wedding. Plan flowers that will be seasonally available or use silk flowers.

Photographer — Plan this carefully in advance. The pictures will be the lasting memory of the event. Suggest that he dress in keeping with the general wedding attire.

Video Tape Producer — If he is to tape the ceremony, he must be discreet. An experienced amateur can do this or hire a professional.

Gift Receivers — Two minimum. One at the door to receive gifts, one to carry them to a designated storage area, preferably out of sight.

Reception Personnel — As needed: 2 cake servers, coffee, punch, tea servers.

Guest Book Attendant

Managing the Rehearsal

● Decide in advance whether the consultant or minister will manage it.

● The consultant should have the following items with her: masking tape, detailed outline of entire ceremony, seating, reception details.

● The minister should begin with prayer and then the consultant reviews verbally every detail of the wedding. This is not the time to make decisions. That should have been done weeks in advance.

● Start the rehearsal with everyone in position on the platform. Mark each place with masking tape. Rehearse the entire service from the beginning.

● Practice the recessional. Bride takes groom's arm. Ushers offer their arms to the bridesmaids. Keep about four pews apart.

Managing the Wedding

● The consultant should have the following items with her: masking tape, matches, scotch tape, pins, safety pins, needle and thread in colors of bridesmaids' dresses.

● She should be there at least two or three hours prior to the wedding. She should assist the photographer if pictures are being taken before the ceremony.

● She should make sure rings have been given to best man and maid of honor, or sewn lightly on the ring pillow.

● She should give appropriate flowers and corsages to the right people.

● She should assist in the flow of the guest book line. The guest book line will determine the start of the service. If it's important to the bride to begin on time, cut the line off several minutes before the start of the service so everyone can be seated. Announce that people can sign at the end of the ceremony.

- Everyone must be seated before the lighting of the candles, which the coordinator cues.
- She should line up the special seating people while candles are being lit, then line up the bridesmaids in descending order and start each person down the aisle at the right time.
- She should signal the organist when the bride is at the door, straighten out the train prior to going down the aisle.
- After the ceremony she should direct the bridal party to the "holding room" and assist with pictures as needed.

Managing the Reception
- The wedding coordinator should help in organizing the reception line, bride's mother at the head of the line, bride at the right of the groom and greeted before the groom.
- She should help with any of the following as needed: entertainment, toasts, cake-cutting and serving, transportation of the gifts to the designated location.

Bibliography
Both Christian and secular publishers have produced many books about wedding planning. One of the best is Goble & Shea's *Complete Wedding Planner*. In addition to being published by a Christian publisher, this comprehensive guide is packed with helpful month-by-month planning calendars and checklists. It would be a perfect gift for a just-engaged woman.

Gibson, Betty. *Planning Your Christian Wedding*. Nashvillle, Tenn.: Abingdon Press, 1987.

Goble, Kathleen and Cecily Shea. *Goble & Shea's Complete Wedding Planner: For the Organized and Relaxed Bride*. Sisters, Ore.: Questar Publishers, 1989.

Muzzy, Ruth, and R. Kent Hughes. *The Christian Wedding Planner*. Wheaton, Ill.: Tyndale House, 1984.

Ministries to Single Women

There are many excellent "how to" books available on singles ministries (see the bibliography at the end of this material). The information contained in them won't be repeated here. But I would like to make a few suggestions regarding working with single women.

Single women constitute more than one third of the adult population in America. They are single for a number of reasons: many by choice, many because of life circumstances. The singles in your church may be:

- college-age
- young professionals
- never-married
- divorced or separated
- single parents
- widows
- senior citizens

Usually a singles ministry is geared for both women and men. However, the needs of single women are different from those of men and they will benefit from having some of their needs addressed separately. How these needs are met and by whom will vary according to the structure and size of your church. You may be able to adjust your existing singles ministry. Or you may want to develop a new program for single women only. This ministry could be handled by a singles coordinator or it might come under a branch of women's ministries.

Change Your Attitude

The first step in beginning a ministry to single women may be to change your church's attitudes about them. Some people just don't see singles and their needs. What they don't see they don't care about. Increase your congregation's awareness of the large numbers of singles in your community who need to be reached. Suggest to your pastor that he preach one or more sermons dealing with the key issues singles face. Address these issues in other programs like women's Bible studies and support groups.

See singles as a mission field; most do not attend any church. You can't minister to them if they aren't around. A variety of factors can keep a single woman from being assimilated into church life. She may view herself in a "holding pattern" until she finds a mate and afraid of making commitments. She may not have a specific friend with whom she can attend church activities. Or the church may be so family oriented it has no programs for singles.

If a woman isn't assimilated she won't stay. Statistics indicate that unless a newcomer makes seven significant friendships in the first six months, she probably will leave the church.

Take Action
Plan a meeting of those interested in ministering to single women. At that meeting identify the single women in your congregation. If your church is small you should be able list them all by name. Larger churches can get information by inserting a card into the Sunday bulletin and asking singles to give their names, addresses, phone numbers, plus ideas they have for a singles ministry, and a list of the needs they feel should be addressed. If you have too few singles to build a program, consider coordinating with other churches.

Once you begin, make sure you vary the program's content. Use speakers on topics helpful to singles. Mix sports with musical and cultural events. Outdoor activities like swimming, hiking, picnics and indoor activities like videos, movies, and dining out, can be enjoyed as a group.

Include a spiritual emphasis. Your focus should include evangelism, edification, and meeting felt needs. Use speakers, testimonies, and prayer partners to foster growth. Do studies about single people in the Bible, but also teach and model basic life skills.

Focus on Fulfilled Living
Encourage and equip the single woman to be self-sufficient, to make her house or apartment into a home, to develop hospitality skills. Singles often eat out or microwave packaged meals. Share favorite recipes and prepare them together. Have a progressive dinner so that they can show off their homes.

Get someone to teach basic home maintenance skills. Ask a mechanic in the congregation to teach a seminar on basic auto maintenance. Encourage singles in their financial responsibilities by providing training in budgeting, long- and short-term financial planning, buying life insurance, saving for a home, etc.

Expect singles to be givers of ministry, not just receivers. Plan service activities to minister to others outside the singles group. Encourage activities that mix singles with couples, families, and children. As the ministry grows develop the necessary leadership from within the group itself.

Bibliography
Fagerstrom, Douglas L., ed. *Singles Ministry Handbook.* Wheaton, Ill.: Victor Books, 1988.

Talley, Jim. *Too Close Too Soon.* Nashville, Tenn.: Thomas Nelson, 1981.

Talley, Jim. *Reconcilable Differences.* Nashville, Tenn.: Thomas Nelson, 1985.

Talley, Jim. *Life After Divorce, a Single Mother's Guide.* Colorado Springs: NavPress, 1990.

Single on Sunday: A Manual for Successful Single Adult Ministries. Minneapolis: Concordia Press, 1979.

National Association of Single Adult Leaders, 777 E. Beltline, Grand Rapids, MI 49506 (616) 956-9377.

Ministries to Mothers of Young Children

Helping New Mothers

The head of the nursery or preschool department may be the logical person to organize this ministry in your church. Any woman with the time and interest to help new mothers can be involved, whether she's a grandmother, or a mother of preschoolers with a vivid memory of her own childbirth experiences.

The needs of new mothers in your congregation will vary. Does a particular woman live far away from her parents and siblings? Will her own mother be able to help her? Is communication with her family poor due to past family problems? Is she a single mother? Whatever her circumstances a new mother needs nurturing support. She may need:

• physical help with housework, shopping, errands, meals, caring for her older children
• emotional encouragement through postpartum changes and learning to care for the baby
• spiritual support to keep her focus on God
• financial aid, especially if she's a single mother
• peer, pastoral, or professional counseling
• friendship with other new mothers. This is particularly true if she recently quit work in order to have her first baby.

One way to show concern for a new mother and learn about her needs is to visit her in the home. Those who visit should have basic peer counseling skills and understand the stresses a new baby can cause in a marriage.

Everything goes better if it's planned and visiting new mothers is no exception. So pre-plan and pre-pray your visit.

Planning Your Visit

There may be more visits to be made than there are hours to make them. The first step is to maintain a prioritized list of potential visits divided into two categories: Urgent and Important. Make the urgent visits first, but don't keep shifting the important ones to the end of the list.

Call ahead for an appointment. A surprise visit will rarely be pleasant for a new mom. Bring a homemade entree that can be frozen and served later. Also bring refreshments for a coffee break to share with her.

If your church presents a standard gift from the nursery department to the new mother, bring the gift along. Consider giving a very helpful but less traditional gift such as: professional diaper service, housekeeping or laundry service for a period of time, or a magazine subscription.

If two women visit together it can provide a training opportunity for the second woman. It also builds more friendship bridges to the new mother and makes conversation easier, especially if the mother is shy or perhaps new to the church.

Don't overstay your welcome, particularly in the first two weeks after childbirth. Limit your visit to thirty minutes. It's better to plan a return visit than stay too long.

After the visit is completed, make specific plans to meet any needs discovered. Stay in touch. Phone the new mother regularly to see how she's doing. When you call, always ask, "Is this a good time to talk?"

What to Do

Observe and assess practical needs. Is the house in a reasonable state of order, or is there chaos everywhere? Is the mother's fatigue overwhelming her or is it appropriate, considering her circumstances? Are siblings demonstrating normal behavior? Is there ample food in the kitchen for the family? Is the family making ends meet financially? Did their health insurance cover all hospital costs?

Ask about her relationship with her baby. Does she need advice or help with nursing or feeding? Is the baby abnormally fussy? How is the mother handling it? Is she depressed? Apathetic? Lonely? (If she was working outside of the home before the birth it can be quite a change to be home all day with an infant.) If she's a working mom, discuss her feelings about leaving the baby with a sitter so she can return to work. What does she have planned for child care? If she's already returned to work, how is the child care going? How is work itself going? Is she experiencing guilt over returning to work?

Inquire about her relationship with her husband. Do they have any time alone? Are they able to talk about problems as they occur? Pre-existing marital problems often become worse with the addition of a baby to the family. Is she attempting to keep her husband number one in her life even though the baby makes so many demands?

Ask about her spiritual life. Is she spending time daily reading the Bible and praying? Assure her that God still loves her even if she can't spend focused time with Him. Encourage her to listen to quality teaching tapes or radio programs while caring for the baby. If your pastor's sermons are recorded, provide her with tapes.

Many women are open to discipling at this turning point in their lives. If the mother is interested in being discipled, pair her with an older mother who can be a mentor and role model (see chap. 11 for details on mentoring).

Most mothers need a four- to six-month leave of absence from ministry responsibilities following the birth of the baby. If she's been involved in ministry, encourage her to take some time off from outside commitments. Assure her this is normal and perfectly all right.

Organizing Nursery and Preschool Ministries

People looking for a church to attend want sermons that aren't boring, no pressure to give money, and well-run nurseries and children's programs. Gone are the days when a basement room with a worn carpet, old rocker, and cast-off toys will suffice as a church nursery. Your church doesn't need to spend top dollars, but you do need to provide a pleasant, secure environment for young children. Any money spent in this area will be more than recovered through the new families you attract.

Quality child care is a ministry to parents as well as children. Parents can attend classes or participate in worship services knowing their children are being well cared for. Here are some suggestions for your ministry to young children according to age-group.

Crib room — birth to twelve months

Adult supervision. Minimum of one adult per six infants. Regardless of the number of children, a second person should be on duty to summon help in case of an emergency. The same person or persons on duty in the crib room during all services gives mothers confidence and children a strong sense of continuity. A paid worker may help maintain this continuity.

In all but the smallest churches, the crib room should use a secure child identification system to prevent strangers from taking infants. The worker receiving the child should issue a number to the parent and tape or safety pin the same number on the child's clothing, bottles, and diaper bag.

Supplies and equipment. The crib room supervisor should see that the room always is equipped with:

- disposable diapers — several sizes — hypoallergenic wipes, Kleenex
- plastic bags with wire closures
- saltine crackers (always get parent's permission before giving solid food to an infant)
- bottled baby apple juice
- cloth diapers for burping and cleanup
- changing surface with washable pad, wash cloths; blankets, one per child
- cribs — one per four infants, sheets — two per crib
- mechanical swings — one per four infants, playpen
- toys that rattle, squeak, roll, or make noise, plastic books, check all toys for safety and age appropriateness
- audio tape player with quiet tapes
- first aid kit

Toddler care — twelve to thirty months

Adult supervision. Minimum ratio of one adult per six toddlers. If your goal is teaching rather than child care, you will need extra staff to handle crying children and younger toddlers. Caring for children up to age two primarily consists of meeting needs and handling problems.

Supplies and equipment. The toddler room supervisor should order the same supplies as the crib room (except that diapers should be toddler size). The room should also have:

- mats or blankets — one per toddler
- sturdy, low-to-the-ground riding toys; large, soft balls; large stacking toys (including blocks and Duplo)
- sturdy plastic slide for older toddlers
- non-tearable books

Early preschool — thirty months to four years

Adult supervision. You will need one adult per six children; more if you have a troubled child with a short attention span.

Supplies and equipment. Early preschoolers are ready for structured teaching and directed play periods. Quality materials can be obtained from many sources such as:

David C. Cook Publishing, 850 N. Grove Avenue, Elgin, IL 60120. 1-800-323-7543, Alaska, 1-312-387-5856, Canada, 1-800-387-5856.

Gospel Light Publishing, 2300 Knoll Drive, Ventura, CA 93009, Outside California, 1-800-235-3415, California: 1-800-227-4025.

Scripture Press Publications, Inc., 1825 College Avenue, Wheaton, IL 60187, 1-800-323-9409.

Standard Publishing, 821 Hamilton Avenue, Cincinnati, OH 45231, 1-800-543-1301.

Teaching components should include:
- take-home papers
- chalk or vinyl writing board
- Bible activity pages
- large pictures for story telling
- flannel graphs
- music
- hand or finger puppets

Craft supplies should include:
- newsprint and construction paper
- water soluble pens, tempura paint, large crayons
- white glue and glitter
- play dough
- popsicle sticks
- masking tape

Appropriate toys for this age are:
- bean bags
- wooden puzzles, wooden blocks, and Duplo blocks
- books
- dolls
- plastic kitchen utensils for playing house
- balls, trucks, cars, planes, trains,
- play sets with plastic people figures
- jars of bubbles

Snacks. Most parents prefer their children to eat healthy snacks (apple juice, muffins, raisins, carrot and celery sticks with peanut butter).

Older preschoolers — four years to kindergarten

Adult supervision. You will need one adult per six children; more if you have a troubled child with a short attention span. The grouping of older preschoolers depends on the availability of adult leaders, space, and number of children per age-group. An age grouping that is satisfactory one year may need to be altered the following year. Stay flexible.

Ideally, kindergarten children should have a separate classroom. They can handle a longer, more involved lesson, and require less play time.

Supplies and equipment. The list of supplies, toys, and snacks listed above is appropriate for this age-group as well, with the addition of:

- bluntnosed scissors — one per child
- glue stick — one per child
- regular size crayons, nonpermanent markers

Recruiting and Organizing Helpers

Those currently working with preschoolers should be actively recruiting new workers. But often preschool workers have limited contact with much of the congregation. Thus the women's ministries council should also be involved in encouraging both men and women (and older teens) to serve in this rewarding but tiring ministry.

Some churches will take anybody willing to work in the preschool department. But there are qualifications for good preschool workers just as for other key positions. They should love and enjoy children and be able to produce a positive emotional environment for them. They should be able to work under and respond well to leadership. They should be dependable, gentle, patient, conscientious, and flexible.

Those who work with young children should pour out love and approval at every opportunity. Though few preschoolers are able to make a clear decision to give their lives to Christ, the groundwork can be laid in these years for a lifelong love-affair with the Savior. Keep in mind that the emotional nurture given a young child at church may be the only positive input he or she receives all week.

The person supervising this ministry should plan a three-month schedule and mail it to all preschool workers. It should be noted on the schedule that workers are to arrive at least fifteen minutes before the church service. If a worker is unable to make it on a Sunday she should arrange for her own substitute or inform the supervisor and let her get a substitute, depending on the policy of the preschool department.

Workers should get a reminder postcard or phone call the week before they're to help out in the preschool department. If they are regulars they will enjoy their time more if they're assigned to the same age-group and same head teacher. Post a schedule of the permanent faculty on the door so parents can get to know them by name.

The same primary welcome person should greet the children each Sunday. This provides familiarity for both children and parents.

Each age-group supervisor is in charge of maintaining her own area. She is responsible to see that infant/toddler toys that are put in the mouth are washed weekly, linens are washed weekly, and all toys are washed monthly.

The supervisors should try to stay aware of home situations. Trauma or big changes at home (new baby, illness, divorce, mother returning to work) can upset a child. Keeping an accurate information card for each child will help with this.

Organizing a Baby-sitting Co-op
(This material comes from Arlington Countryside Church in Arlington Heights, Illinois.)
The purpose of a baby-sitting co-op is to provide baby-sitting free of charge through women's ministries. Select several young mothers to administrate this program and appoint a coordinator and secretary. Exercise caution in accepting non-church members into the co-op. Their moral and/or behavioral standards may cause concern among existing members.

General guidelines
- Begin the "co-op" year on a specific date, preferably the first day of a month.
- Each member should baby-sit for as many hours as she uses the service.
- The co-op secretary will keep an updated record of debit (hours the service is used) and credits (hours baby-sat for others).
- A maximum of twelve debit hours are allowed per month (more hours are allowed for unusual circumstances).
- The minimum job is one hour.
- Don't request a sitter for an ill child; don't accept a sitting job if your own child is ill.
- Decide what basic qualifications sitters must have. (Some co-ops require sitters to have a valid Red Cross first aid card.) A car should be available in case of emergencies.

Client guidelines
- Client can request a sitter via the secretary or can arrange her own sitter.
- Client should inform sitter of her approximate time of departure and return.
- Client should call the sitter if she will be more than fifteen minutes later than planned.
- Client should call the co-op coordinator if any problems develop.

Sitter guidelines
- Report earned time to co-op secretary within seventy-two hours.
- If sitter plans to drive a child somewhere, she must inform the client before she does so. Sitter must use seat belts or car seats.

Computing time
- Appointment starts when sitter arrives or client delivers children to sitter's home.
- If client is late, appointment starts at time originally scheduled unless client notifies sitter before appointment.
- Time is computed in quarter-hour blocks.
- Sitter receives half-hour credit for preparing meal. No meal credit is given when client provides the meal.
- Sitter receives half-hour credit if she must transport child.
- Sitter is paid straight time for watching up to two children of same family and time and a half for watching more than two children of the same family.

Inactive status or resignations
- Those in the co-op must notify secretary when they're unavailable to sit (due to illness, childbirth, vacation, etc.).
- They must notify the secretary and coordinator at least a month before anticipated date of resignation from the co-op. Balance out hours (debit or credit). Debit hours should be reimbursed at a rate of $2.00 per hour.

Duties of co-op secretary
- Keep accurate record of each member's debit and credit hours.
- Promptly at the end of her three-month term as secretary, pass accurate and updated record to coordinator.
- As payment for her services as secretary, she receives one-half hour credit from each active member at the end of her term.

Duties of co-op coordinator
- Notify members of new, resigning, or inactive members.
- If co-op secretary is unable to serve her full term, the coordinator gets a replacement and notifies members of the change.
- Handle questions, complaints, or unusual problems.

BABY-SITTING CO-OP MEMBERSHIP FORM

Name _____

Address _____

_____

Phone (Home) _____ (Work) _____

Child's name   Birthdate   Age

_____ _____ _____

_____ _____ _____

_____ _____ _____

_____ _____ _____

Physician's name and phone number(s) _____

_____

Allergies or any other special instructions _____

_____

Foods my child may not have _____

_____

In case of emergency, please contact:

Name _____

Phone _____ Relationship to child _____

My Red Cross First Aid Card expires on this date: _____

I have read the attached guidelines and sign my name in agreement.

Signature _____ Date _____

Ministries to Seniors

Much of this section was adapted from material by Grace Thornton.

In most churches there are twice as many seniors (adults over fifty-five) as there are youth (ages thirteen through twenty). The growth rate of this older group is three times that of the national population. The fields are "white unto harvest." Research shows that many denominations are already seeing the "age wave" crest on their shores. These seniors can be reached and discipled in significant numbers.

Since there are more women than men in this group the efforts to serve them can be spearheaded by women's ministry. The impetus can come from seniors or from younger women. If your church has few seniors, cooperate with nearby churches in developing a program.

Many of the needs of seniors can be addressed through the regular ministries of your church and women's ministry. Specialized needs can be met by additional programs specifically designed for seniors. Here are four suggestions adapted from Dr. Win Arn's, *Growth Report Number 30*, published by Church Growth, 1921 S. Myrtle Avenue, Monrovia, CA 91016 for ministering to the distinctive needs of seniors.

1. Begin by developing a profile of the seniors in your congregation and your community which includes:
   - age-groupings
   - marital and family status
   - mobility and physical condition
   - needs
   - skills, interests, hobbies

Structure your ministries based on the findings. Begin with the seniors in your congregation. A good program will encourage seniors to invite their friends: expect the group to grow.

2. Provide ministry opportunities suited to the experience and interest of the seniors. They make good visitors to the hospitalized, homebound, or lonely singles. Use them in teaching young children who benefit from the love of a surrogate grandparent. Supply the prayer warriors among them with up-to-date information for intelligent praying.

When planning events, remember to include active seniors. If you're planning a church banquet, think of specific jobs seniors can accomplish while sitting.

3. Challenge them to continue growing spiritually. This might be

through a Bible study suited to their needs. Many seniors prefer their own discussion group within the larger context of the Ladies Bible Study. Small Group involvement should be provided. Since many older citizens prefer to stay home in the evening, consider holding their Small Group during the daytime.

Depending on gift and experience, use senior women as disciplers of young women. Use the Titus 2 principle wherever you can. It's God's gift to the seniors to increase involvement with the youth as well as a boon to the youth who need the stabilization seniors can provide. Their spiritual growth should spill over into evangelism. Seniors are most effective in reaching other seniors.

4. Educational and social/recreational development should be encouraged through seminars. Continuing intellectual growth which raises one's self-esteem contributes to mental health. Many of the following suggested topics will stimulate thinking and an increased awareness of the world. Provide recreational, social, and physical activities. Visit interesting places and do interesting things.

The Active Senior
This ministry can be run by a permanent committee or committees can be set up for each area and event. It could include: monthly field trips or programs, needed services such as lawn care and house cleaning, transportation (to church, doctor appointments, shopping), and regular telephone calls to those without immediate family in the area.

Field trips. The destination should be checked for ease of walking, wheel chair access, shade, and shelter in case of rain. Possibilities include visits to historic places, places of scenic beauty, concerts, plays, museums, and trips to shopping malls.

Programs. Suggested topics:
- effective grandparenting
- handling grief
- writing or taping a family history
- personal safety (presented by a police officer)
- health issues, nutrition for seniors, healthy-heart cooking
- financial matters: tips on investing money; wills and estates
- travel films
- missionary speakers
- seasonal parties (Christmas, Thanksgiving, Valentine's Day)
- senior talent show
- exercise for seniors
- craft demonstrations

Always use microphones to aid hearing-impaired seniors. Make sure lighting is adequate. When providing food, carefully plan menus to accommodate those on restricted diets.

Good publicity is a key to successful programs. Telephone each senior in advance of an event. Don't rely on verbal announcements made during Sunday services. Maintain a senior's bulletin board and encourage them to check it often.

When planning field trips or programs select a time schedule that won't tire the seniors. Arrange for transportation to and from the event.

This ministry can be underwritten financially by the church, by individual donors, or by the seniors themselves. Make sure scholarships are available for those unable to pay or on fixed incomes.

The Slowing-Down Senior

This person may need additional help in order to participate in the seniors' activities listed above. She may also need transportation to church, doctor's appointments, grocery store, and to her friends' homes.

She also needs personal contact. Set up a rotating schedule so these seniors receive a phone call from a person in the fellowship at least once every two or three days. On a routine basis have someone provide an occasional meal and company. Many seniors simply don't bother to prepare healthy meals when they eat alone.

If the person has no family nearby, make sure she has a social worker to help her with social security, medicare, and other government programs for the elderly.

The Convalescent Center or Homebound Senior

The resident care or homebound senior can be ministered to in many ways by your church.

Visits. Convalescent homes are filled with lonely people. Establish a visitation ministry to seniors. If possible, visit at mealtime. Sometimes older people who can't feed themselves go hungry because staff members don't have the time to help each individual. When visiting a specific person, you usually meet a dozen others who never have visitors. Plan extra time to talk and share the Gospel with these needy people on the edge of eternity.

If a senior is sleeping when you visit, wake her up! She can sleep anytime and would hate to miss a visitor.

Personal touches. Institutional food is nutritious but bland. Ask the senior if there's a particular food you could bring her (many seniors are on restricted diets so check with the staff before bringing food). Celebrate birthdays. Bring a cake, a small gift, and a card signed by as many church members as possible. Ask Sunday School teachers to have their classes draw birthday pictures for the party.

Affirmation. Let the senior know she's important to God and to the church. Emphasize her value as a prayer warrior. Keep her supplied with information and let her know you're feeling the effects of her prayers. Have those who have been touched by her life (e.g., kids she taught in Sunday School or women she helped in various ways) visit or write to let her know she made a difference in their lives.

Ministry to the Terminally Ill
The purpose of this unique ministry is to find and train volunteers to minister to the spiritual and practical needs of the terminally ill in your congregation and your community.

Starting a support group
Schedule a meeting for those church members interested in working with the terminally ill. Find out what groups already provide terminal illness support. Contact other churches to determine their interest in forming an interchurch support network. Gather the information you need to design a program.

When you have a core team of committed people, arrange for community health care professionals to provide them with information and training. Include an oncology nurse, a pharmacist, a dietician, and a vocational nurse. Purchase useful resource books and encourage team members to read them to gain more understanding of this sometimes difficult ministry.

Develop a prayer group dedicated to pray for this ministry, its leaders and caregivers, and the families to whom they will be ministering.

Making the initial home visit
A significant part of this ministry consists of making visits in the home. If the person being visited isn't from your church introduce yourself, your church, and this special ministry. If they are open to your help assess their needs by reviewing the following checklist:

• Determine the primary caregiver in the home.
• Determine what specific support is already being provided and what support is needed.
• Determine whether the person needs financial assistance, and if so, how much.
• Ask the person specifically what the doctor has said about her diagnosis. Ask how she feels about the quality of her medical care.
• Assure her you'll visit the following week. Phone her regularly.

Once you have determined the needs do what you can to help meet them. But don't allow yourself to be controlled by the person or victimized by the situation. Set boundaries on the amount of support offered.

Build a partnership among support system members to keep any one individual from burning out. On the second visit, introduce other team members. Say "Somebody [not "I"] will visit you next week."

Remember, you are visiting as a *believer*, bringing a spiritual dimension into the lives of the family as well as the patient. On the first visit, clearly state that you expect the person to develop spiritually through this experience and that your purpose is to help her with spiritual and emotional needs as well as physical needs.

Share the Gospel casually, or if the patient and circumstances warrant, present the Gospel more forcefully (see chap. 14 for some helpful suggestions on personal evangelism).

When the person dies, assist as needed with the funeral arrangements. Provide a list of reputable lawyers and other professionals if the family wants help in settling the estate. Continue visiting the family to help them through the grieving process if they want you to.

Respite Care

(This material is from Heather Andrews. It is in the section on seniors, but this ministry should reach out to any woman or family with a home-bound loved one.)

Respite care is voluntary care given freely out of love. It helps provide relief service for those with the continual responsibility of caring for an ill, elderly, or special-needs invalid. Its main ministry is to the caregiver, not the patient. It provides needed opportunities for the primary caregiver to get out of the house for any reason.

One or two women should be selected to organize this ministry. Through a survey they could find those interested in serving. They should recruit volunteers and match them to appropriate situations:

- home-bound infants (babies on monitors, e.g.)
- mentally disabled
- physically handicapped, paraplegic, quadriplegic
- Alzheimer's disease
- terminally ill/hospice
- total care, comatose patient

While giving the primary caregiver a break, the respite care volunteer can minister to the home-bound individual by providing companionship and conversation. Together they can watch TV, read, play games, work on puzzles, look at photographs, or do handicrafts.

If physical care is needed, make sure the volunteer is trained and capable of giving it.

Each volunteer must receive an instruction sheet when he or she arrives with the following information:

- phone numbers of other family members, doctors, and emergency services
  - primary caregiver's location and anticipated time of return
  - medication schedule and special diet restrictions or preferences
  - level of assistance needed for walking, mobility, using the toilet.
  - instructions on how to turn or lift the patient if necessary

Making Christmas Special for Widows

(This material on caring for widows is from Marylin Hoekstra.)

Christmas is an especially lonely time for widows. Women's ministries can express love and care for widows in the church by sponsoring a Christmas basket program.

For the purpose of this holiday ministry, a widow is defined as any senior, man or woman, who is widowed or otherwise alone.

Change the basket/container annually to include large holiday cookie tins, Rubbermaid one-gallon cylinder with cover, decorative metal serving tray, etc. The basket could include things like: stationery and quality ballpoint pen, post-it note pads, Scotch tape, book of postage stamps, candy, pocket calendar, pocket pack of Kleenex.

Many name-brand cosmetic companies offer giveaways during which the purchaser receives various free samples. Encourage women to buy their cosmetics during these giveaway periods so they can include the freebies in the Christmas baskets.

Add one special personal gift, such as a Bible-based novel or her favorite brand of bath powder, perfume, or specialty food.

The above items are just suggestions. You can include whatever you think your seniors would enjoy. Be creative! Seniors trying to make ends meet on a fixed income will welcome many useful items. Why not include a $5 or $10 gift certificate to a local supermarket so they can purchase favorite food items they usually consider a luxury?

The per basket cost of this ministry should be set in advance. It can be covered by women's ministries, by the church, or by personal gifts. Depending on the number of widows you may want to spend between $20 and $30 a basket.

Don't Lose Out

Often, our youth-oriented society closes its eyes to seniors. Youth don't want to be reminded of their own mortality. But in this closing-off process, the wisdom gleaned by seniors during their lives is lost.

The church can't afford this loss. Nor can she ignore her responsibility to minister to those in need (James 1:27), especially to those who have given so much throughout their lives.